WARFARE AND
THE MIRACULOUS
IN THE
CHRONICLES
OF THE
FIRST CRUSADE

WARFARE AND THE MIRACULOUS IN THE CHRONICLES OF THE FIRST CRUSADE

ELIZABETH LAPINA

The Pennsylvania State University Press
University Park, Pennsylvania

An earlier version of chapter 1 appeared in
Viator: Medieval and Renaissance Studies 38
(2007): 117–39.

Library of Congress Cataloging-in-Publication Data

Lapina, Elizabeth, 1979– , author.
Warfare and the miraculous in the chronicles of the First
Crusade / Elizabeth Lapina.
    pages   cm
Summary: "Analyzes how chroniclers of the
First Crusade attempted to represent the enterprise as a
"holy war." Focuses on accounts of miracles, especially
the intervention of saints in the battle of Antioch;
explores how the chroniclers related the crusade to
biblical events"—Provided by publisher.
Includes bibliographical references and index.
ISBN 978-0-271-06670-7 (cloth : alk. paper)
ISBN 978-0-271-06671-4 (pbk. : alk. paper)
1. Crusades—First, 1096–1099.
2. Miracles—History.
I. Title.

D161.2.L37 2015
956'.014—dc23
2015003524

Copyright © 2015 The Pennsylvania State University
All rights reserved
Printed in the United States of America
Published by The Pennsylvania State University Press,
University Park, PA 16802–1003

The Pennsylvania State University Press is a member of
the Association of American University Presses.

It is the policy of The Pennsylvania State University Press
to use acid-free paper. Publications on uncoated stock
satisfy the minimum requirements of American
National Standard for Information Sciences—
Permanence of Paper for Printed Library Material,
ANSI Z39.48–1992.

To ARGANTHAËL *and* BÉATRICE

CONTENTS

Acknowledgments ix

Introduction 1

1
Eyewitnesses of Miracles 15

2
Supernatural Interventions in the Battle
of Antioch: The Origins 37

3
Hostile Appropriations of Byzantine Saints
by the Normans of the South 54

4
The Normans of the South:
From Scourge of God to Chosen People 75

5
Judas Maccabeus: A Jewish Warrior, a Christian
Patriarch, and a Muslim General 97

6
"The West Prepares to Illuminate the East" 122

Conclusion 143

Notes 153
Bibliography 177
Index 203

ACKNOWLEDGMENTS

This book would not have been possible without the help of a great number of people. Gabrielle Spiegel and David Nirenberg were wonderful teachers when I was a graduate student at Johns Hopkins University and they have been very generous in their guidance and encouragements all these years since my graduation. My debt to them should be apparent in every chapter.

I worked on this book while employed, in succession, by four institutions in three different countries. Receiving the Marjorie McLean Oliver Post-Doctoral Fellowship at Queen's University in Kingston, Canada, was a major boon for me, as it allowed me to ease into teaching with a vastly reduced load. Among the faculty at Queen's, I would like to thank especially my mentor, Richard Greenfield, for his unwavering support of my work. Two years as a visiting lecturer at Durham University gave me a rare opportunity to interact with a series of medievalists and crusader specialists in the United Kingdom. Although I received a Leverhulme Early Career Research Fellowship at the University of Kent in Canterbury for another book, this fellowship gave me much needed time to revise the draft of the present one. Once again, at Kent, I was fortunate when it came to my mentor, Barbara Bombi.

Friends and colleagues too numerous to list have helped me over the years with their advice and good cheer. I particularly appreciate the generosity of Steven Biddlecombe, Barbara Bombi, Clare Monagle, Nicholas Morton, Luigi Russo, Katherine Allen Smith, Carol Sweetenham, and Susanna Throop, who took time to read the drafts of various parts of the manuscript. Anonymous reviewers at Penn State University Press went beyond their call of duty to suggest improvements. Ellie Goodman at Penn State Press kept alive the dream of seeing this project in print. Suzanne Wolk weeded out as many errors as was humanly possible.

I am thankful to my parents, Galina Lapina and Alexander Dolinin, for their unwavering support of my career in general and of writing this book specifically. It is a pity that my grandmother, Alexandra Ivanovna Lapina, will not see it.

I still cannot believe my luck in being able to share this journey with Arganthaël Berson and our daughter, Béatrice Anna Maria Berson. For the past decade, Arganthaël has been there for me every moment, whatever adventures came our way. Béatrice tried hard to be understanding of my need to work long hours and was also very good at reminding me that there was more to life than the Crusades. It is a great pleasure for me to dedicate this book to both of them.

INTRODUCTION

When the news of the capture of Jerusalem on July 15, 1099, reached Europe, the entire Latin world applauded and marveled at the incredible achievements of its soldiers. Robert, a monk in Normandy and author of a chronicle of the First Crusade, claimed that no "more miraculous undertaking" had taken place since the beginning of history, with just one exception: the incarnation.[1] Clearly, there was more to the enterprise for contemporaries of the First Crusade than a military triumph. Even though his statement is exceptional, Robert's position regarding the First Crusade was not: many others appear to have believed that the crusade spelled one of the greatest gifts—perhaps even the greatest—of God to humanity since the sacrifice of Christ. Guibert of Nogent, also a monk in Normandy and also an author of a chronicle of the First Crusade, claimed that God was the "sole leader" and the "king" of the crusading army: "he brought things from their beginning to their conclusion." The personal involvement of God in a military campaign instituted a new type of warfare. According to Guibert, "God ordained holy wars in our time, so that the knightly order and the erring mob, who, like their ancient pagan models, were engaged in mutual slaughter, might find a new way of earning salvation. Thus, without having chosen (as is customary) a monastic life, without any religious commitment, they were compelled to give up this world; free to continue their customary pursuits, nevertheless they earned some measure of God's grace by their own efforts."[2]

The belief that the exercise of violence could be not only sinless but actually salvific—or, in other words, the notion of penitential warfare—was a radically new development. The Christian Church never advocated absolute pacifism, and in many instances its representatives actively promoted and sometimes even engaged in warfare. However, as two eleventh-century examples demonstrate, in general, the church tended to be cautious about celebrating violence. In 1062, Peter Damian described a land dispute between an abbot and a secular lord: "After the supporters of each had engaged in protected quarrels and threats, both sides at length decided to fight it out." The abbot, however, forbade his supporters to defend the abbey, but he himself advanced together with his monks, all of them unarmed, toward the enemy lines. The opponent was flabbergasted: when he, "as he had hoped, saw nothing of weapons but beheld something like a heavenly and angelic array approaching, such a dreadful fear of God gripped him and all his men that, dismounting from their horses, they at once threw down their arms, prostrated themselves humbly on the ground, and begged to be forgiven."[3] In Peter Damian's eyes, this was a perfect victory, achieved without the display of weapons, let alone bloodshed, but culminating in the repentance of the guilty party. To give another example, soon after the victory of William the Conqueror at Hastings in 1066, Norman bishops issued an ordinance imposing penances on the combatants. Those who had fought for gain had to do penance for seven years. Those who had fought for justice still had to do penance, but for only three years.[4] In stark contrast, there was no stigma associated with the shedding of blood by participants in the First Crusade. On the contrary, the very act of fighting was seen as a legitimate way of serving God. As both Robert and Guibert appear to have believed, this was not a one-time exception but a new opportunity for all present and future knights. Indeed, the conviction that certain wars could be salvific became part of the medieval landscape and reemerged in an ever-expanding number of contexts, both on the frontiers of Latin Christendom and in its hinterlands.

Among the sources that reflect the shift toward the sacralization of warfare that took place during and in the immediate aftermath of the First Crusade, chronicles are the most revealing. No fewer than four participants have left records of the events. In the half century after the capture of Jerusalem, numerous chroniclers and poets used some combination of these four works, as well as other written and oral sources, to produce a series of additional narratives. For the Middle Ages, the existence of such a large assembly of sources—which describe the same events but were written by authors from different backgrounds, living in different countries, displaying or concealing different agendas, and working in different styles—is truly exceptional. The possibility of comparing several narratives of exactly the same events allows one to note omissions, additions, free paraphrases, and shifts of emphasis, all of which make each text unique. Although some of the discrepancies could be either accidental or merely stylistic, others point clearly to the heterogeneity of interpretations. Each narrator of the First Crusade probably hoped that his perspective on the event would become the standard one, superseding all others.

In general, as Gabrielle Spiegel has demonstrated, the "communication of factual information" was hardly ever the goal of the medieval author.[5] Most medieval works of history were also interpretations and arguments, often idiosyncratic and controversial. Chroniclers of the First Crusade like Robert or Guibert, however, stand apart from most other writers of history in the Middle Ages because of their belief, which they must have shared with many of their contemporaries, that God was involved in the enterprise in a much more literal sense than ever before, with the possible exception of the wars of the Israelites. Perhaps even more important, this was the first war believed to have actually transformed the meaning of warfare. But it was not enough simply to say, as Robert did, that the First Crusade was the most important event since the incarnation; it was necessary to prove it. The chroniclers found two ways to adduce proof of the exceptional nature of the crusading enterprise. First, they placed miracles at the center of their narratives. Second, they developed ingenious ways to inscribe the First Crusade in the continuum of sacred history. Although the overarching agendas of most of the chroniclers were the same or similar, both the paths that they chose and the conclusions they reached were remarkably different.

Jonathan Riley-Smith was one of the first historians of the Crusades to argue that at least some of the chroniclers had greater ambitions than just to give an account of what had transpired in the East. More specifically, he questioned the reasons behind the decision of Guibert, Robert, and another chronicler working in Normandy, Baldric of Bourgueil, to rewrite the anonymous *Gesta Francorum*, the author of which, unlike them, had participated in the enterprise. Riley-Smith claimed that the three later authors considered the *Gesta* "not theological enough" and strove to give "an intellectual expression" to its "semi-popular ideology."[6] Indeed, although much medieval historical writing overlapped with theology, the transformative nature of the

First Crusade probably made the theological component more central in its chronicles than ever before.

The chasm between the *Gesta* and the later chronicles, however, was perhaps not as profound as Riley-Smith suggests; the *Gesta* is only marginally less "theological" than the other works. More significantly, the differences among all of the chronicles, even when they draw upon the same source and their authors come from similar backgrounds, were numerous and noteworthy. These differences allow the modern historian better to appreciate the complexity of the process of sacralization of crusading warfare in the decades of the First Crusade, when a series of explanations competed against one another.

The stakes involved in recording the First Crusade are apparent in the bitterness with which Guibert, Robert, and Baldric criticized the *Gesta*. Two monks and one monk-turned-bishop were obviously eager to get right what their predecessor, in their opinion, got wrong. The three authors' decision to rewrite the *Gesta* might have appeared particularly open to criticism, since the First Crusade was not just any military campaign but, as Robert put it, the most "miraculous undertaking" since the incarnation. The author of the *Gesta* was thus an active participant in a miracle. But Guibert, Robert, Baldric, and some others who did not take part in the enterprise managed to turn the miraculous nature of the First Crusade to their advantage. As chapter 1 demonstrates, they argued that, in contrast to an ordinary military campaign, the crusade was important first and foremost not because of the facts of what happened on any particular day, no matter how amazing, but because of the inner meaning behind these facts. They minimized the role of eyewitnesses, such as the author of the *Gesta*, and emphasized that of the examiner or interpreter, who could either reject or accept any testimony that came down to him while also explaining its meaning, including to eyewitnesses themselves. This approach presented historical reality as akin to a biblical text with several (much more important) layers of meaning buried beneath the literal one.

In the eyes of many authors, miracles that occurred during the First Crusade gave the best proof that the the capture of Jerusalem was made possible "neither by created nature nor by the will of the creature but by God alone."[7] Arguably, the most important miracle of the First Crusade was the intervention of saints in the battle of Antioch of June 28, 1098. In many of the chronicles, the battle of Antioch functioned as a synecdoche for the entire enterprise. Crusaders' defeat in the battle was almost a certainty, but, thanks to supernatural help, they achieved a resounding victory. According to the *Gesta Francorum*, three saints, George, Mercurius, and Demetrius, were at the head of a supernatural host that joined the crusaders. Since it became an integral part of crusader lore, it is difficult to appreciate the audacity of the narrative of saints appearing on a battlefield. Yet there could hardly be a more powerful statement regarding the sacred nature of the war. George, Mercurius, and Demetrius were early Christian martyrs who became saints by willingly suffering violence. Here, in contrast, they engaged in active resistance to evil in the form of Muslim troops. To some extent, the two types of resistance, which had heretofore been opposites—one through fighting and another through martyrdom—had now become alternatives. Indeed, the narratives of this miracle complement the attempts made by some chroniclers to equate death on the battlefield with martyrdom.[8]

Desire to represent combat as sacred, whether in participants or propagandists, contemporaries or descendants, is timeless. Behind this desire is a need to believe (and to make others believe) that the carnage has a higher meaning. Throughout history, a claim that some sort of supernatural being—a god, a saint, an angel, a deceased hero—appeared on the battlefield was one of the most effective ways to sacralize warfare. If a supernatural being deigned to join the fray, then there could be no doubt that the fight was worth fighting. There could also be little doubt that any setbacks were temporary and, in the end, that victory was assured.

Although the claim that otherworldly beings took part in warfare is timeless, expressions of that desire changed over time.[9] Carl Erdmann was the first to use narratives of visible interventions of saints as one of the key markers of the degree of sacralization of warfare.[10] Thus, as I demonstrate in chapter 2, despite the visceral nature of the need to believe in divine interference in military encounters, the miracle of supernatural interventions in warfare has a history. In antiquity, references to the visible appearance of supernatural agents were rare. Deceased heroes intervened much more often than gods. Many authors expressed skepticism about stories of visible interventions, although Cicero, after presenting both the believers' and the skeptics' side of the argument, refused to pronounce decisively on the subject. Christian narratives of saintly interventions grew out of pagan accounts and in competition with them from the third century on. Attitudes toward warfare developed along different lines in the East and the West. In Byzantium, narratives of supernatural interventions on the battlefield multiplied, especially in connection with the titanic struggle against Persia. Erdmann argues that in the West, at least before the Viking invasions, "only rarely do we hear of a saint appearing in battle to protect his church and the faithful."[11] As numerous studies have demonstrated, Erdmann overstates the "aloofness" of the Latin church toward war.[12] Several Western examples of saintly interventions predate the period of invasions. However, Erdmann is correct in emphasizing the relative importance of the miracle in Byzantium and its resurgence in the West in the context of resistance to the Vikings.

The main difference between the accounts of saints' intervention in the battle of Antioch and earlier accounts of similar miracles is that earlier narratives tended to be confined to specific local contexts. In contrast, the miracle reported at Antioch came to be celebrated throughout Europe, and its fame long outlived the First Crusade. Perhaps more important, this type of miracle was transferred to a variety of situations, including, for example, the battle of Mons in the First World War.[13]

A rare and radical type of miracle would never have become so widely acceptable had the ground not been prepared for it. Chapters 3 and 4 demonstrate how the crusaders and the chroniclers of the First Crusade actively engaged with some of the direct and indirect precedents for the miracle. The search for the immediate inspiration for the narrative of the miracle leads us to the cultural sphere of the Normans of the South. Thus some of the origins of the impulse to present the First Crusade as a holy war are located in the same cultural sphere. The Normans of the South provide an important missing link between the First Crusade and the two earlier clusters of accounts of the miracle. First, the Normans of the South appear to have made the earliest attempt to "borrow" the miracle from the Byzantines during the invasion of the Balkans by Robert Guiscard and his son Bohemond, the future hero of the First Crusade. Their "borrowing" was not an admission of cultural inferiority but a statement of political superiority. It was a question not just of acquisition on the part of the Normans but also of loss on the part of the Byzantines. While the first attempt by the Normans to "borrow" Byzantine saints left only a faint trace in the sources, the second one seems to have succeeded beyond all expectations. The Normans made this second attempt when Bohemond claimed that Antioch belonged to him and not to the emperor Alexius. In both cases, the borrowing of Byzantine saints was hostile and resembled plundering more than imitation.

Second, the Normans of the South were particularly interested in preserving the memory of saintly intervention in battle in defense of monasteries attacked by the Vikings. Although ethnically, linguistically, and culturally, these Normans had little to do with the Vikings, they and their monastic propagandists insisted that they did. For obvious reasons—military prowess was a cause of pride regardless of the circumstances—their supposed past as ruthless raiders was a crucial component of what made a Norman a Norman, or, in other words, of *Normanitas*.[14] The Normans appropriated a past that was only tangentially theirs in order to promote an image of themselves as inspiring fear. They did not ignore the stories of the intervention of saints against the Vikings, but they interpreted them as God's attempt to direct their might toward a more legitimate goal. The Normans emerged as God's chosen people, as manifested in the interventions both against them and for them. Thus the Normans of the South were not only more familiar than other crusaders with earlier narratives of the miracle of saintly intervention, but they had at least two cogent reasons to appropriate such narratives.

It was not enough, however, for most chroniclers simply to include a miracle or two in their works in order to transform the military campaign in the Middle East into a "holy war." Many of them felt the need to make sense of this "holy war" by inscribing it in a wider context of sacred history. The chroniclers were confident that the First Crusade was fundamentally different from any previous military campaign. At the same time, however, medieval thinkers believed that few things were ever entirely new. Behind the messy reality of history there was a sequence of confrontations between good and evil, right and wrong, order and disorder, justice and crime. Although both good and evil could assume a variety of guises, the struggle, which would end only with the final battle of the Apocalypse, remained the same. Therefore, in order to explain the meaning of the First Crusade, chroniclers searched for biblical precedents of what they perceived as basically the same conflict.

This meant establishing a symmetrical relationship between the First Crusade and other key events of sacred history, narrated in both the Old and New Testaments. Medieval authors (and, in all likelihood, crusaders themselves) perceived three biblical stories as particularly relevant to the crusade. First, they drew comparisons between crusading warfare and the struggles of the Israelites. Second, in many sources, crusaders feature as new apostles, the First Crusade being their new mission.[15] Third, desire for vengeance for the death of Christ was one of the key motivations of crusaders.[16] The present work addresses the first and the second of these symmetries: that of crusaders as the new Jews and that of crusaders as the new apostles. The existence of these symmetries is well known, but the mechanisms of their construction are insufficiently understood.

Although the chronicles of the First Crusade abound with references to the Bible, the Maccabees play an especially significant role. The placement of references to the Maccabees is perhaps even more important than their number, as at least two of the chroniclers explicitly acknowledged the similarities between the intervention of saints in the battle of Antioch and that of angels in the wars waged by Judas Maccabeus. The Maccabees thus play a part in the narratives of the key episode of the First Crusade, when divine intervention was most apparent. As chapter 5 demonstrates, the chroniclers diverge in their use of the Maccabees. In fact, even the two chronicles that cite the Maccabees in connection with the battle of Antioch pursue diametrically opposite goals. Some chroniclers indeed used the Maccabees and other biblical prototypes to endow the First Crusade with sacred meaning. Others, however, found that comparisons of crusaders to the Israelites or, more specifically, to the Maccabees were theologically unsound and even dangerous. They proposed that the crusaders and the Israelites should be compared and contrasted, with both similarities and differences clearly spelled out along the lines of traditional Christian attitudes toward Christianity's Jewish heritage.

Many chroniclers of the First Crusade positioned the crusaders as heirs of the Israelites, either equaling or superseding their forbears. At the same time, many chroniclers also positioned the crusaders as heirs of the apostles. The aim of chapter 6 is to analyze references to cardinal points, especially to east and west, in order to gain a better understanding of the chroniclers' attempt to prove that crusaders were "new apostles." These references are relatively few and are only comprehensible in the context of the tradition of interpreting the interrelations between "the East" and "the West" in late antiquity and the early Middle Ages. From the very inception of the binary, "East" and "West" did not denote direction but were cultural constructs. In other words, they were part of the interpretation as much as of the narrative. This is true of the chronicles of the First Crusade as well, which conceived of the relationship between "the East" and "the West" in terms of debt and repayment. As apostles brought Christianity from the East to the West, so crusaders were bringing Christianity back to the East from the West.

The Sources

In recent decades, many of the chronicles of the First Crusade have benefitted from new editions. In addition, a number of scholars have examined the question of the interrelation of these sources and of manuscript transmission, drawing attention both to understudied and, in some cases, utterly ignored sources. These ongoing developments have already transformed and will continue to transform the field of crusader studies. In the present book, whenever possible, I have profited from the most recent editions, but I have not participated in uncovering the history of the production of the narratives of the First Crusade. The following overview serves merely to help the newcomer to crusader studies navigate the book more easily.[17] The overview includes only the works referred to in the present volume. As a consequence, it does not take into account a large number of rewrites and abridgments, the usefulness of which for the study of the Crusades is gradually becoming more apparent, or, with one exception, the sources composed after circa 1160.

At least four participants in the First Crusade wrote chronicles of the enterprise. The *Gesta Francorum et aliorum Heirosolimitanorum* is the earliest of the four. The *Gesta Francorum*'s anonymous author, most probably of southern Norman origin, was likely to have begun working on his narrative during the course of the expedition and to have completed it shortly after the fall of Jerusalem. Historians have long believed that the author was a knight, although most now concur that he was a cleric.[18]

A closely related chronicle, the *Historia de Hierosolymitano itinere*, is attributed to Peter Tudebode, a priest from Civray in Poitou. The relationship between the *Historia* and the *Gesta Francorum* has been subjected to considerable debate. Traditionally, scholars considered the *Gesta* the earlier version and the *Historia* its copy. A number of scholars, most recently Jay Rubenstein, have proposed that the *Historia* and the *Gesta* are both based on a now lost source.[19] However, Marcus Bull's recent examination of a heretofore ignored manuscript related to these two chronicles, *Peregrinatio Antiochie* (St. Catharine's College, Cambridge 3), has demonstrated that the *Gesta* is indeed "the earliest surviving narrative telling the course of the First Crusade," from which the other two, the *Historia* and the *Peregrinatio*, as well as many others, descended.[20]

The other two crusader-chroniclers of the First Crusade were Raymond of Aguilers and Fulcher of Chartres. Raymond of Aguilers took part in the crusade in his capacity as a chaplain of Raymond of St. Gilles, count of Toulouse, but he used the *Gesta Francorum* extensively, especially for the events that had to do with Antioch. Raymond wrote his chronicle certainly before 1105, the year when Raymond of St. Gilles died, and perhaps as early as late 1099.[21]

Fulcher of Chartres, the author of *Historia Hierosolymitana*, was present at the Council of Clermont in November 1095 and went to the East in the company of Duke Robert of Normandy, Count Stephen of Blois, and Count Robert II of Flanders. In October 1097, he joined Baldwin of Boulogne, future prince of Edessa and later king of Jerusalem. He stayed with Baldwin in Edessa and participated in neither the siege of Antioch nor that of Jerusalem. Fulcher finished the first version of his chronicle by 1106 or 1107. He continued working on it, both rewriting and extending it to cover the history of the early decades of the Latin kingdom, until 1127.[22]

In the first decade of the twelfth century, three monks living in Normandy, Baldric of Bourgueil, Guibert of Nogent, and Robert the Monk, rewrote the *Gesta Francorum*. Baldric was the first to do so, composing his *Historia Ierosolimitana* around 1105. Baldric, in turn abbot of the wealthy monastery of Bourgueil and archbishop of Dol, was probably the highest-ranking chronicler of the First Crusade. In addition to the chronicle, Baldric composed poetry that has attracted considerable scholarly attention and a series of saints' *Lives*. Baldric was a witness of the event that set the First Crusade in motion, the Council of Clermont in 1095.[23]

The second chronicler in the group, Guibert of Nogent, wrote his *Dei gesta per Francos* slightly later than Baldric, in 1107–8, and continued to edit it for at least another decade. In modern historiography, Guibert, like Baldric, is more famous for his other works, especially his autobiographical *Monodies*, than for his chronicle of the First Crusade. While Guibert had only the anonymous *Gesta* at his disposal when he composed the first version of the chronicle, he later came across Fulcher's *Historia Hierosolymitana*. Jay Rubenstein has noted similarities between Guibert of Nogent's *Dei gesta* and Albert of Aachen's *Historia Ierosolimitana* and has suggested that the two must have heard similar oral accounts.[24]

Baldric's work survives in twenty-four manuscripts, while Guibert's is preserved in eight.[25] In contrast, there are no fewer than eighty-four manuscripts of Robert the Monk's *Historia Iherosolimitana*. Although the import of these numbers should not be overstated, it is safe to say that Robert the Monk's *Historia* was the most widely read narrative of the First Crusade. Robert took part in some of the events that he describes, since, like Baldric, he attended the Council of Clermont of 1095. Although he has traditionally been identified with the abbot Robert of the monastery of Saint-Remy in Reims, there are good reasons to doubt that they were the same person. There is a possibility, though it is also based on insufficient evidence, that

Robert went on a pilgrimage to Jerusalem in the wake of the First Crusade. Although Robert relied primarily on the *Gesta Francorum*, he might have come across Guibert of Nogent's version as well. Robert completed his chronicle around 1110.[26]

Hystoria de via et recuperatione Antiochiae atque Ierusolymarum is another narrative of the First Crusade based on the *Gesta Francorum*. In this case, however, the line of descent is not immediately apparent, so a number of scholars, including the chronicle's editor, Edoardo D'Angelo, advocate a common source. The chronicle survives in only one manuscript, preserved at Montecassino, and was written much later than the three Norman ones, between 1130 and 1153.[27]

Some of the sources based on the *Gesta Francorum* have produced their own rewrites. One of these likely "thirdhand" narratives, the *Historia vie Hierosolimitane*, is a composite work written by Gilo of Paris and an anonymous author conventionally called the Charleville poet (so named because the sole manuscript of his work is found in the library of Charleville-Mézières), who added four books to Gilo's poem and also made a series of insertions and alterations. According to Christopher Wallace Grocock and Elizabeth Siberry, we no longer possess the source or sources used by either Gilo or the Charleville poet and can only note resemblances.[28] Damien Kempf and Marcus Bull have argued, in contrast, that Gilo's work is based on Robert the Monk's *Historia Iherosolimitana*.[29]

Gilo was a cleric in Paris at the time of the writing and went on to become a monk at Cluny and a cardinal in Rome. He probably wrote the *Historia* in the first decade of the twelfth century and almost certainly before 1120. We know very little about the Charleville poet, although Grocock and Siberry speculate that he must have been a teacher. The Charleville poet mentions King Baldwin I of Jerusalem, who died in 1118, in the past tense, which provides a *terminus post quem* for his part of the work. The Charleville poet's decision to rework the earlier text has to do, at least in part, with his desire to glorify Godfrey of Bouillon, the first ruler of the kingdom of Jerusalem, who must have been a local hero (Charleville-Mézières is located within twenty miles of Bouillon).

Orderic Vitalis is another "thirdhand" chronicler. Book IX of his *Ecclesiastical History* is largely an epitome of Baldric of Bourgueil's *Historia Ierosolimitana*. Baldric's chronicle was Orderic's only source, even though Orderic mentions Fulcher's *Historia Hierosolymitana* in the preface. Although Orderic follows Baldric's account closely, he also augments it with information drawn from oral accounts. Book X of the *Ecclesiastical History* is devoted to the crusade of 1101 and the early years of the kingdom of Jerusalem and the principality of Antioch, and it seems to be based exclusively on oral accounts. Both book IX and book X appear to have been written in 1135.[30]

Like Orderic Vitalis, William of Malmesbury also incorporated a narrative of the First Crusade in a much longer work. William's major work, *Gesta Regum Anglorum*, covers the period from late antiquity until about 1125. While the focus is on England, William also addresses some of the key events that took place elsewhere, including the First Crusade. In fact, William's narrative of the crusade is as long as a number of freestanding chronicles, including the *Gesta Francorum*. William's account is based primarily on Fulcher's *Historia Hierosolymitana*, although he consulted other sources, including Bernard the Monk's *Itinerary* and the anonymous *Gesta Francorum*. He also had an opportunity to consult the participants in the First Crusade and included some of their oral accounts in his work.[31]

Henry, archdeacon of Huntington, also included an account of the First Crusade in a much longer work. Henry's *Historia Anglorum* begins with the Roman invasion of England and ends with the coronation of King Henry II of England in 1154. At twenty-five hundred words, Henry's account of the First Crusade is much shorter than the one found in Orderic Vitalis's or William of Malmesbury's works. It traces its lineage primarily to the *Gesta Francorum*, although it also includes material recorded by other authors, such as Baldric, Ralph of Caen, and William of Malmesbury, as well as some details not found anywhere else.[32]

A series of sources are entirely independent of the *Gesta Francorum* or other accounts written by participants. Ralph of Caen, the author of the *Gesta Tancredi*, relied exclusively on oral testimony. Ralph had studied in Caen in Normandy under the tutelage of Arnulf of Chocques, future patriarch of Jerusalem. In 1106, while in the West, Bohemond recruited him to serve as his chaplain. The following year, Ralph accompanied Bohemond to the eastern Mediterranean. Sometime before Bohemond's death in 1111 and probably shortly after Bohemond's fiasco during his campaign in the Balkans in 1108, Ralph journeyed to Antioch, where he entered the service of Tancred, the regent of the principality during Bohemond's absences and, upon Bohemond's death, during the minority of his son, Bohemond II. Ralph began writing his *Gesta Tancredi* after Tancred's death in 1112 and completed it at some point before 1118, when Arnulf, to whom the work is dedicated, died. Although most of the text focuses on the First Crusade, the narrative continues to around 1105.³³

Abbot Ekkehard of Aura was a member of the Bavarian nobility and a participant in the unsuccessful crusade of 1101. In or shortly before 1117, he finished his *Chronicle*, which, as the author admits, is largely a revised compilation of earlier sources. An appendix to the *Chronicle*, the *Hierosolymita*, is based on a continuation of Frutolf of Michelsberg's *World Chronicle*. The continuation, which dates from 1106, has crusading as the dominant theme for the years 1099–1101. The author of the continuation might or might not have been Ekkehard himself.³⁴

We know nothing about the author of the *Historia Ierosolimitana* attributed to Albert of Aachen, except his place of residence, Aachen, and, with a degree of uncertainty, his name, Albert. Albert appears to have composed the first six books early in the twelfth century and the rest sometime in the 1120s and 1130s. The narrative itself continues until 1119. There is no conclusive evidence that Albert used any written sources, but there are similarities between his work and the vernacular *Chanson d'Antioche*.

Caffaro di Rustico, lord of Caschifellone, stands out among other authors of narratives of the First Crusade in being a Genoese layman. In the summer of 1100, he boarded one of the ships of the Genoese fleet en route to the Holy Land. In 1101, Caffaro made this event the starting point of his *Annals* of Genoa. Around 1155, Caffaro dedicated a separate work to the Crusades titled *De liberatione civitatum orientis*, which begins with the discussion of the origins of the First Crusade and ends with the capture of Tripoli in 1109.³⁵

It might appear strange to include a vernacular *Chanson d'Antioche* (*Song of Antioch*) in the overview of chronicles. However, although different conventions, aims, and patterns of transmission of these two types of sources must be taken into account, they are less different than might at first appear. On the one hand, many of the early chronicles "contain material that reflects closely the conventions of the *chanson de geste*," such as, for example, a conversation between a Muslim general and his mother.³⁶ On the other hand, the *Song of Antioch* reveals numerous parallels with the chronicles of Albert of Aachen and Robert the Monk. The *Song*'s recent translators, Susan Edgington and Carol Sweetenham, argue that the author appears to have been using a no longer extant epitome of Albert of Aachen's work and a copy of Robert the Monk's. As Edgington and Sweetenham admit, however, we know very little about the genesis of the *Song*, except that there have been two versions. The tradition of associating the first—oral—version with Richard le Pèlerin and the second with Graindor de Douai rests on shaky foundations. The first version, in some form, was in existence by the end of the twelfth century. The second version, the one that has come down to us, dates from the early thirteenth century.

Although the present work refers to a wide variety of narratives, it privileges the family of chronicles related to the *Gesta Francorum*. More specifically, it gives more attention to Guibert of Nogent's *Dei gesta per Francos* than to any other source. There are two reasons for this. First, as his entire oeuvre makes apparent, Guibert was less concerned than an average medieval chronicler with concealing his opinions. Second, and more important, Guibert was the most accomplished theologian among the chroniclers, so he was able both to push further than the rest the "theological refinement" of the First Crusade and to appreciate the associated problems.

EYEWITNESSES OF MIRACLES

In the *Etymologiae*, an encyclopedic work written in the seventh century, Isidore of Seville argued that historians had to be eyewitnesses: "Among the ancients, no one would write history unless he had been present and had seen what was to be written down, for we grasp with our eyes things that occur better than what we gather with our hearing, since what is seen is revealed without falsehood."[1] Isidore drew on a long tradition of considering the sense of sight a more reliable source of information than that of hearing, although the idea that eyewitness accounts were always true appears to be his own.[2] Most modern historians have argued that Isidore's viewpoint on eyewitnesses was universally accepted in the Middle Ages. Bernard Guenée claims that firsthand testimonies "remained certain."[3] Jeanette Beer has asserted that, from Isidore on, "the eye-witnessing of events was the best source and the best guarantee of historical truth."[4] Peter Damian-Grint concurs: "an extraordinarily high degree of authority was accorded to eyewitness accounts in the historiographical tradition of the middle ages."[5] Finally, Peter Ainsworth has affirmed that at the time of Jean Froissart, in the fourteenth century, firsthand testimony "still was deemed entirely dependable."[6]

The only possible qualification for the reliability of eyewitnesses was their sound reputation. Guenée has argued that in the case of contradictions between firsthand narratives of events, chroniclers decided on the best one by comparing not the credibility of accounts but the authority of those who conveyed them.[7]

Isidore of Seville would have approved of the fact that four of the chroniclers of the First Crusade had participated in the enterprise. Damian-Grint has noted the importance of these accounts for medieval historiography: "the early twelfth century had seen an upsurge of interest in eyewitness narratives (in Latin) of contemporary events. The role of the crusades in this interest should not be underestimated."[8] Ainsworth agreed: "the First and Second Crusades had a major impact upon the development, in Latin first of all, of eyewitness historiography."[9]

Few historians have remarked that the problem of eyewitnesses in the chronicles of the First Crusade is a complex one. Marcus Bull calls eyewitness accounts "a term so embedded in the crusade historian's lexicon that it tends to obscure how problematic it is on the basic level of what in fact is the nature of 'witness.'"[10] Indeed, complications are many. Most obviously, so-called eyewitness chroniclers did not always witness the events they wrote about. The author of the *Gesta Francorum*, for example, does not admit to having witnessed the miracle of the intervention of saints in the battle of Antioch but refers to the accounts of others. At the same time, some of those who did not participate in the First Crusade, and thus were not "eyewitness chroniclers," saw some of the events with their own eyes. For example, both Robert the Monk and Baldric of Bourgueil attended the Council of Clermont, which launched the First Crusade in 1095.

Yuval Noah Harari has addressed the problem of firsthand accounts of the First Crusade in the greatest detail, arguing that we should not consider all accounts written by eyewitnesses actual eyewitness accounts. According to Harari's narrow definition, the authors of such accounts had to demonstrate awareness of the significance of the fact that they had been both observers and participants. Harari also addresses some of the secondhand chroniclers, arguing that they "were not necessarily either interested or skillful in sifting eyewitness accounts from other sources." He explains this by the habit of relying on "imaginative inventions."[11] These conclusions presuppose that medieval chroniclers shared the goals of modern historians but had inferior techniques. Indeed, some chroniclers of the First Crusade demonstrate a casual attitude toward firsthand testimony. However, this attitude was not only fully conscious but was also an integral part of their understanding of history and how it should be recorded—an understanding that was very different from the modern one.

With few exceptions, such as that of Harari, modern historians seem to be largely in accord that in the Middle Ages firsthand testimony was infallible, or at least that it always carried more weight than secondhand narratives. This assumption is valid on a superficial level only. It is true that a claim of having seen the events with one's own eyes, or a reference to reliable and numerous eyewitnesses, boosted an account's credibility. At the same time, however, many medieval authors reveal a nagging suspicion that the senses were unreliable and that eyewitnesses could fall victim to deception or illusion. Even more significantly, many of them (especially secondhand chroniclers) shared a conviction that even when eyewitnesses reported events correctly, they did not necessarily understand their meaning. One of Guenée's proclaimed goals was to add nuance to the ingrained conviction that medieval writers of history lacked *esprit critique*.[12] It is possible to go a few steps further and argue that medieval chroniclers were largely free to alter or reject firsthand testimony if the logic of their narratives seemed to warrant it.

A key to understanding the role accorded to eyewitnesses in the chronicles of the First Crusade lies in the symbiotic relationship between theology and history in the Middle Ages. The source of this relationship is the mystery of the incarnation, revealingly represented by John Scotus Eriugena, writing in the ninth century, in terms of "an eagle descending from the summits of theology into the deep valley of history."[13] While most modern scholars view the problem of eyewitnesses in medieval chronicles as purely historiographical, it is intimately related to the concept of "witness" in theology. In the New Testament, the notion is of paramount significance, and the word μάρτυς and its derivatives occur there no fewer than 170 times. As Jean-Louis Chrétien has demonstrated, there are both literal and figurative interpretations of the concept of "witness."[14] On the one hand, apostles and others testify to having seen Jesus, both before and after the Resurrection. In Acts, for example, Peter asserts, "And we are witnesses of all that he did. . . . God raised him on the third day and made him to appear, not to all people but to us who had been chosen by God as witnesses, who ate and drank with him after he rose from the dead" (Acts 10:39–41). On the other hand, on numerous occasions the New Testament minimizes the importance of firsthand observation. In the Gospel of John, Jesus tells his disciples, "When the Spirit of truth comes, he will guide you into all the truth" (John 16:13). Saint Augustine explained this passage to mean that the apostles testified not only (and not even primarily) because they had known Jesus during his lifetime but because the Holy Spirit revealed the truth to them.[15] It logically follows that all those who came after the apostles could testify with equal merit if the Holy Spirit guided them "into all the truth." Søren Kierkegaard clearly explained this exceptional characteristic of Christian perspective on witnessing: "There is not and cannot be any question of a follower at second hand, for the believer (and only he, after all, is a follower) continually has the *autopsy* of faith; he does not see with the eyes of others and sees only the same as every believer sees—with the eyes of faith."[16] The theological notion of witness had a significant impact on medieval historical writing. This particular point of convergence between theology and history is one of the most original (and one of the least appreciated) innovations of medieval chronicles.

The problem of eyewitnesses came to the fore in the chronicles of the First Crusade with the discovery of the holy lance.[17] Although many details of this discovery are unclear, the sources generally agree that while the army of Kerbogha besieged crusading troops in Antioch in June 1098, Peter Bartholomew, a low-ranking crusader from Provence, reported a vision in which he learned of the whereabouts of the lance. Extensive digging led to its unearthing, at which Raymond of Aguilers, one of the staunchest supporters of the authenticity of the lance, was present. He described the moment of discovery: "Finally, prompted by His gracious compassion, the Lord showed us His Lance and I, Raymond, author of this book, kissed the point of the Lance as it barely protruded from the ground."[18]

Not everybody was convinced that Peter Bartholomew's find was the holy lance, and a vocal minority contended that it was a hoax. Writing two decades after the fact, Ralph of Caen went into the most detail when he described the moment of the supposed discovery:

> They dug. But nothing appeared. For the upturned earth could not return what had never been placed in or accepted by it. But Peter had secreted the iron point from an Arab spear that he had found by chance. He had picked it up as the means of carrying out his trickery. It was rough, worn, old, and dissimilar in form and size to what we use. He felt that because of the novel shape of the spearhead, people would believe his story. Peter therefore seized the moment for his deception. Picking up a hoe, he jumped into the ditch and turned towards a corner. While digging he said, "here it is, here lies that for which we have been searching. . . ." Then, adding more and more blows, he struck the lance which he had fraudulently placed in the ditch. The trickery was aided by the shadow, the shadow by the crowd of people, and the crowd by the narrowness of the place.[19]

Ralph created an extensive argument against the authenticity of the lance, putting it into the mouth of Bohemond. Bohemond questioned the reputation of Peter Bartholomew, whom he accused of immoral behavior, and found it suspicious that the visionary himself, and not the others involved in the digging, found the relic. He expressed doubt that the real holy lance could have made its way to Antioch from Jerusalem, the place of the Crucifixion, since Longinus was in the service of Pontius Pilate, who had never visited Antioch. Finally, he argued that the lance in question was not Roman but Arabic.[20] In short, according to Ralph, a thorough investigation, based on common sense and historical knowledge, was sufficient to invalidate eyewitness testimony.

Using Bohemond as his mouthpiece, Ralph explained why he paid so much attention to the matter: "Because the Provençals ascribe 'our' victory, which is from above, like light from the Father, to their piece of iron."[21] The Provençals, led by Raymond of Toulouse, used the lance to try to establish their primacy among the crusaders, something the Norman Ralph found highly objectionable. However, it is also possible to examine the passage from a different perspective. Throughout the *Gesta Tancredi*, Ralph was sparing in his references to supernatural occurrences, so that, for example, he omitted any mention of the putative intervention of celestial troops at the battle of Antioch. Instead, Ralph believed that God helped crusaders by diverting the eastern wind that was blowing smoke into their eyes.[22] According to Ralph, the success of the First Crusade came "from above," but not from any prodigies that would conflict with the laws of nature. One reason for Ralph's rejection of eyewitness testimony with respect to both miracles seems to be that it clashed with his overall vision of the enterprise.

Both Raymond and Ralph developed their respective positions on the lance in their report of Peter Bartholomew's ordeal by fire in April 1099, in consequence of which he died. According to Raymond, the main reason for the ordeal was distrust of firsthand testimony. He cited Peter, who said before the trial, "I offer to do this because I see that no one believes in revelations or witnesses" (*Video enim quia nec signis nec testibus creditur*).[23] By recording Peter's complaint, Raymond revealed his awareness that some of his contemporaries did not consider firsthand testimony infallible. Still, he authenticated his account of the trial almost exclusively via references to eyewitnesses. As in his report of the discovery of the lance, Raymond professed that he took an active part in the ceremonies surrounding the ordeal: "As the fire was started and flames shot into the air, I, Raymond, in the presence of the crowd declared: 'If Omnipotent God talked to this man in person ... let him walk through the fire unharmed; but if this is a lie, let Peter Bartholomew and the Lance he carried be consumed by fire.'"[24] Raymond named three other eyewitnesses—Ebrard, a priest, Guillelmus Bonofilius, "a respectable and excellent knight of Arles," and Guillelmus Malus Puer, "a respected knight from Béziers"—who saw ancillary miracles accompanying the ordeal. These miracles included a bird plunging into the flames and a man "dressed in priestly garments" walking into the flames before Peter Bartholomew.[25] Raymond acknowledged that not all of those present had seen these miracles, explaining that "in the huge crowd many things were not seen."[26] Although Raymond conceded that being present did not necessarily mean being able to see, he asserted that the evidence he presented was enough, and that three witnesses were "sufficient for all judgments."[27] According to Raymond, Peter Bartholomew suffered only minor burns but died because the crowd of onlookers, upon seeing him emerge from the fire unharmed, rushed upon him and accidentally broke his backbone. Raymond also discussed several visions that demonstrated that the doubters of the miracle risked punishment both in this life and in the next.[28] One of these visions revealed that Adhémar of Le Puy had to spend some time in hell as a punishment for his initial misgivings about the lance.[29] Mistrust of "witnesses and revelations" was not merely inapposite but actually sinful.

Ralph of Caen had a very different vision of the trial; in contrast to Raymond, he claimed that Peter's burns were fatal: he "fell burned ... and died on the following day." He averred that the vast majority of eyewitnesses agreed on the outcome. "The people," he wrote, "upon seeing what was done, confessed that they had been deceived by his wordy guile, were sorry that they had erred, and testified that Peter was a disciple of Simon, the magician." According to Ralph, only those profiting from the hoax, such as Count Raymond, obstinately persisted in their veneration of the relic.[30]

Fulcher of Chartres shared Ralph's opinion regarding the lance. According to Fulcher, Adhémar thought that the lance was a forgery from the start, and the ordeal proved the skeptics right: "they saw that he [Peter Bartholomew] was guilty, for his skin was burned and they knew that within he was mortally hurt." The majority of the observers of the trial agreed; "since everyone had venerated the lance for the honor and love of God, when the ordeal was over those who formerly believed in it were now incredulous and very sad." Count Raymond was one exception to the general consensus, preserving the relic "for a long time afterward."[31]

In emphasizing Raymond's obstinacy, Ralph and Fulcher reveal that the controversy continued long after the trial of Peter Bartholomew. Similarly, albeit without referring specifically to the relic, Raymond of Aguilers claimed in the introduction to his chronicle that his goal was to dispute alternative narratives of the First Crusade: "This task, [I have] chiefly undertaken because misfits of war and cowardly deserters have since tried to spread lies rather than truth."[32] It is more than probable that, from Raymond's perspective, some of the "lies" concerned the holy lance. An anonymous scribe who bound several chronicles under one cover in the mid-twelfth century realized that Fulcher and Raymond had disagreed on the authenticity of the relic. He decided to side with Raymond, adding the following title to the chapter about the discovery of the relic in Fulcher's chronicle: "Where the Lance was found, about which Raymond's book speaks better and more truthfully than does Fulcher's."[33]

Although a number of authors acknowledged the differing opinions concerning the relic, Guibert of Nogent was the only one to argue explicitly against the side he opposed. Guibert was a supporter of the authenticity of the lance, and he built an extensive case against the skeptics, such as Fulcher, to whom Guibert referred by name. First, Guibert evoked "recent testimonies" of eyewitnesses and stressed that Fulcher, in contrast, was not present at Antioch: "Will the cleverness of the priest Fulcher, who, while our men were suffering from starvation at Antioch, was feasting at ease in Edessa, prevail over the inspired work of the wise men who died at the time that it was found?"[34]

In this case, Guibert used the traditional argument that firsthand testimony was intrinsically more reliable than any other supposed evidence. He supported it by claiming that not only was Fulcher absent during the discovery of the lance but also, "feasting at ease," he did not partake in the salvific suffering of crusaders. Thus, according to Guibert, Fulcher was neither a witness nor an authority. In fact, Guibert described him as similar to the Israelites, whose wars, even when they were just or even holy, still lacked a spiritual dimension. While Fulcher argued that Adhémar of Le Puy had been suspicious of the lance from the beginning, Guibert claimed that he had in fact accepted its authenticity. "Was the worthy Bishop of Puy so foolish," Guibert asked, "as to have carried a lance of questionable authenticity with such reverence when he went out to fight Kherboga?" Raymond and Guibert were of the same opinion that Peter Bartholomew had discovered the genuine holy lance, and they both observed that the relic had accompanied Adhémar of

Le Puy as he rode into battle. However, while they agreed on the basic sequence of events, they differed on how to buttress the veracity of their accounts, disagreeing on the relative importance that they accorded to eyewitnesses as opposed to an authoritative observer. Raymond based his narrative squarely on firsthand testimony, and made Adhémar's initial doubts and final approval of the lance largely irrelevant by arguing that the legate's judgments were not impeccable. Guibert, by contrast, made no reference to Adhémar's doubts but claimed that the acceptance of the relic as authentic by such an authoritative figure should be sufficient to allow others to follow suit. For Raymond, eyewitness testimony was key; for Guibert, Adhémar's judgment was more important.

In addition to emphasizing Adhémar's reverence for the lance, Guibert felt obliged to evoke written evidence in support of his position, arguing that "the most pious ancient writers" described the lance being venerated at Antioch before the Turkish invasion. Like Ralph, who traced the history of the lance back to the time of Pontius Pilate, Guibert connected the discovery of the relic to earlier events. However, whereas Ralph wrote that the lance was unlikely to have made its way from Jerusalem to Antioch, Guibert alleged that, according to "ancient writers" (whom he did not name), it had. For him, the discovery of the lance completed a story arc. Christians worshipped the relic before the Turkish invasion, and they began worshipping it again after the First Crusade. The crusade became the opposite of the invasion, restoring the normal order of things after a disruption.[35]

For Ralph and especially for Guibert, firsthand testimony became one type of evidence among others. One had to evaluate it in the context of other facts, or if it presented too many difficulties, one could simply shrug it off. Guibert refused to interpret the outcome of the ordeal of Peter Bartholomew. "No one is certain whether he was harmed by the flames," he wrote, and he compared the ordeal to an inexplicable event described in the *Dialogues* of Gregory the Great.[36] There is little doubt that Guibert was aware of different interpretations of Peter's demise, but he refused to discuss them at any length, indicating instead that he considered the entire matter of minor significance. For Guibert, inscribing the lance in the unfolding of sacred history was largely independent of the figure of Peter or the details of his ordeal. The discernment of a larger picture trumped witnessing specific events.

In another context, Guibert offered a different example of the limited value of eyewitness testimony. In a digression on his own experience, Guibert described eyewitnesses misinterpreting a natural phenomenon: "I swear by God that I saw, when I was living in Beauvais, in the middle of the day, clouds approach each other somewhat obliquely, so that they scarcely seemed to form anything other than the shape of a crane or a stork, when suddenly many voices from everywhere in the city cried out that a cross had been seen to them in the sky."[37] In this case, eyewitnesses who were numerous and who came up to the same conclusion independently from each other (the voices came from "everywhere in the city") were wrong, and there was no cross in the sky.

Several paragraphs later, describing an event in the Holy Land, Guibert recounted another occurrence: "a brilliant red light, like a fire, shone in the night above the army, and it also unmistakably took the form of a cross. Some of the wise men there related the fire to future battles, and said that the appearance of a cross was a sign of certain salvation and victory to come. We do not call this an error, for many witnesses confirm this testimony."[38] In this case, eyewitnesses were right; a cross had actually appeared in the sky. It is possible that in putting the two examples relatively close together in his text, Guibert invited the reader to juxtapose them. After all, the basic scenario, with numerous eyewitnesses observing a cross appearing in the sky, is the same. Apparent similarities, however, mask profound differences. In the first case, there was merely a cloud, while in the second there was something of a more unusual nature, a "brilliant red light, like a fire" shining in the night. In the first case, a cloud taking fanciful shapes could support different interpretations (a crane, a stork, a cross), while in the second case only one interpretation was possible ("unmistakably" a cross). The most important difference, however, is the reference to "wise men" in the second case. These "wise men" argued that the cross predicted future events (victorious battles), which did in fact take place with the capture of Antioch and Jerusalem. Guibert did not mention any prophetic meaning that could be attached to the cross seen by people of Beauvais.

In these two passages, Guibert represented the roles of eyewitnesses and interpreters as complementary. Although eyewitnesses were the unavoidable source of information, they could "lie," being misled by their visual experience. In addition, most of them were also incapable of going beyond observed reality. "Wise men" (among whom Guibert must have counted himself), in contrast, were unlikely to be carried away by general enthusiasm or duped by optical illusions. In addition, they were capable of interpreting the data conveyed by the senses with the help of their rational faculties. In juxtaposing the two "signs," one bogus and the other genuine, Guibert subtly subverted the status of eyewitnesses as the source of truth and thereby shifted the center of gravity toward the role of an interpreter.[39]

While Guibert described Christians succumbing to an optical illusion, two other chroniclers of the crusades represented self-deception as one of the weapons that God used against "infidels." Walter the Chancellor gave a revealing example. In describing the battle of Tall Danith, fought in 1115, Walter argued that the crusaders' victory was largely due to the delusions of "infidels": "At once the prince's banners came into view, and by God's guidance they were seen by Persians spread out in such a way that they believed from the banners that the very land was clothed all around with white-clad knights."[40]

Fulcher of Chartres related a similar story about the Turks, who, during the battle of Ascalon, fought on August 12, 1099, decided that the number of crusading troops was significantly greater than it really was. "One day," according to Fulcher, "when the Franks were scouring around Ascalon and awaiting battle they discovered considerable booty in oxen, camels, sheep, and goats. When our men had gathered these beasts near their tents at the end of day, our leaders decreed by strict proclamation that the men should not drive their quarry with them on the morrow, when battle was expected." Although the proclamation was obeyed, the animals refused to stay behind: "You might have seen the animals mentioned above advancing of their own will to the right and left of our formation as if by command; yet they were driven by no one. In this way many of the pagans, at a distance seeing the animals proceeding with our soldiers, concluded that the whole array was the army of the Franks."[41] Fulcher does not make clear what effect this vision had on the Turks or what role it played in their eventual defeat.

When he rewrote Fulcher's account, William of Malmesbury added no factual information. However, he transformed Fulcher's narrative, which merely hinted at a miracle, into an account that proclaimed and celebrated it, and he placed the Turks' delusion at the center of their defeat: "So when morning came, and the army advanced, you would have seen the cattle, as though by some heaven-sent instinct, walking alongside the knights with their horns held high, and refusing to be driven off by any use of force. When the enemy saw this from a distance, with their eyes dazzled by the rays of the sun, they lost heart before the battle began, thinking their adversaries were without number."[42]

Raymond of Aguilers recounted the same episode. Unlike Fulcher, he did not hesitate to argue that the behavior of the animals was a deciding factor in the crusaders' victory: "We moved forward in nine ranks ... and God multiplied his army to the point that we seemed to equal the Arab forces. This miracle came when the animals we had freed formed herds, and without a directing hand followed us, stood when we stood, ran when we ran, and marched forward when we marched forward."[43] Raymond then proceeded to recount the booty the crusaders seized from the enemy.

In both cases—at Ascalon and Tall Danith—divine intervention influenced natural agents in order to mislead the "infidels." Although the Turks were deceived by their visual experience, however, they were not entirely wrong. From the chroniclers' point of view, crusading armies, helped by God, were indeed greater than they seemed to be. This further emphasized the importance of the invisible reality beyond the visible one.

In another example, drawn from further afield, "infidels" demonstrated a correct understanding of the basic course of events but a faulty interpretation. An anonymous author of a chronicle of the Third Crusade titled *Itinerarium Peregrinorum et Gesta Regis Ricardi* extols the valor of a Templar, Jakelin de Mailly, killed in the battle of the Spring of Cresson on May 1, 1187. When the "infidels" finally overcame the knight, they rejoiced because they thought they had killed Saint George: "Death is sweet when the victor lies encircled by the impious people he has slain with his victorious right hand. And because it so happened that the warrior had been riding a white horse and had white armor and weapons, the gentiles, who knew that St George had this appearance in battle, boasted that they had killed the Knight of Shining Armor, the protector of the Christians."[44]

Confused by the physical resemblance between Jakelin de Mailly and Saint George, the "gentiles" made a mistaken interpretation of their empirical experience. Once again, however, their vision of events, erroneous to the point of being ridiculous, contained a grain of truth. While the "gentiles" were wrong in thinking that they had killed Saint George, they were right that he often helped crusaders on the battlefield. Their ignorance made their testimony that much more credible. Unaware of even such a rudimentary notion that a saint, already martyred once, could not be killed again, they were unlikely (in contrast to the residents of Beauvais in Guibert's chronicle) to invent a miracle.[45] While eyewitnesses' interpretation of their immediate experience could be wrong, others—such as a Christian author and reader of the chronicle, who would be aware of the reality beyond the visible world—could use it in order to understand some of the mechanisms of divine intervention in human affairs. In this case, eyewitnesses served as oblivious transmitters of knowledge to be used by secondhand interpreters.

In light of these examples, it is beyond any doubt that not everyone was immediately convinced upon reading the declaration of the anonymous *Gesta Francorum* about celestial troops intervening in the battle of Antioch: "This is quite true, for many of our men saw it."[46] This supposition is supported by the fact that a number of chroniclers who rewrote the *Gesta* either significantly changed the narrative of the miracle or added a few sentences to shore up its credibility. Baldric of Bourgueil, for instance, preempted the question of why only some observers saw the saints when he wrote that it was God's decision to whom to reveal the miracle. Baldric also emphasized that he did not make up the story, that he recorded what he had heard from returning crusaders and that the resulting account was "true."[47]

Guibert of Nogent expanded the original statement found in the *Gesta* to read, "These things were seen by many of our men, and when they told what they had seen to others, their words were taken in good faith as true." With this seemingly minor addition, Guibert shifted the burden of proof from eyewitnesses to "others," a body of listeners, presumably himself included, who could decide the veracity of firsthand narratives. In his account of the miracle, Guibert deviated from the *Gesta Francorum* on another important point. According to the author of the *Gesta*, crusaders recognized the saints in the heat of the battle. Guibert offered a different version of events. "After the battle," he wrote, "they [crusaders] thought that these glorious leaders were, in particular, the martyrs George, Mercurius, and Demetrius."[48] That is, in his view, participants in the battle did not immediately identify these particular three saints but decided that they had seen them only retrospectively. Once again, Guibert shifted the emphasis from raw experience to post factum interpretation.

Similarly, William of Malmesbury gave an original slant to the story of the intervention of saints at the battle of Antioch. He deviated significantly from his main source, Fulcher's *Historia Hierosolymitana*, and came closer to the *Gesta Francorum*: "They [crusaders] were convinced that they saw those ancient martyrs who had been knights in their own day, and who by their deaths had purchased the crown of life, St George and St Demetrius, with flying banners come charging from the hill-country, showering missiles on the enemy, and aid upon themselves."[49] In comparison to the *Gesta Francorum*, William replaced the categorical "they saw" (*viderunt*) with the more indecisive "they were convinced that they saw" (*persuadebantque sibi videre*). Jean-Claude Schmitt has made the same observation about medieval accounts of appearances of *revenants,* or ghosts, where such ambiguous expressions as "he seems to have seen" (*visum est sibi* or *videtur sibi videre*) appear much more frequently than the active "he saw" (*vidit*). According to Schmitt, a preference for the former type of phrasing denotes doubt about the ontological status of the object observed.[50] After introducing a trace of doubt into his account, William argued that the miracle was credible because it had biblical precedents: "nor can we deny that martyrs have aided Christians, at any rate when fighting in a cause like this, just as angels once gave help to the Maccabees."[51] According to Guibert and William, the *Gesta Francorum*'s declaration that "many" saw a miracle was no longer sufficient to establish the truth. A knowledgeable interpreter, who, for example, would be familiar with the second book of the Maccabees, was needed to demonstrate that a miracle was plausible.

Several chroniclers claimed that the Turks also saw the saints. For example, Baldric of Bourgueil wrote, "Many Christians saw them, and so, it is thought, did many gentiles."[52] This authenticated the miracle, since the ignorance of the "gentiles" made them incapable of inventing it and since, even if they were capable, it was not in their interest to do so. Robert the Monk, who rewrote the anonymous *Gesta Francorum,* however, was unique in depicting one Turk, Pirrus, as the main eyewitness. Robert discussed at length the friendship conceived between Pirrus and Bohemond while the crusaders were besieging Antioch. During one of their meetings, Pirrus told his Christian interlocutor about an unusual contingent of knights riding white horses, wearing white armor, and carrying white shields and banners. After describing their ravaging of the Turks in battle, Pirrus begged Bohemond, by his "faith in Jesus," to tell him the location of their camp. "Inspired by the Holy Spirit," Bohemond realized, Pirrus had witnessed the intervention of a celestial army. With this perfunctory mention of the Holy Spirit, Robert referred to the scriptural tradition, discussed above, of arguing that true knowledge comes not from firsthand observation but from above. Bohemond told Pirrus that the troops descended directly from the sky, as they were made up of those who "suffered martyrdom for the faith of Christ and fought against unbelievers across the earth." Robert, however, reveals the limitations of Bohemond's interpretation by making Pirrus dumbfound him with a question concerning the material side of the intervention of the saints, namely, the source of so many white horses, shields, and standards. Bohemond, stumped, answers that these things are "beyond his understanding" and calls on his chaplain for help. The chaplain explains the miracle to Pirrus from a different perspective: "When the all-powerful Creator decides to send his angels or the spirits of the righteous to earth, they assume the bodies of air so that they can appear to us, because they cannot be seen in their essential spiritual form." The chaplain introduces greater sophistication to the discussion, abandoning Bohemond's military vocabulary and introducing God as the fundamental cause of the miracle. His interpretation satisfies Pirrus, who replies, "You describe wonderful and credible things stemming from him whom you say is the Creator, things which we had never heard of before."[53]

It seems that Robert deliberately juxtaposed three interpretations of the miracle: those of an "infidel," a Christian knight, and a priest. Despite the fact that Pirrus was the only one of the three to have witnessed the miracle, his grasp of the event was the least complete. Robert demonstrated that the Turk was not conscious of any reality beyond the physical appearance of the miracle, whereas Bohemond, albeit inspired by the Holy Spirit, understood only the basics of the transcendent; only the chaplain was capable of providing an exhaustive interpretation within the broader theological context. Robert's implicit claim seems to be that the majority of eyewitnesses, "infidels" and Christians alike, were capable of only partial understanding of the mechanisms of divine intervention in human affairs. Only the better educated members of the clergy, regardless of whether they were firsthand observers, were capable of presenting the miracle as not merely "marvelous" but also "credible." It is possible that Robert saw a parallel between Bohemond's chaplain, interpreting Pirrus's account, and himself, rewriting a chronicle of the First Crusade. Pirrus and the author of the *Gesta* (who actually saw the events) provided raw details, while the chaplain and Robert (who only heard or read about them) interpreted them and explained them to others, including the eyewitnesses themselves.

In this episode, Robert clearly separated the role of a truthful but guileless eyewitness from that of a knowledgeable interpreter. However, in developing the account of the same miracle, he suggested a symbiotic relationship between the two. In his description of the battle of Antioch, Robert allotted a particularly important role to Adhémar of Le Puy. He wrote that the bishop was the first to see a "legion of saints" and to announce the news to his fellows.[54]

Henry of Huntington went a step further than Robert, implying that clergymen and monks were the *only* witnesses of the intervention of saints in the battle of Antioch: "The bishops, priests, clerks, and monks, dressed in sacred vestments, chanted hymns to God upon the city walls. Thus they saw the heavenly army, with white horses and sun-gleaming arms, whose leaders were George, Mercurius, and Demetrius."[55] Henry did not specify whether lay crusaders also witnessed the miracle, possibly because he considered this detail of secondary importance. Clergymen's participation in the regular miracle of the Eucharist, their role as intermediaries between this world and the next, and their traditional responsibility of authenticating and explaining miracles made it implausible that they would give an incorrect interpretation of their empirical experience. According to Robert and Henry, clergymen made particularly good eyewitnesses because they were trustworthy and well-versed interpreters.

The Narratives of the two greatest miracles that occurred during the First Crusade, the *inventio* of the holy lance and the intervention of celestial troops in the battle of Antioch, give indirect evidence that medieval writers of history reflected on the problem of eyewitnesses. In addition, some sources contain explicit discussion of the subject. Fulcher of Chartres and Raymond of Aguilers emphatically stressed their individual role, so that asides involving "ego Fulcherus" or "ego Raimundus" appear in both texts.[56] Thus Fulcher wrote at the beginning of his work, "I, Fulcher of Chartres, who went with the other pilgrims, afterwards diligently and carefully collected all this in my memory for the sake of posterity, just as I saw it with my own eyes." On another occasion, Fulcher emphasized that the testimony of eyewitnesses could involve senses other than sight. Describing the waters of the Dead Sea, he wrote, "It is so salty that no beast or bird of any kind whatsoever can drink from it. This I, Fulcher, learned by experience when I dismounted from my mule into the water and took a drink with my hand, testing it by the taste and finding it to be more bitter than hellebore." According to Fulcher, an eyewitness not merely saw but also experienced the reality that he reported. Most important, the chronicler stressed that he shared in the suffering of the crusaders: "I saw many people who had no tents die from chills from the rains. I, Fulcher of Chartres, who was with them, saw many persons of both sexes and a great many beasts die one day because of these freezing rains."[57] Similarly, Walter the Chancellor indicated that personal experience of hardship was one of his credentials as a chronicler: "I myself, Walter the Chancellor, having experienced both sorts of fortune and knowing therefore that prosperity of the flesh is more harmful for the soul than adversity to the body, have taken pains to describe that part of the second war as it gave way to contrary fortune."⁵⁸ Walter does not specify the "adversities" he endured, but modern historians have argued that he refers to his having been taken prisoner in the disastrous battle of the Blood, in which Roger of Antioch was killed.⁵⁹

Other chroniclers stressed their close connection to miracles. Raymond of Aguilers claimed to have carried the newly discovered lance during the battle of Antioch and to have witnessed that, miraculously, no one in his vicinity was killed, wounded, or even shot at by arrows.⁶⁰ Peter Tudebode called attention to his participation in a ceremony of penitence during which a different miracle occurred. He described a procession of crusaders around the walls of Jerusalem during the siege of the city and the sudden death of a cleric upon entering the church of the Virgin. The chronicler interpreted this event as a sign of divine favor to the cleric, whose soul would "dwell with Christ through eternity," and, by synecdoche, to crusading troops at large. He concluded his report with the following self-reference: "This was believed by him who first wrote this, since he was in the procession and saw it with his worldly eyes—namely, Peter Tudebode."⁶¹ By emphasizing their participation in crusaders' suffering and their connection to miracles, eyewitness chroniclers claimed to have taken an active part not merely in a military campaign but in a salvific exercise ordained by God.

Chroniclers who had not participated in the crusades were aware of their considerable disadvantage in comparison to eyewitnesses, and some expressed doubts about their ability to narrate the events adequately. William of Malmesbury wrote in his account of the First Crusade, "Let no man who enjoys fuller knowledge of the facts upbraid me with lack of pains, for in our distant lair beyond the British Ocean, scarcely a rumor comes to enlighten our ignorance of events in Asia."⁶² To some extent, this was a demonstration of the virtue of humility, more or less obligatory for any medieval chronicler. However, the decision to demonstrate humility in this particular fashion is significant. Orderic Vitalis similarly spoke of his inability to discuss events that had occurred in a faraway land, affirming that he would relate only the events that he had seen or that happened in the vicinity of his monastery: "For although I cannot explore Macedonian or Greek or Roman affairs and many other matters worthy of telling, because as a cloister monk by my own free choice I am compelled to unremitting observance of my monastic duty, nevertheless I can strive with the help of God and for the consideration of posterity to explain truthfully and straightforwardly the things which I have seen in our own times, or know to have occurred in nearby provinces."⁶³

Revealingly, however, Orderic did not keep his promise; he included an extensive narrative of the First Crusade in his chronicle. Finally, in his *Liber quo ordine sermo fieri debeat*, composed in the 1080s, Guibert of Nogent wrote that an account by a participant in battle had infinitely more value than that of someone who had merely listened to others talk about battles: "Any idle person who has never engaged in military exercises can say several things about battle, if he has seen warriors or heard talk of battle, but how differently does someone who has fought and who has been fought against in battle, who has undertaken military affairs and who has suffered because of military affairs, how differently does he recall battle?"[64]

Guibert's early statement pays tribute to the hierarchy according to which witnessing events ranked above hearing about them. Yet in the first decade of the twelfth century, Guibert and his peers, eager to show that their chronicles had as much value as those written by eyewitnesses, began to question and subvert the time-honored convention. In his chronicle of the First Crusade, Guibert wrote, "If anyone objects that I did not see, he cannot object on the grounds that I did not hear, because I believe that, in a way, hearing is almost as good as seeing."[65] The same desire to undercut the traditional view of seeing versus hearing is evident in the writings of Baldric of Bourgueil. Baldric admitted outright that he was not a crusader. "I was not worthy to be among that blessed knighthood," he wrote, "and I have not told of what I have seen."[66] He argued, however, that he had invented nothing but had only supplemented the *Gesta Francorum* with what he had heard from those returning from the Holy Land.[67]

Both Guibert and Baldric argued that an eyewitness's oral account became no less truthful when written down by someone else. Guibert offered further support for this conclusion. Jacques Fontaine has argued that Isidore of Seville derived his statement about eyewitnesses, quoted at the beginning of this chapter, at least in part from a statement in the Gospel of John: "He who saw it has borne witness—his testimony is true, and he knows that he is telling the truth—that you also may believe" (John 19:35).[68] Guibert, in contrast, referred to a series of biblical passages that put seeing and hearing on an equal footing. He wrote in an introduction to book IV of his chronicle, "who doubts those historians who wrote the lives of the saints, who wrote down not only what they saw with their own eyes, but what they drunk up from what others have understood and told them? For if the narrator is reliable and, as one reads, 'testifies to what he saw and heard,' then stories told by those who speak the truth about events no one has seen are clearly acceptable as true."69 Guibert's reference here to hagiographical writing is hardly accidental. For him, the First Crusade was at once a military campaign and a spiritual quest. While those who took part in the First Crusade were in the best position to describe its military facet, they were not necessarily more competent to write about its spiritual import, which transcended the boundaries of the visible world.

Secondhand chroniclers further undermined the prestige of eyewitness reports by emphasizing that even the best accounts were incomplete. As mentioned above, Guibert belabored the point that Fulcher's participation in the First Crusade was limited and that, technically, he was an eyewitness only of its earliest phase. Robert the Monk justified his decision to write his chronicle by arguing that the anonymous *Gesta Francorum* was deficient, in that it did not mention the Council of Clermont. Robert, as a participant in that council, was in a perfect position to fill the gap. He wrote that his superior, Abbot Bernard, instructed him "to add the beginning which was missing."70 Orderic Vitalis admitted that he based his account of the First Crusade on Baldric's chronicle but claimed also to have included stories he heard from returning crusaders: "I have added a few things not mentioned by him, for the benefit of posterity, truthfully, just as I learned them from men who took part in these toils and dangers."71 Other chroniclers emphasized in more general terms that omniscience was impossible.72 Guibert made this case with particular vigor. "We do not think it possible," he wrote, "for anyone to tell what happened at the siege of Antioch, because, among those who were there, no one can be found who could have seen everything that happened everywhere in the city, or who could have understood it entirely in the order in which it happened."73 Both "eyewitness" and secondhand chroniclers agreed that participants in an event possessed only a partial knowledge of what they were describing.

Eyewitnesses' knowledge of events was incomplete from another perspective as well. While Guibert acknowledged that chroniclers after the fact were more likely to make mistakes than those who had been there, he declared that all writers of history shared the same problem of deducing the motivations behind actions. "How can it be surprising if we make errors," he asked, "when we are describing things done in a foreign land, when we are clearly unable not only to express in words our own thoughts and actions, but even to collect them in the silence of our own minds? What can I say then about intentions, which are so hidden most of the time that they can scarcely be discerned by the acuity of the inner man?"74 Guibert adroitly shifted the reader's attention from the visible reality ("things done in a foreign land") to the invisible one (the "silence of our own minds" and the "intentions" that even "the inner man" had trouble determining). His chronicle makes clear that he considered his essential task the exploration of such intentions. As Jay Rubenstein has argued convincingly, the major subject of Guibert's *Dei gesta per Francos* is the crusaders' quest for spiritual improvement and self-knowledge. Rubenstein demonstrates that Guibert relied in his chronicle on the Old Testament and brought to the subject the skills of a moralist that he had honed in his commentaries on the book of Genesis.[75] Guibert paid greater attention than any other author to the spiritual transformation of crusaders and went further than the rest in using the scriptures to explain the enterprise. In this context, Guibert's evocation of the "inner man" can be read as an attempt to minimize the importance of actions. Guibert lamented that he had not taken part in the crusade, but he implied that this did not matter.

Most of the time, the chroniclers' defense of the legitimacy of their work against claims that it was derivative or unreliable was implicit rather than explicit. However, the three monastic writers, Guibert, Robert, and Baldric, apparently independently of one another, complained that the anonymous *Gesta Francorum* was badly written.[76] Robert the Monk argued that the chronicle "did not make the best of the sequence of wonderful events it contained and the composition was uncertain in its style and expression."[77] Baldric was also deeply disparaging, writing, "I do not know which anonymous author had published a little book on this affair which was very crude. He contrived to tell the truth, but because of the uncouthness of his writing he cheapened a noble subject and the inelegant and artless language turned the more guileless away from it at once." Baldric presented his work as a revision of the *Gesta Francorum* that would please Christian readers of the future by preserving the events for posterity more surely and effectively.[78]

While Baldric feared that the *Gesta Francorum* might displease the "guileless," Guibert, taking exactly the opposite position, wrote that he was afraid that it would displease the more sophisticated: "A version of this same history, but woven out of excessively simple words, often violating grammatical rules, exists, and it may often bore the reader with the stale, flat quality of its language. It works well enough for the less learned, who are not interested in the quality of the diction, but only in the novelty of the story, nor is it the case that the author should have spoken in a way that they do not understand."[79]

Although the three chroniclers claimed that they were dissatisfied with the style of the *Gesta Francorum*, it seems that their goal was more ambitious than merely to write with greater care. In improving the style of the *Gesta*, the chroniclers made a statement about the First Crusade. "The style of writers should fit the status of the events," Guibert wrote; "martial deeds should be told with harsh words; what pertains to divine matters must be brought along at a more controlled pace."[80] The author of the *Gesta Francorum* used "harsh words" to convey the harsh reality of the First Crusade, which he had observed with the eyes of the flesh. In this way, he depicted the crusade as merely a "martial deed." Guibert, by contrast, told the story of the First Crusade in a more elevated style, "at a more controlled pace," as he envisioned it with the eyes of the spirit. He could thus portray the crusade as a "divine matter." Just as there were two ways to perceive reality, there were two corresponding styles of writing about it.

In the conclusion to his chronicle, Guibert laid out a coherent and assertive defense of his undertaking. He began by reporting that in the early stages of the siege of Jerusalem, a certain anchorite had a vision that the city would be taken on Easter, at the very hour when Christ was crucified. Guibert then turned again to the problem of eyewitnesses: "For the rest, if anyone thinks that we have not laid things out as diligently as Julius Caesar and Hirtius Pansa did in the history of the Gauls, Spaniards, Pharsalians, Alexandrians, and Numidians, he should carefully consider the fact that the same people who waged the wars wrote them down. As a result, nothing general or particular that happened is omitted from their accounts."

Guibert admitted that he, unlike Caesar and Pansa, was not capable of giving detailed information about the battles of the First Crusade:

> They tell how many thousands of men there were, how many from each region, who the princes were, to whom power was delegated, who the leaders and princes were on the other side, what the cavalry, what the lightly armed troops did, how many shields were pierced by javelins, and, if I may use their own words, "after the consuls and their officers had sounded the retreat," how many men were missing and wounded at the end of the battle. Since another profession detains us who write this history, and our confidence is not strengthened by what we saw, we have decided, in reporting what we have heard, to exercise restraint.[81]

In an article on Guibert as a writer of history, Jacques Chaurand commented on this passage, "A vrai dire les précisions qu'il regrette de ne pouvoir nous fournir... n'auraient pas été pour nous d'un intérêt majeur."[82] It is true that the excluded information does sound rather unexciting, except to a military historian. It seems, however, that Guibert intended it to sound insipid in order to minimize the importance of the military aspects of the First Crusade. Once again, Guibert's expression of regret that he was not there seems intended, at the same time, to forestall criticism and to make an implicit argument that one need not have fought in the crusade to produce a valid account of the experience.

The placement of the story of the anchorite—just before the digression about the problem of eyewitnesses—supports this interpretation. Guibert appears to be juxtaposing two types of knowledge: that of a Christian visionary and that of a pagan eyewitness. The anchorite, a resident of Bethania, was absent at the capture of Jerusalem, but he knew about it even before it happened. Even more important, he could establish a direct connection between the capture of the city and Christ's Crucifixion, thereby proving that the First Crusade was divinely ordained. Eyewitnesses to the siege of Jerusalem could give a clearer picture of the unfolding of events, but the anchorite knew what was of real significance.

The interpolation between the story of the anchorite and the discussion of Caesar and Pansa shows Guibert inviting a comparison between the visionary from Bethania and himself. "We thank God," he wrote, "for having composed these deeds with his own spirit, through our mouth."[83] Like the anchorite, Guibert had a better understanding of the First Crusade than the crusaders themselves. Claiming divine inspiration for his work, Guibert emphasized that he was not a mere intermediary between eyewitnesses and subsequent readers. Rather, his role complemented that of the actual participants in the First Crusade. If God used crusaders' military capacities to take Antioch and Jerusalem, he relied on Guibert's abilities to record these events.

As noted above, in the New Testament, the Holy Spirit was the source of a particular type of knowledge that was otherwise unattainable. With his reference to "God's spirit" as the source of inspiration for his work, Guibert made the case for two parallel genealogies. In the first were prophets, apostles, the anchorite of Bethania, and the chronicler himself, to all of whom the Holy Spirit had granted superior knowledge. In the second were Caesar, Pansa, and the firsthand chroniclers of the First Crusade, who had all witnessed the events they were describing. There can be no doubt about which of the two groups, from Guibert's perspective, had a better understanding of history.

As Gabrielle Spiegel has demonstrated, for medieval thinkers history was of both greater and lesser consequence than it was for their Greek and Roman predecessors. It was more important because it contained clues about the reality beyond, and less important because this reality beyond was what truly mattered.[84] One's attitude toward eyewitnesses was at the center of this tension. The vast majority of writers of history agreed that mere observation of events did not suffice for their proper understanding and recording. Participants may have argued that eyewitness observation conferred a considerable advantage, but nonparticipants rejected this claim.

Most of the eyewitness chroniclers of the First Crusade contended that they had not merely seen the incidents they were describing but had taken an active part in purifying suffering and miraculous occurrences. Their physical contact with the transcendent allowed them not just to narrate events but also to explain divine intentions. Many of the secondhand chroniclers, more attuned to the theological concept of "witness," refused to allot as much significance to empirical experience. They strove to demonstrate that most eyewitnesses were incapable of going beyond the microcosm of visible reality to the macrocosm of providential history, and that this limitation made their narratives unreliable. Thus, in an original and daring move, several secondhand chroniclers of the First Crusade, confined in monasteries thousands of miles from the Holy Land, made the case that they could appreciate, and convey to others, the real significance of the crusade better than those who saw the capture of Antioch and Jerusalem with their own eyes. True witnesses were not those who saw but those who understood.

SUPERNATURAL INTERVENTIONS IN THE BATTLE OF ANTIOCH: THE ORIGINS

As crusaders proceeded on their march toward Jerusalem, they halted for nine months at the walls of Antioch until, thanks to help from inside, they finally captured it on the night of June 2–3, 1098.[1] Within days, an army assembled by Kerbogha of Mosul (who hurried to relieve Antioch but arrived after crusaders had taken it) besieged the city. Both as besiegers and besieged, the crusaders suffered from low supplies and low morale, which led to numerous desertions. It is even possible that they tried to negotiate a surrender, which Kerbogha declined to grant.[2] After three weeks of languishing in the already depleted city, on June 26 the crusaders decided on a sortie and a battle. The decision was a desperate one, as Kerbogha's forces, according to modern estimates, could easily have been two or three times their number.[3] Moreover, many crusading knights had lost their horses and were, in the words of one chronicler, "reduced to weak and helpless footmen," which further tipped the scales in Kerbogha's favor.[4] Without doubt, the crusaders came close to a defeat that would have spelled the end of the entire enterprise. Yet they won an overwhelming victory with relative ease.

Modern historians offer several explanations for this victory. For the most part, they follow Muslim sources, particularly Ibn al-Athir, and focus on wrangling in Kerbogha's camp. R. C. Smail, for example, describes the battle as having been won before it began: "The Turks, whose morale had been sapped by the desertion of many Turkmen auxiliaries and by quarrels among the leaders, fled with little resistance to the Latin charge."[5] Jay Rubenstein takes this interpretation a step further and suggests that the crusaders may have known that circumstances actually favored them: "It may be that Kerbogah's followers not only deserted him in the battle but also that Bohemond, and perhaps the other crusader princes, knew—or at least suspected—that this would happen."[6] John France, in contrast, refuses to blame the defeat on Muslim dissenters and points out that there was plenty of discord in the crusaders' camp as well. France attributes the crusaders' victory to Kerbogah's tactical mistakes and the mindset of crusaders, who were "fired by religious fervor and the desperate need for food."[7] Thomas Asbridge largely concurs, writing, "Zealous conviction, gifted generalship and a healthy dose of luck brought them victory against all the odds."[8]

Medieval Christian explanations of the events revolve around the element that most modern historians understandably sideline, namely, miracles. The anonymous *Gesta Francorum* reports that shortly before the battle, Christ appeared in a dream to a certain priest and promised to send "mighty help." Christ fulfilled his promise, and in the midst of battle there appeared "a countless host of men on white horses, whose banners were all white," according to the *Gesta*, which adds, "This is quite true, for many of our men saw it."[9] James MacGregor argues that the addition was evidence of incredulity on the part of some participants in the First Crusade, suggesting that "perhaps some crusaders found the story too fantastic or, as seems more likely, some were unfamiliar with the idea of saintly intercession on the battlefield."[10]

Indeed, many of the sources are surprisingly silent about the miracle. Only one letter—addressed by the clergy and people of Lucca to all the faithful and claiming to transmit an account by a certain crusader named Bruno—includes a variation on the story of the intervention of saints.[11] The narrative of saintly intervention is entirely absent from other early crusading letters, including the ones written in Antioch in the aftermath of the battle, the first by Anselm of Ribemont in July and the second by the crusading princes together to Pope Urban II in September 1098.[12]

If one considers the chronicles written by participants in the First Crusade, the narrative is found in only two of them: the *Gesta Francorum* and the closely related *Historia de Hierosolymitano itinere* written by Peter Tudebode.[13] It is absent from that of Fulcher of Chartres. The fourth chronicler, Raymond of Aguilers, claims that deceased crusaders joined their comrades in battle against Kerbogha.[14] The image of dead soldiers fighting shoulder to shoulder with their live counterparts has some affinities with, but is distinct from, that of saints intervening on the battlefield. While Raymond did not explicitly mention saints on the occasion of any battle, he alluded to their appearance during the battle of Dorylaeum that took place on July 1, 1097, and the capture of Jerusalem on July 15, 1099.[15] Similarly, there was no unanimity among the later chronicles regarding any miracle that took place during the battle of Antioch. Some of them gave accounts similar to that found in the *Gesta Francorum*, while others included a different combination of saints, omitted the miracle of saintly intervention altogether, or associated it with the battle of Dorylaeum or the siege of Jerusalem.[16] Clearly, the hesitation regarding the credibility of the miracle extended beyond the participants in the First Crusade to their contemporaries and near contemporaries.

This hesitation must have been due to the fact that the miracle was, as MacGregor puts it, "unfamiliar." But although this type of miracle was new to many crusaders, it is found in earlier sources. This chapter provides an overview of the precedents in ancient Greece and Rome, as well as in the early Christian and Byzantine traditions. The following two chapters explore the Byzantine influences on the narratives of the battle of Antioch (chapter 3) and analyze some of the precedents produced in western Europe (chapter 4). Almost all of the narratives examined in the present chapter are part of the genealogical tree of the intervention of saints in the battle of Antioch, meaning that it is possible to reconstruct, with some degree of plausibility, lines of descent. All of them demonstrate that the concepts of warfare and the supernatural were not always easy to bring together in a historical narrative.

Attribution of victory to divine assistance is common enough in a variety of traditions. Reports of the appearance of supernatural agents in a military setting (before, during, or after the actual military encounter) are much rarer. One of the earliest is found in what is also one of the earliest narratives exclusively dedicated to warfare: Homer's *Iliad*. There is no direct connection between *The Iliad* and the narratives of saintly intervention in the battle of Antioch, and the differences between the two are numerous. Most obviously, at the walls of Troy, gods fought on both sides, while at Antioch, the Christian God sent his agents to help one side against the other. However, the very differences throw into sharper relief one basic similarity: the radical nature of the claim that mere mortals could see supernatural beings in the context of war.

Most of the time, while gods protected their favorites or caused the demise of their enemies among the Achaeans or the Trojans, they remained invisible.

In only one exceptional case does Athena allow Diomedes, the king of Argos and one of the best fighters in the war, to distinguish the gods. In book 5 of *The Iliad*, she tells him:

> And I have removed the mist with which your eyes
> Were darkened, that now with ease you may distinguish
> The god from the man.[17]

Upon receiving Athena's gift, Diomedes rushes into battle with such valor that Aeneas begins to suspect that he is "some wrathful god, angry with Trojans because of neglected offerings" (90). Pandarus, fighting alongside Aeneas, is less sure:

> He looks very like Diomedes, for I know his shield
> And crested helmet, and those are his horses too.
> Still, I don't really know: he may be a god! (91)

In his fury, but also with Athena's permission, Diomedes does not hesitate to spear Aphrodite, who is carrying wounded Aeneas from the heat of the battle, and afterward to warn her to keep away from the battlefield (95). Apollo takes the relay from Aphrodite in protecting Aeneas, which does not stop Diomedes from pursuing Aeneas. He charges at him four times, even though he sees that "Apollo himself was holding his arms above him." Apollo warns him not to try

> To equal the gods in spirit and valor, for the race
> Of immortal gods is by no means the same as that
> Of earth-treading men! (98)

Diomedes backs away, but not enough to satisfy Apollo, who addresses Ares:

> Won't you go into battle and withdraw this man
> Diomedes, who now would fight Father Zeus himself? (99)

With Athena's encouragement, Diomedes wounds Ares as well (111). Ares complains to Zeus, who, in response, scolds him for his bloodthirstiness (112).

This episode in *The Iliad* elucidates some of the reasons why the narratives of visible interventions of supernatural forces in battle were relatively rare in

Greco-Roman antiquity and beyond. The result of Athena's gift to Diomedes was an effacement—however conditional and temporary—of the dividing line between the human and divine realms. On the one hand, his human opponents began to mistake Diomedes for a god. On the other hand, the visibility of the gods diminished or even annulled the awe that Diomedes was supposed to feel before them. He began treating his divine opponents as if they were mere mortals and made it clear that even if they shed ichor instead of blood, they were vulnerable to the blows delivered by a human hand. A mortal challenging the gods on the battlefield alarmed Apollo, who felt the need to remind Diomedes that mortals and gods were not the same. Apollo need not have worried, however, for Diomedes was in fact an obedient tool used by Zeus and Athena to humiliate Aphrodite and Ares and keep them in their place. What appeared to Apollo to be a challenge to the power of the gods was a reinforcement of Zeus's authority. Still, the ability to see gods in the middle of a fray could only be an exception, granted to one person in particular circumstances. Otherwise, instead of gods taking a close interest in human affairs, there would be two armies in which gods and humans intermingled freely.

The majority of later narratives of visible supernatural intervention in warfare in the Greco-Roman tradition feature not gods but heroes—Heracles, Theseus, and the twin brothers Castor and Pollux—who returned posthumously to activity familiar to them during their lifetime. The four heroes straddled the gap between the two spheres of humans and gods from their conception. Although competing stories of their descent exist, at least some accounts claim that all four were products of a union between a mortal mother and a divine father. Heracles and the Dioscuri were sons of Zeus, while Theseus managed to have two fathers, Poseidon and a mortal. Eventually, traditions honoring all four as demigods developed, although they did not enjoy equally wide popularity.

None of the accounts concerning the four heroes makes an explicit claim that all of those on the battlefield saw a supernatural being. Rather, the number of eyewitnesses is often limited, or the visible evidence is indirect. In one case, for example, the deceased hero eager to join the fray remained invisible but left visible evidence of his intervention. Xenophon (ca. 430–354 B.C.) recorded that just before the battle of Leuktra, fought between the Thebans and the Spartans in 371 B.C., "all the temples were opening of themselves" in Thebes, foreshadowing victory. Moreover, weapons disappeared from the sanctuary of Heracles in the same city, indicating that the hero "had gone forth to the battle." Although the deified Heracles did not make a visible appearance, his borrowing the weapons from the sanctuary, obviously to wield them once again in battle, was an exceptional case of an overlap between the human and divine spheres. Xenophon, however, noted that some of his contemporaries suspected that the entire affair was a hoax: "Some, to be sure, say that all these things were but devices of the leaders."[18] From the very start, then, instances of disbelief accompanied accounts of supernatural intervention in war.

In antiquity, the heyday of narratives concerning supernatural interventions appears to have been the first century B.C.–first century A.D. *The Nature of the Gods*, a philosophical treatise by Cicero (106–43 B.C.), contains not just a narrative of a supernatural intervention on the battlefield but an analysis of its plausibility. Admitting that the subject was "particularly difficult and obscure," Cicero framed the discussion as an imaginary dialogue between three historical figures: Velleius (representing the Epicureans), Quintus Lucilius Balbus (representing the Stoics), and Gaius Aurelius Cotta (representing the New Academy).[19] Balbus argues that the reports of the Dioscuri being seen in battle were true, while Cotta supports the opposite viewpoint. Velleius ends up siding with Cotta.

Balbus gives two examples of apparitions, which "have compelled each and everyone who is not dull-witted or sacrilegious to admit that gods were at hand" (49). The first is that of Castor and Pollux in the battle between the Romans and the Latins at Lake Regillus, which took place in the late sixth or early fifth century B.C. According to Balbus, at Lake Regillus, "Castor and Pollux appeared fighting on horseback in our [the Romans'] battle-line" (49). The hoof marks supposedly left by Castor's horse became a local attraction (112).[20] Balbus also mentions that in the wake of the battle of Pydna (168 B.C.), fought in Greece between the Romans and the Macedonians, "two young men mounted on white horses"—once again, obviously, Castor and Pollux—announced the Roman victory in Italy. They appeared to a certain Publius Vatinius, who "reported this to the senate" and was "thrown into prison for making reckless claims about state business," but, when the news was confirmed, was released and rewarded generously. Balbus buttresses the credibility of his story by specifying that Publius Vatinius was the grandfather of a man known to the participants in the dialogue.

Cotta discounts these reports as "old wives' tales" and wages a two-pronged attack to undermine the credibility of reports of celestial interventions. First, Cotta questions Publius Vatinius's reliability as an eyewitness, asking why Castor and Pollux would announce the victory to him rather than to a higher-ranking official. To this, Balbus replies that the Senate considered Publius Vatinius reliable enough and even issued a decree in his honor.

Second, Cotta asks how plausible it is that those enjoying eternal life would actually take part in earthly affairs: "You must surely prefer to believe what is susceptible to proof, that the souls of outstanding men ... are divine and eternal, rather than that, having been cremated once and for all, they could have ridden horses and fought in the battle-line" (112). Cotta accuses Balbus of repeating vague tales and demands a rational explanation. Balbus replies that the weight of tradition makes the accounts of apparitions credible. In the end, Cotta manages to convince Velleius but not, apparently, the narrator: "Cotta's argument seemed to Velleius to be more truthful, but in my eyes Balbus' case seemed to come more closely to a semblance of the truth [*ad similitudinem veritatis propensior*]" (146). Modern historians, however, have emphasized the lack of conviction in this statement and have found Cicero's position difficult to gauge.[21]

In the following century, many writers apparently agreed with Balbus rather than with the skeptical Cotta. The story of Castor and Pollux's intervention in the battle of Lake Regillus is found in a number of texts.[22] Plutarch (ca. A.D. 46–120) recorded a different yet clearly related tradition, according to which Theseus took an active part in the battle of Marathon (490 B.C.) between the Greeks and the Persians. According to Plutarch, the Athenians "saw an apparition of Theseus in arms rushing on in front of them against the Barbarians [the Persians]." This event contributed to the Athenians' decision "to honor Theseus as a demigod."[23]

Some authors, however, shared Cotta's skepticism about the accounts of Castor and Pollux intervening in battle. For instance, in the chapter of *Stratagems* aptly titled "How to Arouse an Army's Enthusiasm for Battle," Sextus Julius Frontinus (ca. A.D. 40–103) described the Dioscuri's appearance at Lake Regillus as a ploy used by Postumius, the leader of the Romans, to inspire courage in his soldiers. He argued that Postumius made use of his soldiers' credulity to convince them that victory was at hand: "When two youths, mounted on horseback, appeared in the battle which Aulus Postumius fought against the Latins, Postumius roused the drooping spirits of his men by declaring that the strangers were Castor and Pollux. In this way he inspired them to fresh combat."[24]

According to Frontinus, other generals employed the same tactic. For example, in the fifth century B.C., Archidamus II, the king of Sparta, "set up weapons in camp, and ordered horses to be led around them secretly at night. In the morning, pointing to their tracks and claiming that Castor and Pollux had ridden through the camp, he convinced his men that the same gods would also lend them aid in the battle itself."[25] Pericles, also in the fifth century B.C., was behind the most elaborate staging of a "miracle," this time aimed at tricking both sides. Pericles chose a soldier of "enormous stature," clothed him in purple robes, had him mount a chariot "drawn by gleaming white horses," and placed him in a grove consecrated to Pluto and located near the site of the impending battle. Frontinus relates that "this man was instructed to drive forth, when the signal for battle should be given, to call Pericles by name, and to encourage him by declaring that the gods were lending their aid to the Athenians. As a result, the enemy turned and fled almost before a dart was hurled."[26]

Early Christian authors were undoubtedly familiar with accounts of demigods' having intervened in this or that battle through either oral or written traditions. Lactantius, writing in the early fourth century, reacted directly to such accounts. He included the reports of the appearances of Castor and Pollux in his list of "false things" that ancient authors, "reputable ones at that" (a possible jab at Cicero), had handed down to posterity. Lactantius argued that the existence of a long tradition made such accounts no less false: "Those who have gone before us in time have not . . . gone before us also in wisdom."[27]

Other authors, however, instead of rejecting the accounts of supernatural intervention in battle outright, Christianized them. The Romans believed that Castor and Pollux had performed a variety of functions posthumously, each of which passed on to a pair of Christian saints. Peter and Paul supplanted them as helpers at sea; Cosmas and Damian replaced them as healers.[28] Similarly, two saints took over their function as abettors of victory. The fifth-century *Ecclesiastical History*, written by Bishop Theodoret of Cyrrhus, described the apostles John and Philip aiding Emperor Theodosius in the battle fought by the Frigidus River against the usurper Eugenius in 394.[29] Eugenius had allied himself with the pagans, which made it possible for Theodosius to present himself as the defender of Christianity. The sacred nature of the power of Christian Emperors made the transformation of the narrative easier. In Byzantium, the emperor's office was to become "arguably the most sacred" of all, before that of the patriarch.[30] Thus the emperor was already breaching the divide between the sacred and the profane, so it made sense for narratives of saints' intervention on the battlefield to be associated with him.

There are clear resemblances between Theodoret's account of John and Philip and earlier narratives dealing with Castor and Pollux. Like the Dioscuri, the apostles formed a pair and rode white horses. But Theodoret must have based his account not just on pagan legends but also on a foundational Christian narratives. The book of Revelation describes two apocalyptic battles between the forces of good and evil. In the first battle, "[Archangel] Michael and his angels fought against the dragon, and the dragon and his angels fought back" (Rev. 12:7). Before the second battle, the narrator "saw heaven opened, and behold a white horse; and he that sat upon him was called Faithful and True, and in righteousness he doth judge and make war.... And the armies which were in heaven followed upon him upon white horses, clothed in fine linen, white and clean" (Rev. 19:11, 19:14).[31] However, the biblical narrative, in contrast to that of Theodoret, does not challenge the line separating this world from the next, since the events take place after the end of time.

The accounts of the battle of Milvian Bridge, fought in 312 between Emperor Constantine the Great and Maxentius, provided another precedent for Theodoret's narrative. As with Theodosius and Eugenius, this was, from the victor's point of view, a standoff between a rightful emperor and a usurper. Although the battle of Milvian Bridge involved no intervention on the battlefield, the narrative is the earliest example in the Christian tradition of a victory credited to divine arbitration, and as such it paved the way for all subsequent attempts to sacralize warfare. Eusebius of Caesarea addressed the battle of Milvian Bridge in several of his works, adding new details over time. In his *Vita Constantini*, left unfinished at the author's death in 339, Eusebius narrated two specific miracles preceding the battle. Before the battle, the entire army saw a cross in the sky with the inscription in Greek "conquer by this." In addition, Christ appeared to Constantine in a dream and told him to make a copy of the sign that he had seen and put it on the standard, *labarum*, of the legions.[32] To summarize, Theodoret's account of two saints charging into battle stems from three different sources: pagan accounts of Castor and Pollux, the apocalyptic battle of the book of Revelation, and Eusebius's attempts to create theological underpinnings for the new Christian empire.

Augustine, an older contemporary of Theodoret, was the Christian counterpart of Cicero in that he too tried to understand the mechanisms of supposed supernatural intervention on the battlefield. In fact, it seems probable that Augustine was responding to Cicero's treatment of the subject in his

The Nature of the Gods. Augustine's "De cura pro mortuis gerenda" (On Care to Be Had for the Dead), written around 421–24, contains the earliest extant mention in a Christian source of a supernatural agent making an appearance in a military setting. According to Augustine, credible witnesses had reported that Felix appeared when the barbarians attacked the town of Nola.[33] Augustine used this episode to illustrate his discussion of the possibility of interventions by the dead, both saintly and "ordinary," in the affairs of the living. Augustine combined the certainty that the saints did help the living with hesitation about how exactly they operated. He argued that the appearance of Felix was a remarkable exception to the usual order of things, a miracle nearly equaling those performed by Christ. He claimed, moreover, that Felix or any other saint could not intervene in human affairs merely by his own volition, for only God could make such interventions possible.[34]

Like Cotta in Cicero's *The Nature of the Gods*, Augustine also wondered exactly how celestial interventions worked. He vacillated between two possibilities: either saints performed the miracles themselves, or angels took on the appearance of saints. Augustine found support for the second possibility in the Old Testament, which contains narratives of angels intervening in affairs of the living—for example, in the battle fought by Judas Maccabeus. When it came to the "ordinary dead," Augustine did not hesitate, arguing that any specter is an *imago*, a purely spiritual image that had nothing to do with either the body or the soul of the deceased. Angels, acting as intermediaries, presented these images before the "eyes of the soul" of the living. Thus if Augustine was willing to admit, albeit reluctantly, the prospect of saintly intervention in human affairs, he emphatically denied the possibility that the "ordinary dead" could do the same. Throughout his discussion, however, Augustine stressed his uncertainty about the mechanics of saintly interference in the affairs of the living, admitting that the question surpassed his power of understanding.[35]

Augustine's acceptance of the story of Saint Felix coming to rescue Nola from barbarians was the earliest in a line of similar narratives, in which saints protected "their" cities, both in Byzantium and in the West. In Byzantium, the most famous of them had to do with the Virgin and the capital city, Constantinople. Once again, this Christian tradition grew out of pagan narratives. In the late fifth or early sixth century, Zosimus, a pagan, described apparitions of Athena and Achilles saving Athens from Alaric, king of the Visigoths. According to Zosimus, "When Alaric and his whole army came to the city, he saw the tutelary goddess Athena walking about the wall, looking just like her statue, armed and ready to resist attack." When he mounted an attack, Alaric also saw "the hero Achilles, just as Homer described him at Troy when in his wrath he fought to avenge the death of Patroclus. . . . These apparitions were too much for Alaric who, giving up his attempt against the city, sent heralds to treat for peace."[36] The choice of supernatural agents was logical. Athena was the tutelary goddess of Athens, while Achilles—like the four heroes discussed above—was of mixed descent, born of an immortal nymph and a mortal. Zosimus was writing after Augustine and Theodoret, so it is likely that he was not only continuing the pagan tradition of attributing victory to supernatural intervention but also competing against the emerging Christian one.[37]

The statue to which Zosimus refers was a colossal bronze figure of Athens, sculpted by Phidias and known as Athena Promachos, that dominated Athens. In the late fifth century, the statue was transported to Constantinople. Although Athena, a pagan goddess, could not be a protector of the capital of the Christian empire, Theotokos (the Mother of God), who became the titular saint of Constantinople in the sixth century, acquired some of her traits. A number of sources dedicated to the siege of Constantinople by the Persians and the Avars in 626 depicted her "as a warrior-maiden, a reminder of Athena Promachos."[38] In these sources, the Virgin's "active belligerence, linked to her perpetual virginity, echoes qualities of the virgin warrior Athena."[39]

Perhaps the turning point of the siege of Constantinople was the destruction of the enemy fleet in the Golden Horn, across from the church of the Virgin at Blachernae. A number of accounts of supernatural interventions in the siege were composed in the 630s, probably at the court of Patriarch Sergius, during the period of jubilations following Emperor Heraclius's defeat of the Persians. According to the *Chronicon Paschale*, the *khagan* of the Avars reported the following vision during the siege of Constantinople: "I see a woman in stately dress rushing about on the walls all alone."[40] Theodore Synkellos gives an even more prominent role to Theotokos, "who appeared everywhere, winning uncontested victory and inflicting horror and fear on the enemies. She was giving strength to her servants and protecting the subjects from harm, on the one hand, and destroying the enemy on the other."[41]

If Constantinople had Theotokos, other Byzantine cities had their own protectors. For example, during the reign of Emperor Nikephoros I (802–11), Saint Andrew was reported to have intervened in favor of the city of Patras, besieged by the Slavs, accompanied by "African Saracens." When the inhabitants attacked their besiegers, they saw the first-called apostle [Saint Andrew], revealed to their eyes, mounted upon a horse and charging upon the barbarians, yea, and he totally routed them and scattered them and drove them far off from the city and made them to flee. And the barbarians saw and were amazed and confounded at the violent assault upon them of the invincible and unconquerable warrior and captain and marshal, the triumphant and victorious first-called apostle Andrew, and were thrown into disorder and shaken, and trembling gat [i.e., got] hold upon them and they fled for refuge to his most sacred temple [the church of Saint Andrew].[42]

In some cases, it was not saints but other kinds of apparitions that supposedly saved cities from being sacked. The *Chronicon Paschale*, mentioned above, includes an account of an angel who took the form of the absent Emperor Constantius II and saved the city of Nisbis from the Persian shah Shapur I (240/42–270/72). When "the wall had sustained a very large cleft and the city was on the point of surrendering," Shapur saw "a man running around on the walls of Nisbis," in whom he recognized the emperor. Yet during the negotiations with Shapur, the citizens of the city claimed that they had no right to hand over the city in the absence of their leader. Shapur accused them of lying: "With my own eyes I behold your Emperor Constantius running around on the walls of your city." After his siege met with many reversals, Shapur turned for an explanation to the magicians who accompanied him. The magicians explained that he had seen not Constantius, who was indeed absent, but an angel. Shapur "was afraid and ordered that the war-engines be burnt and that all that he had prepared in respect of military equipment be destroyed."[43]

What Theotokos was to Constantinople, Demetrius was to Thessaloniki.[44] According to a miracle story compiled by John, who became archbishop of Thessaloniki during the reign of Emperor Phocas (602–610), Demetrius rescued the city as it was being besieged by barbarians. Although the "barbarians" remain anonymous in the source, it is possible that the narratives reflect a historical attack on Thessaloniki by Avars and Slavs in 586. According to one miracle, in the midst of the siege, Demetrius, "just as he is depicted in paintings," appeared to a certain shipmaster named Stephen on the island of Chios and told him to sail to Thessaloniki. At first, Stephen refused, claiming that the city was about to be taken by barbarians, but Demetrius reassured him that the city would be saved. Indeed, the barbarians abandoned the siege.[45]

Another miracle story resembles the narratives of saintly intervention on behalf of crusaders at Antioch in 1098 particularly closely. When a barbarian army besieged Thessaloniki and was on the brink of capturing it, there exited from the city gates, "like a swarm of wasps," a group of armed men. At their head was a certain red-haired youth, holding a cross in his hand and riding, once again, a white horse. The barbarians fled, with the exception of those who, overcome by fear, were unable to move. The citizens of Thessaloniki asked them why their companions were fleeing without any apparent reason. The barbarians replied, "The crowd of men whom you hid, together with their most brave commander, put our companies to flight." The citizens realized that it was Demetrius at the head of an army of angels.[46]

A man who had visited the church of Saint Demetrius before the battle confirmed this conjecture. While he was in the church praying, "a great tiredness came over him," so that he was "neither entirely asleep nor . . . wholly awake." At that moment, two youths entered and asked the guardian to take them to "the lord of this temple." After a proper evocation, Saint Demetrius appeared, and the two youths told him that their lord (evidently Christ) had asked them to convey the following message to him: "Hurry out and come to me, since your city is being surrendered to its enemies." Demetrius, greatly saddened, prayed to Christ, saying, "What life will I have when my citizens have been destroyed? Just as I was with them in spirit when they were prospering, so I will not desert them when they are in danger." Christ rescinded his decision and spared Thessaloniki from destruction.[47]

In the eleventh century, John Skylitzes returned to the tradition of crediting the protection of Thessaloniki to Saint Demetrius. According to John, when the Bulgarians besieged Thessaloniki in 1041, the residents spent a night praying on Demetrius's grave, and the following day rode out of the city and engaged the enemy. Unprepared for this sudden attack, the Bulgarians were defeated. Captured prisoners testified that they had seen a young horseman who had led the Byzantine army and exuded "a fire that burnt up the enemies."[48]

In the Byzantine tradition, saints made visible appearances almost exclusively while defending "their" cities during sieges. However, there is at least one case of a saint aiding an emperor in a pitched battle, in continuation of the tradition going back to the account of the intervention of apostles John and Philip in the battle of the Frigidus River. Leo the Deacon wrote an account of the battle of Dorostolon, fought in 971 between Emperor John Tzimiskes and Svjatoslav, a pagan leader of the Rus', shortly after the events. Leo describes a successful attack by the "Scythians" on the "Romans." On seeing his troops in flight, John Tzimiskes decided to engage in battle personally, together with his closest companions. Other "Romans" then turned their horses around and charged the enemy. Suddenly, a simultaneous rainstorm and sandstorm filled the eyes of the enemy with dust. At that moment, a warrior riding a white horse appeared and, miraculously, put the enemy's lines in disarray. Nobody saw this warrior either before the battle or afterward, when the emperor tried to seek him out. Afterward, all grew to believe that the warrior was Theodore, to whom the emperor had prayed to protect his troops. At the same time, a certain woman in Byzantium saw the Virgin, surrounded by "dazzling warriors," in a dream. The Virgin asked Theodore to protect her favorite, Emperor John Tzimiskes.[49]

The saints' special relationship with the emperors extended not only to aiding good leaders but to punishing bad ones. The two most famous regicides were committed by Saint Theodore (credited with assassinating Emperor Valens) and Saint Mercurius (who was believed to have killed Emperor Julian). Both Julian and Valens perished under uncertain circumstances either in the heat of battle or in its immediate aftermath, the first in 363 and the second in 378. Although these miracles are different from those of saintly intervention in a siege or a battle, there are at least two elements in common: the exercise of violence by a saint and the military setting. Also, in at least some of the accounts of these assassinations, the avenging saint becomes visible, although usually in a vision or dream. That the same saint, Theodore, was credited in different sources with helping one emperor in one battle and assassinating another in another battle is further indication that the two types of miracle were complementary.

The claim that Saint Mercurius killed Julian was earlier than the claim that Saint Theodore was behind the death of Valens.[50] It emerged in the context of competition between several explanations. In the first century after Julian's death in battle against the Persians, both Christians and pagans attributed his death to a human agent (a Persian or an Arab ally of the Persians; a Christian unhappy with Julian's persecutions; a Roman soldier eager to return home from a disastrous campaign).[51] In the fifth century, the theory that a supernatural being was behind the death of Julian gained ground. Socrates Scholasticus listed several theories regarding Julian's assassination:

some believed that Julian's assassin was a Persian who hurled the javelin and then fled; others argued that he was a member of Julian's own camp; still others claimed that the emperor was slain by a demon. Socrates commented on the last hypothesis, "This is possibly a mere poetical fiction, or perhaps it was really the fact; for vengeful furies have undoubtedly destroyed many persons."[52]

Salminius Hermias Sozomen, also writing in the fifth century, argued that Julian's assassination by a supernatural agent was "fact" rather than "poetic fiction" and also that there was nothing demonic about him. Quite the contrary, two saints had come back to life to slay the emperor. While they remained invisible on the battlefield, two people—a friend of Julian's and a philosopher from Alexandria—saw them in a dream. Julian's friend fell asleep in a church, where he took refuge on a journey, and saw apostles and prophets deliberating on how to take vengeance on Julian for persecuting the Christians. The deliberations ended when two of the assembly volunteered to take care of the matter. Julian's friend stayed in the church for another night and had a second dream, in which the two returned and announced the emperor's death.[53] It is possible that the Christians turned on its head the pagan accusation that a Christian had assassinated Julian. They "admitted" to the deed with the caveat that the assassin was a saint who had come back from the dead.

While in Sozomen's account the two assassins remained anonymous, in the sixth century the saint responsible for the assassination of Julian, this time acting alone, acquired a name. An anonymous Syriac source describes the future emperor Jovian (Julian's successor) dreaming of Mercurius, armed with a bow and three arrows. Mercurius tells Jovian that he will kill Julian in three weeks, and at the appointed time the emperor was indeed slain by an arrow.[54]

In his *Chronographia*, John Malalas also identified Saint Mercurius as the regicide. Malalas described both Julian and the future Saint Basil, bishop of Caesarea, who had suffered from the emperor's persecution of Christians, having dreams or visions that prophesied the emperor's death. In his first dream, Julian, while at Antioch preparing for his campaign in Mesopotamia, saw a young blond man who told him that he would die in a place called "Asia." In his second dream, Julian, sleeping in a town called "Asia" in the vicinity of Ctesiphon, saw a man approach him and pierce him with a lance. When Julian awoke, he asked for the name of the town and understood that his end was near. Indeed, he was killed in battle soon afterward. On the day of the emperor's death, the future Saint Basil had a vision that complemented Julian's dreams. In the vision, Christ ordered Saint Mercurius, who was wearing a shining iron plate, to slay the emperor, "an enemy of the Christians." After a short period of time, the saint returned and reported that the deed was done.[55]

Finally, in the so-called *History of the Patriarchs of the Coptic Church of Alexandria*, the date of which is uncertain, Saint Mercurius finally makes a visible appearance on the battlefield rather than in a vision or dream. The *History* recounts the death of the emperor: "He [Julian] saw in the night an army which came down upon him from the air, and one of the soldiers struck him with a lance on the head so that it pierced him through the body."[56] In this case, however, Emperor Julian appears to be the only eyewitness of the celestial intervention.

This brief overview of the Greco-Roman, early Christian, and Byzantine narratives of supernatural intervention in warfare supports several conclusions. First, the intervening agents tended to straddle the divine and human realms. In antiquity, they were not gods but deceased heroes. In the Christian era, they were not angels but Theotokos and a select group of saints. Second, this was a very rare type of miracle that tended to be recorded only in connection with particularly dramatic moments in history: either battles or sieges in which the stakes were particularly high and victory was uncertain or even improbable, or persecutions against Christians. A cluster of sources deal, for example, with the standoff between Byzantium and Persia, during which the survival of the former was in question. Third, although the miracle was not easy to believe, as instances of skepticism toward it demonstrate, it was ultimately credible even to the most sophisticated thinkers, among them Cicero and Augustine. Fourth, many of the narratives built upon one another and shored up their credibility by incorporating details from earlier versions, which were sometimes centuries old. In some cases, the borrowing from earlier traditions was hostile and suppressed those traditions in favor of new ones. This applies above all to the transition from pagan heroes to Christian saints as supernatural agents intervening in battle. Fifth, although the majority of narratives deal with the rescue of besieged cities, there is also a strand, undoubtedly going back to Constantine, that associated the miracle with the emperor as a military commander fighting in defense of the realm. The saints would, of course, help only worthy emperors. In the case of unworthy emperors like Valens and Julian, the saints could turn against them. These two roles—imperial protector and regicide—were complementary, in that both reflected the saints' close interest in the person ruling the empire.

The narratives of the intervention of saints in the battle of Antioch, as recorded in the *Gesta Francorum*, provide a new development in the patterns established in earlier texts. As in the majority of earlier narratives, the miracle takes place in the context of a siege (in this case, of Antioch). The narrative is closest to the one in which Demetrius saves Thessaloniki from barbarians by riding out of the gates to engage the enemy. It also has affinities with the accounts of Saints John, Philip, and Theodore intervening in pitched battles, although in this case, unlike earlier ones, no emperor is present. The color white features prominently in earlier narratives, beginning with those about Castor and Pollux, and this is also the case in the *Gesta Francorum*. In comparison to the accounts surveyed in this chapter, the *Gesta*'s version clearly presents the miracle at its most radical, in that the saints actually appear on the battlefield before many eyewitnesses, rather than in a dream or vision. Finally, Saints Demetrius and Mercurius, who had already appeared in Byzantine narratives, also play key roles in the *Gesta*. The following chapter addresses both the lines of transmission from the Byzantine tradition to the crusading tradition and the implications of this borrowing.

THREE

HOSTILE APPROPRIATIONS OF BYZANTINE SAINTS BY THE NORMANS OF THE SOUTH

According to the *Gesta Francorum*, three saints intervened in the battle of Antioch: George, Mercurius, and Demetrius. Peter Tudebode, in his *Historia de Hierosolymitano itinere*, based largely on the *Gesta Francorum*, gave a similar list, but he replaced Mercurius with Theodore.[1] The four saints featured in the two earliest chronicles of the First Crusade were essentially Byzantine saints and belonged to the cohort of so-called warrior-saints. In Byzantium, the function of warrior-saints was to defend the Byzantines against their "human but demonically inspired" enemies and, in particular, to protect "the emperor and his armies."[2] George, Demetrius, Theodore, and Mercurius were among the most famous of all Byzantine warrior-saints. In his pioneering study on the subject, Hippolyte Delehaye placed three of them (he excluded Mercurius, whom he considered more minor) in what he called an "état-major," a general staff of celestial forces.[3]

Despite their fame in the East, the four were relatively little known in the West, and it is surprising that the crusaders would have expected these saints to intervene on their behalf. As chapter 4 will show, the idea of saints making an appearance on the battlefield was not completely foreign in the West. But earlier narratives of saints participating in warfare tended to include universal or widely familiar saints, or saints closely associated with the location where the miracle took place, usually through their relics' being preserved there, which was not the case here.

It is true that none of the four saints was completely unfamiliar in the West before the First Crusade. The degree of the infiltration of their cults varied, being greater for George and Theodore and smaller for Mercurius and Demetrius. Liturgical texts provide perhaps the weightiest evidence of the veneration of saints, who in several cases feature specifically in connection to warfare. For example, an early eleventh-century *ordo* for the consecration of knights, part of a pontifical of Cologne, refers to George.[4] George, Mercurius, and Theodore feature in several of the so-called *laudes*, liturgical acclamations of both secular and ecclesiastical leaders.[5] However, *laudes* feature a large variety of saints and do not single out these three in any way.

An exceptional piece of evidence is found in *Liber miraculorum sancte fidis* (*Book of Sainte Foy's Miracles*), probably composed in the first third of the eleventh century by Bernard of Angers. According to the author, a monk and prior of the monastery of Saint Foy named Gimon "kept in the dormitory a cuirass, a helmet, a lance, a sword, and all kinds of instruments of war," and did not hesitate to employ them against any who attacked the monastery. Bernard uses the story of Saint Mercurius's posthumous use of violence to justify the use of force by Gimon: "Don't we read that after Saint Mercurius had already been martyred he punished the emperor Julian the Apostate by piercing him through with a lance? Therefore he who raised Mercurius from death in revenge against his own adversary was also able to arm Gimon well in defense of his own Church."[6] In other words, if a saint could fight, so could a monk. According to Carl Erdmann, however, Bernard's knowledge of Saint Mercurius derived from "book learning" rather than from any popular oral tradition.[7]

The *Ecclesiastical History* of Orderic Vitalis contains another important piece of evidence concerning the cult of the four saints, particularly among knights, in the West. According to Orderic, a certain clerk named Gerold at once entertained and instructed the knights at the court of Hugh of Avranches in the Welsh March in the 1070s in the following manner: "He [Gerold] told them vivid stories of the conflicts of Demetrius and George, of Theodore and Sebastian, of the Theban legion and Maurice its leader, and of Eustace, supreme commander of the army and his companions, who won the crown of martyrdom in heaven."[8] Orderic's list contains the three saints who are also found in Peter Tudebode's chronicle: George, Demetrius, and Theodore. The date when the text was written, however, puts the authenticity of this testimony in doubt. Orderic was writing some sixty years after the events that he described, i.e., some thirty years after the capture of Jerusalem. In fact, his *History* includes a narrative of the First Crusade based upon Baldric of Bourgueil's *Historia Ierosolimitana*, which in turn was based upon the *Gesta Francorum*. Like the *Gesta*'s, the *History*'s account of the battle of Antioch mentions Saints George, Demetrius, and Mercurius.[9] Even James MacGregor, who believes that the account is largely a faithful rendition of what happened at the court of Hugh of Avranches in the 1070s, accepts that in making the list of saints Orderic might have come under the influence of crusading sources. According to MacGregor, it is the presence of Demetrius that raises concern: "In seeking to understand why Orderic included the name of St. Demetrius in his account of Gerold's ministry, it is highly likely that his reporting was coloured by the impact of the First Crusade on his historical imagination."[10]

In sum, when it comes to the cults of the four saints in the West, we have only scraps of evidence. It is safe to say that the majority of crusaders had no habit of devotion to them and perceived them—especially Mercurius and Demetrius—as quintessentially foreign. With the exception of Saint George, they remained so even after the First Crusade. Carl Erdmann remarks in passing that the transformation of "explicitly Byzantine saints" into "patrons of warfare in the West" was a matter of "considerable importance."[11] Indeed, an explanation of why Byzantine saints were believed to have made an appearance at Antioch is crucial for understanding the nature of Eastern influence on the ideology of war in the West.[12]

As Jonathan Riley-Smith has demonstrated, the choice of the saints mentioned in the chronicles of the First Crusade "did not reflect the personal predilections of the crusaders."[13] No specific leader was clearly behind the choice of the saints. Christopher Holdsworth has attempted to explain the growing popularity of Eastern military saints in the West in general by noting that they "were not associated by birth with any one of the successor kingdoms of the west."[14] When it comes to the First Crusade, however, this does not explain why these specific foreign saints were singled out.

Riley-Smith proposes a more cogent interpretation: "The bias towards eastern saints [at Antioch] was a consequence . . . of a sense of geography."[15] In other words, crusaders believed that the East was the sphere of influence of Eastern saints. Yet the ties that connected three of the four saints to Antioch specifically were slim or nonexistent. Although the center of his cult was at Lydda, George is the only possible exception. One of the gates of Antioch, in the northwest corner, was named the Gate of Saint George.[16] Most of these associations, however, postdate the battle of Antioch. According to Raymond of Aguilers, while encamped in the city after having defeated Kerbogha, crusaders found a chest containing relics that no one was able to identify. The natives suggested that "they belonged to Saint Mercurius, while others gave the names of various other saints." George then appeared in a vision to a priest by the name of Desiderius and identified the relics as his own.[17] At least by 1101, there was a church dedicated to George in the vicinity of the city.[18]

So, although the evidence is hardly conclusive, the participants in the First Crusade might have perceived Antioch as the city of George and expected his involvement in the affairs there. Mercurius and Theodore had at best a tenuous connection to Antioch. The natives' misidentification of the relics of George as those of Mercurius in Raymond of Aguiler's chronicle is perhaps the strongest piece of evidence. At the end of the eleventh century, the cult of Theodore was particularly strong among Byzantine military commanders in the regions of Antioch, Edessa, and Cilicia.[19] As far as I have been able to ascertain, there was no special relationship whatsoever between Demetrius and Antioch. Following the theory of the "localization of saintly power," it would have made more sense for crusaders to expect Saint Peter, the first bishop of Antioch, to appear on the battlefield than any of the other four saints.

Part of the reason why these specific saints were credited with helping crusaders is that, in addition to all four being Byzantine "warrior-saints," three of them were credited with visible appearances on the battlefield before the First Crusade. The exception is Saint George, although there are narratives of his interventions in warfare while remaining invisible.[20] As the previous chapter established, in Byzantium there were close—in the case of Demetrius and Theodore, very close—precedents for the narrative of the intervention of saints in the battle of Antioch. These posthumous miracles were little known in the West before (or, for that matter, after) the First Crusade. This means that those who claimed that Mercurius, Demetrius, and Theodore appeared in the battle of Antioch possessed knowledge about the Eastern saints that was difficult to obtain in northern Europe.

The origin of this knowledge is not immediately clear. One hypothesis is that crusaders learned about Eastern saints while passing through Byzantine lands en route to the Holy Land. Many of them took Via Egnatia, the road that connected Durazzo (Dyrrachium) on the Adriatic coast to Constantinople and that passed through Thessaloniki, the center of the cult of Saint Demetrius.[21] At Constantinople, they must have come across the church of

Saint George of Mangana, rebuilt by Emperor Constantine IX (r. 1042–55) and described by Michael Psellus as being of "exceptional beauty."[22] The Greek clergy that accompanied the crusaders could also have served as a crucial source of information.[23] Indeed, Saints George, Theodore, and Demetrius (and also Blaise) appear in a letter written in January 1098 by the Greek patriarch of Jerusalem and the bishops accompanying the crusaders "to the West."[24] This explanation, however, may place too much emphasis on the receptivity of the crusaders to Byzantine culture. One doubts that crusaders were capable of readily adopting foreign saints as their patrons in preference to familiar ones so quickly after first learning about them. As the following chapter will demonstrate, all of the Western narratives of saintly intervention in warfare feature either universal saints or the saints whose cult was predominant in the conflict zone.

Huguette Taviani-Carozzi has approached this question in her analysis of Geoffrey Malaterra's narrative of the battle of Cerami, a key encounter of the Norman conquest of Sicily, in which Saint George was reported to have intervened. She noted that Geoffrey might have known the account involving a different saint, Theodore, reported to have intervened on the side of the Byzantines in the battle of Dorostolon. Taviani-Carozzi argues that the Greek clergy of southern Italy served as a conduit for transmission of this narrative.[25] Indeed, if most crusaders came into contact with the Greeks only when marching across the Balkans, the Normans had been living side by side with them in southern Italy and Sicily for decades before the First Crusade. However, when discussing the adoption of Saint George in the West, Erdmann has proposed perhaps the most plausible explanation, arguing that "the Normans and other mercenaries who served in the Byzantine army" acted as intermediaries.[26] While fighting for the Byzantines, the Normans had an opportunity to become familiar with Byzantine saints not in general terms but "in action," as they were supporting or at least were expected to support the emperor and his troops. They probably developed the desire for the saints to fight on their—the Norman—side against whatever enemy they faced, including the Byzantines.

By the time of the First Crusade, at least two generations of Normans had served the Byzantines.[27] It suffices to mention that in the immediate family of Robert Guiscard, the duke of Apulia and Calabria, four—possibly five—close relatives fought for the Byzantines at one point or another. In 1038, Robert Guiscard's two older brothers, William and Drogo, and possibly a third brother, Humphrey, participated in the Byzantine invasion of Muslim

Sicily. Robert Guiscard's nephew, known as Constantine Humbertopoulos, made a career in the Byzantine military and actually fought against his uncle in the battle of Durazzo in 1081. From 1085 to at least 1097, Guy, Robert Guiscard's son and Bohemond's half brother, was fighting for the Byzantines. According to Anna Comnena, when Bohemond himself passed through Constantinople during the First Crusade, he asked the emperor to make him "the Domestic of the East."[28] Recent research has demonstrated that Bohemond's interest in the imperial service is entirely credible.[29]

In sum, the frontier between Norman Italy and Byzantium was extremely porous. Some—albeit "very few"—Norman mercenaries ended up assimilating: they learned Greek, married into Byzantine families, and converted to Eastern Orthodoxy.[30] Although the majority did not become Byzantines, all Norman soldiers for hire must have come under the influence of Byzantine traditions to a greater or lesser degree. This was made easier by the fact that most of the inhabitants of southern Italy and Sicily had probably mastered at least the rudiments of Greek: "Greek, albeit of a rough and ready sort, seems to have been the *lingua franca* of these habitués of fringe areas of the Byzantine world."[31] In the 1070s, the ties uniting the Normans and the Byzantines were about to become familiar.

After prolonged negotiations, Guiscard made a treaty with Emperor Michael VII, arranging the marriage of his daughter, Olympias, to the emperor's son Constantine Doukas. The prospect of marriage "boosted Robert's prestige," helping him in his dealings with the papacy, the Holy Roman Empire, and his own subjects, both Greek and Norman.[32] Michael in his turn hoped to secure Norman aid against the Seljuks in the East and the Turkophone bands in the Balkans.[33] In 1076, Olympias arrived in Constantinople, where she changed her name to Helena, but the marriage never took place because of the deposition of Michael VII. The Norman Olympias/Helena spent nearly two decades in Constantinople.[34]

Relations between the Normans and the Byzantines, however, were not always mutually beneficial. Amatus of Montecassino explains that Michael VII's desire to forge a marriage alliance with Guiscard stemmed from fear for his throne: "Because the empire of Constantinople had been deprived of lordship over all of Apulia and Calabria by the power of Duke Robert Guiscard and his brothers, the emperor . . . in order that he might not [also] be driven from the lordship over the empire, sought the duke's daughter to be the wife of his son." Robert initially refused, in order to obtain "even greater gifts and promises," which led Michael to fear his prospective son-in-law's intentions even more: "he thought that the duke did not want to become related to him because the duke intended to take the empire from him and become the emperor." Amatus does not explain whether Michael's fears were justified or whether Guiscard was merely using his signature Norman cunning to outwit the emperor and obtain greater gifts.[35] These marriage negotiations were characteristic of Norman-Byzantine relations in the second half of the eleventh century, when the Byzantines maneuvered at once to dispel the Norman threat and to harness the Norman military might to serve their own agenda.

In 1078, Nikephoros Botaneiates overthrew and imprisoned Michael VII and proclaimed himself emperor. In April 1081, Alexius I Comnenus overthrew Nikephoros III in his own turn. Apparently, by the time of this second overthrow, Guiscard was planning a campaign against Byzantium in earnest.[36] As part of his preparations, he began promoting pseudo-Michael, a monk claiming to be Michael VII escaped from confinement. The expedition, which began in the late spring of 1081, initially went well for the Normans, who captured, among other territories, the island of Corfu and besieged Durazzo. Alexius's attempt to relieve Durazzo ended in disaster for the Byzantine army, the near capture of the emperor, and, eventually, capitulation of the town to the Normans. From Durazzo, Via Egnatia led to Thessaloniki and from there to Constantinople. Unsuccessful on the battlefield, Alexius achieved a diplomatic coup by encouraging the invasion of Italy by Holy Roman Emperor Henry IV. Guiscard left to defend his domains, while Bohemond stayed in the Balkans and continued campaigning, with mixed success, until he too left for Italy in 1083. In 1084, Robert Guiscard and Bohemond made another attempt against Byzantium, which ended in Robert's death and the Normans' loss of Durazzo.

Historians debate whether, during the campaign of 1081–84, Guiscard and his son merely wanted to extend the Norman domains into the Balkans or had farther-reaching ambitions. According to Anna Comnena, Guiscard announced that his plan was "to plunder cities and lands, collect much booty in this way, and then return to Apulia." In reality, however, "he coveted the throne of the Roman Empire."[37] Historians are still unsure whether to take Anna's testimony at face value.[38] But there is little doubt that by the time of Robert and Bohemond's campaign, the Normans were thoroughly familiar with Byzantine military culture, in which military saints played a significant role. Moreover, on the eve of the battle of Durazzo, the Normans were already presenting themselves as supplanting the Byzantines as objects of patronage of Eastern military saints. According to Anna Comnena, just before the battle, Robert "with all his forces ... arrived at the sanctuary built long ago by the sea in honor of the martyr Theodore. All that night the Normans, in an attempt to propitiate the Deity, were partaking of the holy and divine mysteries."[39] If Anna Comnena's account is accurate, the Normans were praying to a Byzantine saint to help them against a Byzantine emperor. Thus, already at this early date, the Normans were trying to drive a wedge between the Byzantines and one of their most important warrior-saints.

Byzantine military culture had more in its arsenal than just saints. Normans were aware of this and tried to appropriate other symbols of power. In his *Ecclesiastical History*, Orderic Vitalis narrated another symbolically charged moment preceding the battle of Durazzo. He described Bohemond's engagement with the advance guard of Emperor Alexius:

> The Greeks, unable to stand up to the Norman onslaught, turned tail abandoning much booty. On this occasion they lost the bronze cross which the Emperor Constantine had had made when he set out to fight Maxentius, after seeing a cross in the sky. Consequently when the Normans returned from the fray they spread jubilation and high hopes of victory among their comrades, whereas the Greeks were filled with sorrow and misgiving because they had lost their Lord's cross, and strove desperately to redeem it by offering a great sum of gold.[40]

The identification of this cross as the one purportedly carried by Constantine in the battle of Milvian Bridge is unlikely. According to John Haldon, "both central and provincial forces were accompanied from the fourth century by crosses of varying patterns and sizes from simple wooden constructions to much larger and more elaborate bejeweled examples." From the ninth century on, these crosses played an important part in warfare against Muslims, as is evident from the efforts spent to capture and restore them.[41] However, the actual origin of this specific cross was a nicety that Orderic could easily ignore.

The Normans, of course, refused to sell their newly won relic. Orderic suggests that the capture of the cross meant that divine favor had shifted from the Byzantines to the Normans. In the ensuing battle, "the Lord in Heaven, having regard for the faithfulness, perseverance, and small numbers of the western pilgrims, granted the victory to them."[42] Also, although Orderic does not elaborate on this, the capture of Constantine's cross must have allowed the Normans to claim that the Byzantines had lost the right to call themselves heirs of the first Christian Roman emperor—and that the Normans had gained this right.

In addition to Theodore, two of the saints who would later be reported at Antioch feature in Anna Comnena's account of the campaign that Guiscard and Bohemond waged in the Balkans. Before a battle against Guiscard, Emperor Alexius had a dream in which "it seems that he was standing in the sanctuary of the great martyr Demetrius," when "he heard a voice say: 'Cease tormenting yourself and grieve not; on the morrow you will win.'" The emperor believed that the voice was coming from one of the icons of Saint Demetrius.[43] The next day, Alexius indeed emerged victorious. In the Byzantine understanding of war, protecting the emperor in dire straits was exactly what military saints were supposed to do. In challenging the emperor, the Normans had to challenge this connection between the emperor and his supernatural protectors.

When their campaign proved unsuccessful, the defeated Normans negotiated an exit strategy with the Byzantines. They asked that two standards be set up: "one, close to the sanctuary of the great martyr George . . . , the other on the road to Avlona," the port from which they could sail back to Italy. The Normans who decided to serve the emperor then went to the sanctuary of Saint George, while the rest returned home.[44] At this moment, at least, there was a strong association between military service to the Byzantines and Saint George. As we shall see, the Normans would end up attempting to sever this tie.

As the Normans tried to conquer the lands belonging to Byzantium, they elaborated a zero-sum ideology to explain and justify the conquest, asserting that the Byzantines had lost the right to these territories because they had lost divine patronage. The Normans had the right, bordering on a duty, to conquer these lands because God was now on their side. As the public prayer that Guiscard offered to Saint Theodore on the eve of the battle of Durazzo demonstrates, saints played a key role in the construction of Norman ideology early on. So it is not surprising that they would continue to do so in one of the key moments of the Norman challenge to the Byzantines, namely, in the weeks before and after the battle of Antioch.

The development of Bohemond's relations with Emperor Alexius, from their first meeting in Constantinople to the battle of Antioch, explains why the Normans found it opportune to claim that Byzantine saints had intervened in this particular battle.[45] When the leaders of the crusading armies passed through the capital of Byzantium, they, with the exception of Count Raymond of Toulouse, swore an oath that "whatever towns, countries or forts ... which had in the first place belonged to the Roman Empire" (i.e., those recently captured by Seljuk Turks) should be handed over to Byzantine authorities.[46] Apparently, Bohemond was instrumental in ensuring that the crusaders swore this oath, and he was particularly close to Alexius, "acting, or posing, as the emperor's right-hand-man." This was in keeping with the Norman tradition of switching easily between fighting and serving the Byzantines. Bohemond himself did not merely swear an oath but secretly performed liege homage to Alexius, which implied an "unambiguous and highly personal bond of subordination." Bohemond was "almost certainly the only one of the Crusading commanders" to do so, according to Jonathan Shepard.[47] It was at this moment that Bohemond asked to be made "the Domestic of the East," but Alexius refused this request.

If Bohemond could change from an enemy of the Byzantines to a friend, he could easily perform the volte-face once again. Well into the siege of Antioch, Bohemond walked on the razor's edge, struggling to preserve his unique relations with the Byzantines without compromising himself in the eyes of his fellow crusaders. As the conditions in the crusading camp became increasingly dire and the Byzantines made little effort to alleviate them, Bohemond's closeness to Emperor Alexius became more of a liability than an advantage. "His special connection, albeit secret, as liegeman with an increasingly unpopular, seemingly remote and ineffectual emperor began to weigh on him like a ball and chain," writes Shepard.[48] Thus Bohemond orchestrated his first major coup of the siege by forcing the departure of Taticius, a representative of Alexius who accompanied the crusaders. According to Anna Comnena, Bohemond "devised an evil scheme for removing Taticius involuntarily." Bohemond warned Taticius that a rumor was circulating that Alexius was plotting with the "infidels" against the crusaders and that, as a consequence, the Byzantines in the crusaders' camp were in grave danger.[49] Taticius left in February, promising, according to the *Gesta Francorum*, to "send by sea many ships, laden with corn, wine, barley, meat, flour, cheese and all sorts of provisions."[50] According to Raymond of Aguilers, Taticius's professed goal was to join the emperor's army that, as many crusaders apparently believed, was advancing to relieve them.[51] As Shepard has demonstrated, Taticius's departure created a situation highly favorable to Bohemond. If Taticius returned, Bohemond "would still be in imperial favor." If he did not, Bohemond could claim that Alexius had not fulfilled his promises to the crusaders, and that their promise to hand Antioch over to the Byzantines was thus invalid, which would allow Bohemond to claim the city for himself.[52]

Taticius never rejoined the crusaders, bringing "eternal shame to himself and his men," according to Raymond's chronicle.[53] The Byzantines' abandonment of the crusaders allowed Bohemond "to slip out of the role of Alexius' liegeman" and begin plotting a takeover of Antioch.[54] By May 1098 Bohemond had established contact inside the city with a certain Firuz (or Pirrus), who on the night between the second and third of June let the crusader into the city. At some point, Bohemond made the crusading leaders swear a new oath that whoever captured the city would have the right to it. The *Gesta Francorum* describes the event as follows: "All our leaders came together at once and held a council, saying 'If Bohemond can take this city, either by himself or by others, we will thereafter give it to him gladly, on condition that if the emperor come to our aid and fulfill all his obligations which he promised and vowed, we will return the city to him as it is right to do. Otherwise Bohemond shall take it into his power.'"[55] Soon after the capture of Antioch, "Bohemond was acting as if he were the legal authority in Antioch," as shown by a charter in which he donated the church of Saint John to the Genoese.[56]

Yet, according to the *Gesta Francorum*, even after the battle of Antioch was fought and won on June 28, crusaders were hesitant to accept Bohemond's governance over Antioch. As late as July, they sent an embassy "to the emperor at Constantinople, asking him to come and take over the city and fulfill the obligations which he had undertaken towards them."[57] It is probable that the narratives of Eastern saints intervening in the battle of Antioch originated in the Norman camp in the context of Bohemond's struggle to have Antioch recognized as his by right and to refute Alexius's claim to the city. It is not impossible that Bohemond, a skillful storyteller, was personally involved.[58] The spread of news of the miracle was a continuation of part-ideological, part-psychological warfare against the Byzantines that dates back at least to the battle of Durazzo. When Byzantine saints were reported to have intervened on behalf of the crusaders, this implied that they had abandoned the Byzantines. The narrative of the intervention made a powerful statement that the Byzantines were no longer worthy of Antioch and that the right to the city had passed to the crusaders. Since the crusaders had promised to give Antioch to Bohemond if he managed to capture it, this right passed to him. Both the Normans and the Byzantines would have understood this reasoning easily, but it is likely that other crusaders would have been able to comprehend it as well.

Moreover, this adoption of Eastern saints by the crusaders was an attack on Alexius personally, in that the connection with warrior-saints was part of the mystique of the Byzantine emperors. The psalter of Basil II, preserved in the Marcian Library in Venice (Cod. Marc. gr. 17), features a portrait of the emperor surrounded by Saints George, Theodore, Demetrius, Mercurius, and Procopius. With the exception of Procopius, the list is exactly the same as the composite one found in the *Gesta Francorum* and Peter Tudebode's *Historia de Hierosolymitano itinere*.[59] A banner produced during the reign of Constantine IX Monomachos (1042–55) depicted the emperor with Saint George.[60] At the end of the eleventh century, there was a new "militarization of the imperial image." If, before this period, the virtues of an emperor included "righteousness, philanthropy, generosity, chastity, love of truth, and intelligence," with the coming of the Comneni, martial abilities became of paramount importance.[61] As Michael Angold puts it, "war was no longer the business of armchair strategists, but of heroes."[62] The special function of warrior-saints has always been that of "protectors of the emperor and his armies."[63] Even more than their predecessors, the new dynasty of warrior-emperors put forward the claim of benefitting from saintly protection on the battlefield.

Coinage is particularly revealing in this respect. Alexius I was the first emperor to issue coins with a representation of Saint Demetrius. Michael Hendy associates these coins with Alexius's campaign against Guiscard and Bohemond. Alexius used Thessaloniki as "the main base of munitions and supplies" for the war, visiting it three times: twice in 1081 and once in 1083. In all likelihood, the precious mint that began to operate in Thessaloniki in 1081 was set up during one of these visits by the emperor, who must have had a say in the iconography of the coins minted. On these coins, Saint Demetrius, identified by an inscription, is portrayed as a soldier, wearing a short tunic, breastplate, and *sagion* (mantle), and girded with a sword. The saint, represented laterally, hands a labarum (military standard) to the emperor, who stands next to him. Hendy observes that "the Norman war was bitter, the outcome crucial, with the Empire fighting for its very existence. Under the circumstances nothing would be more natural than this iconographical scene."[64] One can imagine Norman mercenaries being paid with these coins and inquiring into the meaning of the image. Eventually, some of them began to claim that the image was wrong, that Saint Demetrius gave his support—symbolized by a labarum—not to the Byzantines but to the Normans.[65]

Norman rulers of Antioch also began to mint coins with a representation of at least one of the Byzantine warrior-saints. From 1115 on, Roger of Antioch (a regent during the minority of Bohemond II, son of Bohemond I) minted copper coins featuring Saint George. On the coin, Saint George, on horseback, pierces a dragon with his lance. The coin recalls the miracle of saintly intervention as the founding moment of the principality of Antioch and also underscores the association of the Norman ruling dynasty with Saint George, much as the Byzantine coins do.[66]

When it comes to narratives of the battle of Antioch, the Normans' claim of greater right than the Byzantines to the patronage of military saints is only implicit. After all, the saints intervened on behalf of all of the crusaders, not just the Normans. Ralph of Caen's account of crusaders' sojourn at Constantinople contains an explicit Norman claim to another Byzantine symbol of power. According to Ralph, after Tancred (Robert Guiscard's grandson and Bohemond's nephew)—like other leaders of the First Crusade—swore an oath to him, Emperor Alexius offered him a gift of his choice, expecting that "he would ask for gold, silver, gems, cloth and similar types of things that were needed for travel or soothed a greedy soul." Instead, Tancred asked for the imperial tent, because "only a piece of the imperial accoutrement would be pleasing to him." The gift, apparently requiring twenty camels to carry, would have been "a useless burden" on a military campaign but "hardly an ignoble sign for the future." An emperor's or king's tent had powerful symbolic value. On the battlefield, it performed a function akin to that of a standard. As long as both leaders' tents are still standing, the outcome of the battle is undecided. For example, in the battle of Hattin, Saladin's son, al-Afdal, began rejoicing at the Muslims' victory, but his father stopped him, pointing at the king's tent: "Be quiet! We have not beaten them until that tent falls." At that moment, the tent fell, and Saladin "dismounted, prostrated himself in thanks to God Almighty and wept for joy."[67]

Ralph compares Alexius's reaction to Tancred's request for his tent to that of Delius (Phoebus/Apollo) when his son Phaeton asks to be allowed to drive his chariot for a day. Alexius grew "violently angry," exclaiming, "The common things are filthy in his eyes and he desires nothing other than my palace, which is unique in the world. What more can he ask except to take the diadem off my head and place it on his own?"[68] In Alexius's eyes, Tancred's demand for the tent suggested that he wanted to usurp his place. Here, the tent fulfills a function similar to that of the cross won by the Normans at the battle of Durazzo. Although Alexius did not grant Tancred the tent, the very request demonstrates the Normans' belief that they had the right to Byzantine appurtenances of power, both secular and religious.

Competition for saints' patronage was not unlike competition for more tangible symbols of power bearing both political and religious significance, such as relics. When it came to the acquisition of relics, the *translatio* of the remains of Saint Nicholas from Myra to Bari in 1087 was one of the most famous examples of *furta sacra* in the eleventh century. Saint Nicholas enjoyed wide fame, but it is likely that the political situation further increased the appeal of his relics. Myra fell to the Turks soon after the defeat of the Byzantines in the battle of Manzikert in 1071. According to Nikephoros, a Barian who composed the earliest account of the *translatio*, after the Turks "invaded that region and cruelly depopulated it," the inhabitants fled Myra and abandoned the sanctuary.[69] Nikephoros blamed the Myrans for reneging on their duty and forsaking the saint. He recounts that Saint Nicholas appeared to the guardians of the church and "admonished them through a vision to inform the inhabitants of the city of Myra, who had fled in fear of the Turks to a mountain twelve *stades* away, that they should return to live and guard the city. Otherwise they should know that he would migrate elsewhere." "Elsewhere" was not just anywhere but somewhere where the saint himself wanted to go. According to Nikephoros, in the past, "many emperors and other potentates" tried to remove the relics, "but they had no luck because the saint of God was unwilling." Myrans did not heed the warning of Saint Nicholas, and when they saw the Barians taking the relics from them, they recognized that God was on the side of the thieves: "The high-thundering Lord has clearly approved this unprecedented act for you; and His most blessed confessor Nicholas, who has left us orphaned, has completely re-established his fatherhood among you unknowns."[70]

It is true that Nikephoros celebrated the Barians rather than the Normans. Also, the Byzantines introduced the Feast of the Translation of the relics of Saint Nicholas from Myra to Bari, probably considering both of these cities only temporarily out of their possession. Patrick Geary is probably correct in interpreting the theft of the relics in the context of competition between Bari and Venice: "The sack of Myra gave the Barians an opportunity to acquire a patron who in the East was at least as important as Venice's Saint Mark."[71] However, it is possible that the Normans interpreted this theft as proof of divine support for their growing importance in the eastern Mediterranean and their ambition to fill the power vacuum left by the Byzantines. According to Marjorie Chibnall, "The Normans were likely ... to have claimed that the translation showed the saint's deliberate choice to leave the place where the Byzantine emperor was unable to give protection."[72] If the Greeks were unable to defend his sanctuary from the Turks, then they were no longer worthy of possessing the body of the saint. The saint naturally chose to join those who could protect him: the Normans.

That the church figures prominently in affairs in the East supports this interpretation. Bohemond obtained control over Bari probably a year after the consecration of the church of Saint Nicholas in 1089 by Pope Urban II.[73] When he returned to Italy in 1105, he donated Kerbogha's tent, captured in the battle of Antioch in 1098, to this church.[74] This must have been a gesture of gratitude but also an affirmation that Bohemond enjoyed the support of Saint Nicholas in his military endeavors against the "infidels." Thus Bohemond thanked what he may have considered a formerly Byzantine saint for helping him become the prince of what was formerly a Byzantine city. In 1107 Bohemond heard Mass in the church before embarking on the expedition to the Balkans against the Byzantines.[75] Once again, his appeal to an Eastern saint for help against Byzantium may have been both deliberate and provocative.[76]

Even in death, Bohemond displayed a predisposition toward the "hostile imitation" of Byzantium. He was buried in a chapel added to the south transept of the cathedral of San Sabino in Canosa di Puglia. At first glance, Bohemond's choice of burial place (it was, no doubt, his own) in a town of secondary importance is odd. The cathedrals of Taranto and Bari and the abbey of the Trinity in Venosa were much more likely candidates to receive his remains. According to Anitra Gadolin, Bohemond "could not ... have been buried at Canosa without causing surprise and even anger among his subjects—unless he had some very good reasons."[77] Gadolin has argued convincingly that Bohemond did in fact have good reasons, having to do primarily with the design of the church, rebuilt in the late eleventh and early twelfth centuries and dedicated in 1101. The plan of the church closely resembles that of the no longer extant church of the Holy Apostles at Constantinople built by Emperor Justinian and dedicated in 548, the second most important ecclesiastical structure in Constantinople, after Hagia Sophia.[78] According to Gadolin, Bohemond, who probably footed the bill for the construction of the church, must have had a say in its design. Having spent almost a month in Constantinople during the First Crusade, he would have been familiar with the church of the Holy Apostles, so it is likely that he suggested it as a model.[79] The cross-in-square chapel added to the south transept of the cathedral, executed after Bohemond's death, probably under the supervision of his widow, Constance, is also clearly reminiscent of Byzantium and incorporates several paleo-Byzantine acanthus capitals.[80]

The church of the Holy Apostles was a particularly prestigious model for imitation, not only as an awe-inspiring structure of venerable age but also as a burial place for Byzantine emperors. Although the last emperor buried in the church was Michael V, in 1042, "the tombs of the Byzantine emperors must have remained a considerable tourist attraction."[81] Some imperial sarcophagi were placed in the church itself and others in secondary structures attached to it, known as the mausoleum of Justinian and mausoleum of Constantine.[82] The desire, even in death, to equal the Byzantine emperors was probably behind Bohemond's choice to be buried in what was essentially a copy of the church of the Holy Apostles in Constantinople. As Gadolin puts it, "On Apulian soil, there could hardly be any worthier resting place for the bones of one who all his active life had fought for the diadem worn by the eastern Caesars."[83] Ann Wharton Epstein reached a similar conclusion, arguing that Bohemond recognized the church "as a surrogate for its prototype."[84]

Bohemond's burial place thus emerges as an example of "aggressive imitation." Bohemond had the right to be buried like a Byzantine emperor if only because he inflicted a series of military defeats on another such emperor, Alexius. Two inscriptions associated with the tomb refer to Bohemond's "conquest" of "Greece." The first, under the cornice of the cupola, reads, "The magnanimous prince of Syria lies under this roof. No one better than he will be born afterward in the universe. Greece conquered four times, the greater part of the world sensed for a long time the genius and strength of Bohemond. He conquered columns of thousands with a battle-line of tens by the rein of his virtue, which indeed the city of Antioch knows." The second inscription, on the bronze door, extols Bohemond in even more vaunting praise: "How noble, how valuable Bohemond was, Greece has witnessed, Syria enumerates. He conquered the former; protected the latter from the enemy. . . . He thundered over the earth. Since the universe submitted to him I can't call him a man; I won't call him a god."[85]

Later in the twelfth century, the pattern of aggressive Norman borrowing of Byzantine symbols of power continued. The mosaic portrait of Roger II—son of Roger I and first cousin of Bohemond—in the narthex of the church of

Santa Maria dell'Ammiraglio (the Martorana) in Palermo, commissioned by Roger's chief minister, George of Antioch, and executed between 1146 and 1151, is a prime example.[86] Roger is wearing a *loros*, a jeweled scarf, draped around his shoulders, waist, and left forearm, over a tunic decorated with gold and pearls. Christ is placing a crown with *pendalia*, tassels with gems, on his head. The attire is "modeled to an amazingly precise degree on the Byzantine emperor's court costume."[87]

There is no consensus among historians regarding the meaning of this image and of other examples of Sicilian art inspired by Byzantine models. According to David Douglas, one of the catalysts for the initial adoption of Byzantine style might have been the desire to please the Normans' numerous Greek subjects.[88] Other scholars, however, interpret it as part of a grander project; Ernst Kitzinger, for example, claims that the representation of Roger in the church of Santa Maria dell'Ammiraglio is "essentially a political manifesto."[89] Kitzinger draws a connection between this image and Roger's far-reaching ambitions in the last decade of his reign. Apparently, Roger demanded that an emissary of Manuel I Comnenus recognize him as the emperor's equal, and in 1147 he took advantage of the Byzantines' being distracted by the Second Crusade and mounted a major expedition against Greece, conquering the island of Corfu and sacking Thebes, Athens, Chalcis, and Corinth.[90] Odo of Deuil records a number of crusaders—probably including himself—approaching Louis VII with a proposal to undertake a joint attack on Constantinople with Roger II.[91] In 1149, after the crusading armies of Louis VII had long since moved on, Norman troops burned the suburbs of Constantinople and even stole fruit from the imperial gardens.[92]

Like the two campaigns of Robert Guiscard and Bohemond in the Balkans, the extent of Roger's ambitions lies at the crux of debates in modern historiography. According to Paul Magdalino, "The episode showed how easily a crusade could turn into a coalition of western kings that would threaten the empire's territorial integrity, its religious autonomy, and the Comnenian dynastic regime."[93] Other historians, however, doubt that Roger was bent on conquest of the empire. Hubert Houben, for example, juxtaposes Roger's campaigns with his uncle's: "In contrast to Robert Guiscard, Roger never sought to conquer Constantinople. The war against Byzantium was of secondary importance to him."[94]

William Tronzo has argued convincingly that the representation of Roger in Palermo reflects Roger's understanding of the meaning of sovereignty, heavily influenced by Byzantium; Tronzo rejects as "too narrow" the theory that it represents "the claim of the king to the territories of the Byzantine state."[95] Still, even if the mosaics do not represent any direct "claim," it is significant that Roger's adoption of Byzantine garb and crown on the wall of Santa Maria dell'Ammiraglio, as well as the Byzantine style of the entire program, roughly coincided with the Norman war against Byzantium. It seems likely that Roger displayed Byzantine trappings of power like a trophy, affirming the Normans' rise and, conversely, the Byzantines' decline.[96]

The quest for prestigious icons provides another analogue to the competition for the patronage of saints. According to the Byzantine historian Niketas Choniates, during the Norman raid on Corinth in 1147, the captain of the Norman fleet was surprised by the ease with which he conquered the impregnable acropolis of the city, declaring that "he had fought with God's help, for only God could have enabled him to occupy such a position." Then, having "taken captive the most comely and deep-bosomed women," the captain "took into his hands the icon of Theodore the Stratelates, the greatest among martyrs, renowned for his miracles, and removed this icon which had been set up in the church of his name."[97] Niketas Choniates represents the Normans as plundering whatever they could, whether women or icons. Perhaps this was his attempt to blunt the power of the statement that the Normans seem to have been making. According to the Normans, Saint Theodore chose not to protect Corinth against an invasion because he wanted the city (and his icon) to be captured. Theodore was no longer a patron of the Byzantines but of the Normans.

The Normans were not the only ones eager to use captured Byzantine icons as palpable proof that the saints were on their side. In 1203, during the Fourth Crusade, a skirmish took place between the crusaders and Emperor Alexius V during which the Byzantines let fall Alexius's imperial helmet, standard, and icon. According to Robert of Clari, the icon "was all of gold and charged with precious stones and was so beautiful and so rich that never was one seen to equal it." The clergy in the camp went out to meet the fighters and "received the icon with great joy." The crusaders decided to donate the icon to the monastery of Cîteaux, "and later it was taken there." First, however, the Franks put the standard and the icon on a galley and paraded them before the city walls.[98] Both the standard (which was likely to have contained religious imagery) and the icon were supposed to convey to both camps the message that the Byzantines had lost and the crusaders had won divine support.[99]

Other neighbors of the empire also used icons representing Byzantine saints as sacred ammunition against Byzantium. At the turn of the year

1185–86, the Vlachs and the Bulgars rebelled against Byzantium, enraged by extraordinary taxes levied by Emperor Isaac II.[100] The leaders of the revolt, the brothers Peter and Asen, built a chapel in honor of Saint Demetrius in order to rally their followers. According to Niketas Choniates, they "gathered many demoniacs," who were instructed to say "that the God of the race of the Bulgars and Vlachs had consented to their freedom [from the Byzantines] and assented that they should shake off after so long a time the yoke from their neck; and in support of this cause, Demetrios, the Martyr for Christ, would abandon the metropolis of Thessaloniki and his church there and the customary haunts of the Romans [the Byzantines] and come over to them to be their helper and assistant in their forthcoming task."[101] If Niketas Choniates's record is accurate, the rebels took advantage of the recent capture of Thessaloniki in 1185 to argue that Saint Demetrius had abandoned the Byzantines and was now willing to support the case of the Vlachs and Bulgars *against* Byzantium. To quote Paul Stephenson, "the galvanizing force employed by the rebels was not a common ethnic identity long suppressed under the 'Byzantine Yoke,' it was a belief borrowed directly from Byzantium: the cult of St. Demetrius." According to a poem written by Theodore Balsamon, Isaac II, in a symbolic gesture, eventually captured an icon of Saint Demetrius from the house of Peter, thereby establishing that the saint was still on the side of the Byzantines.[102]

Another variation on the same process of appropriation of Saint Demetrius by the rivals of Byzantium can be found in *The Russian Primary Chronicle*, written in the late eleventh or early twelfth century. The author reports how during Oleg's siege of Constantinople in 907, the Greeks tried to poison their enemy and, on failing, exclaimed: "This is not Oleg, but Saint Demetrius, whom God has sent against us."[103] Although Oleg, a pagan, had little to do with Saint Demetrius, the chronicler implies that there was some truth in this statement, for, in his view, the army of the Rus was indeed protected by God and Saint Demetrius. Thus a patron of the Byzantines, protecting Thessaloniki, became a patron of the enemies of the Byzantines who were besieging Constantinople. These examples demonstrate that the Normans' ideological warfare was not unique but followed the same pattern as that adopted by many others confronting Byzantium over the course of several centuries.

In the relations between the Byzantines and the Normans, past and present, religion and politics, culture and conquest were intimately intertwined. The traditional explanation of this relationship portrays the militarily superior

Normans (or Latins in general) coming under the influence of culturally superior Byzantium. According to Steven Runciman, when it came to culture, Byzantium tended to overawe "the average Westerner," for whom it was, "though perhaps over-civilized and rather decadent, nonetheless splendid and glamorous."[104] "The average Westerner" then developed feelings of envy and resentment and desire to confront the Byzantines with force of arms. Similarly, Krijnie Nelly Ciggaar writes, "One wonders how many Westerners did not feel at ease when contemplating the wealth of the Greeks, perhaps unjustly feeling inferior to them."[105] Along the same lines, Ruth Macrides describes the reaction of Western visitors to Constantinople in terms of both awe and bitterness. They admired the city and wondered at the number, size, and beauty of the monuments there. In the midst of such grandeur, however, they felt excluded and alienated, which led to "a desire to possess."[106]

Some historians acknowledge that the Byzantines were largely responsible for the feelings of exclusion and alienation experienced by foreigners. Alexander Kazhdan and Ann Wharton Epstein summarize the situation: "in Byzantium one of the strongest inherited prejudices was directed against alien cultures," including that of western Europe.[107] Similarly, Donald Nicol describes the Byzantines' "pride" as "born partly of their ineradicable sense of exclusiveness as the inhabitants of the Christian Roman Empire, partly of their exalted idea of the unique and supreme position of their emperor." Byzantine pride, says Nicol, "must have infuriated western Europeans, especially after they had become conscious of their own military and commercial superiority to the *Graeculi* of the East."[108]

Not all scholars, however, accept this picture entirely. Historians of the Crusades especially have argued in favor of a more egalitarian relationship between Byzantium and the West. Jonathan Riley-Smith, for example, claims that alienation was not the dominant sentiment in crusaders' dealings with the Byzantines. Newcomers from the West realized that Constantinople was the most splendid city in Christendom, but they "did not look on the Greeks as their superiors." Despite frequent tensions between the Latins and the Greeks, "the emphasis in western writings connected with the crusade was on the brotherhood of equals."[109] Writing about late antiquity more generally, Peter Brown has also challenged the view that the Byzantines "civilized" the uncouth Latins:

> Nothing has done more to handicap our understanding of Mediterranean history in the medieval period than the tendency of scholars to

treat Byzantium as a world apart, standing aside and above the destinies of an "underdeveloped" western Europe. Once this view is accepted, the East tends to be treated as a distinct and enclosed reservoir of superior culture from which the occasional stream is released to pour downhill—by some obscure law of cultural hydraulics—to water the lower reaches of the West. Relations between East and West, therefore, tend to be treated as so many "releases" of Byzantine "influence."[110]

Indeed, even in those spheres where they could not equal the Byzantines, the peoples who came in contact with Byzantium were not passive receptacles of Byzantine cultural influences. The Byzantines clearly possessed something that such newcomers as the Normans lacked: a sophisticated vocabulary of power. Thanks to their close contact—in some cases almost to the point of assimilation—with the Byzantines, the Normans fully mastered and then appropriated this vocabulary. Yet this wholesale borrowing of Byzantine symbols of power did not imply a Norman inferiority complex. Nor was this borrowing a neutral action. Rather, the Normans appear to have believed that, thanks to their military prowess, combined with divine support, they had the right to make use of this vocabulary. The Normans understood the devices used by the Byzantine emperors to present their authority as providential, and they assimilated them to make a counterclaim about the providential nature of the defeats that they inflicted on, among others, the same Byzantine emperors. Just as trophies captured in battle, whether of sacred or secular nature, belonged to them by right, so did intangible attributes of their ascendancy, such as the patronage of saints. The claim that Demetrius, Theodore, George, and Mercurius helped the crusaders at Antioch was thus a statement similar to the capture of Constantine's cross at Durazzo. The "fact" of saintly intervention on the side of the crusaders served as proof that the crusaders (and, more specifically, the Norman Bohemond) had gained the right to Antioch that the Byzantines had lost.

THE NORMANS OF THE SOUTH:
FROM SCOURGE OF GOD TO CHOSEN PEOPLE

If one is to trust Geoffrey Malaterra, the author of *De rebus gestis Rogerii Calabriae et Siciliae Comitis et Roberti Guiscardi ducis fratris eius* (*The Deeds of Count Roger of Calabria and Sicily and of His Brother Duke Robert Guiscard*), the appearance of Saint George in the battle of Antioch was not the earliest example of the saint's posthumous military prowess. In his chronicle, Geoffrey describes the saint intervening in the battle fought between the Normans and the Muslims near Cerami in Sicily some thirty years earlier, in 1063. In the battle, the Normans, led by the future Count Roger I of Sicily, were heavily outnumbered, but they still managed to obtain a decisive victory and to capture both slaves and plunder, including four camels that Roger sent to Pope Alexander II. In return, the pope granted a papal banner to Roger and an "absolution for their sins" to all the Norman soldiers. Although the victory of Cerami did not lead to the conquest of Sicily, completed only in 1091, it was significant from a military perspective, because "the Muslims were almost always on the defensive" ever after.[1]

According to Malaterra, after the battle began,

> there appeared a certain knight, magnificent in his armor, mounted on a white horse and carrying a white standard with a splendid cross on it tied to the tip of his lance. It was as if this knight were advancing with our battle line and rushing at the enemy where they were the thickest with a most valiant attack, so as to make our men more confident and

ready to fight. Seeing this, our men were elated, and they called out again and again, "God and Saint George." Struck with the joy of such a vision to the point where they were shedding tears, they eagerly followed the horseman who preceded them. Many also saw a banner containing a cross hanging from the top of the count's lance, a banner which only God could have placed there.[2]

The similarity between this narrative and the one found in the *Gesta Francorum* is striking, as both sources not only have Saint George making a sudden appearance on the battlefield, but they describe him in the same way, as riding a white horse and carrying a white standard. However, there are major differences as well. In the *Gesta Francorum,* two other named saints, Mercurius and Demetrius, and "a countless host of men" follow Saint George into battle. In *De rebus gestis Rogerii*, there is a second standard of miraculous origin on Roger's lance and a cross on both standards. Also, Saint George plays a more active role in Geoffrey's chronicle, actually "rushing at the enemy." The similarities point to a close affinity, but the differences make direct copying unlikely.

The *terminus post quem* of *De rebus gestis Rogerii* is straightforward, for the work ends with a transcription of the bull promulgated by Pope Urban II on July 5, 1098. Establishing the *terminus ante quem* is more problematic. Near the end of the chronicle, Geoffrey mentions Bohemond's departure on the crusade, but there is no reference to the crusaders' achievements, such as the capture of Antioch (June 2–3, 1098) or that of Jerusalem (July 15, 1099), which must mean that Geoffrey finished his work before learning about these events.[3] This would make *De rebus gestis Rogerii* almost exactly contemporary with the *Gesta Francorum*, most of which was written shortly after the capture of Antioch.[4] It is highly improbable that one author read the other's work, so it appears that two remarkably similar accounts of a rare type of miracle were produced at the same time independently of each other.

The common denominator of the *Gesta Francorum* and *De rebus gestis Rogerii*, as Graham Loud has noted, is that their authors were in the service of the Normans of the South.[5] Geoffrey Malaterra, who might or might not have been a Norman himself, wrote his chronicle at the request of Count Roger I of Sicily, the victor of Cerami.[6] We know nothing for certain about the author of the *Gesta Francorum*. However, his close familiarity with the Norman contingent led by Bohemond of Hauteville (a nephew of Roger), and the fact that he refers to him, and not to any of the other leaders, as "dominus" leave little doubt that the author accompanied Bohemond on the First Crusade, at least for a large part of the journey.[7] It is probable that they parted ways at Antioch, where Bohemond stayed, while the author of the *Gesta Francorum* continued on to Jerusalem.

Modern historians debate the extent to which the *Gesta Francorum* is a pro-Bohemond work. John France expressed a long-standing belief when he wrote that "the *Gesta* was very much an account of the crusade from the standpoint of an adherent and admirer of Bohemond."[8] This is also the opinion of Kenneth Wolf, who has analyzed the work as an ingenious attempt to transform Bohemond from an opportunist whose ambitions in the eastern Mediterranean (inherited from his father) predated the First Crusade into a *miles Christi*. Bohemond's behavior on the crusade did not always correspond to that of a model "warrior of Christ." The episode in which Bohemond maneuvered to keep Antioch for himself, in spite of having sworn an oath, while passing through Constantinople, to hand it over to Emperor Alexius if and when he conquered it, is particularly problematic. In his takeover of Antioch, Bohemond had to overcome the reservations of many of his fellow crusaders, especially Raymond of Toulouse, who believed that Alexius had a rightful claim to the city. According to Wolf, the author of the *Gesta* "went to some length" in his narrative of the struggle over Antioch "to show how the oath to the emperor [sworn at Constantinople] had been superseded by a new one, the one sworn by the Latin leaders at Antioch."[9]

Wolf also reviews numerous instances in which the chronicle presents Bohemond as a crusader whose military ability is enhanced by God's favor to him. The author of the *Gesta* includes an undoubtedly fictional account of Kerbogha asking his mother whether Bohemond and his nephew Tancred were "gods." Kerbogha's mother, who plays the role of an "infidel" sage in the chronicle, replies that although they are human, "God loves them exceedingly beyond all others, and therefore he grants them courage in battle."[10]

Other historians, however, have proposed a different reading of the *Gesta Francorum*. Emily Albu argues that the author's attitude toward Bohemond's takeover of Antioch is highly critical, and that "the contrast is stark between the honorable Raymond and Bohemond the opportunist."[11] Jay Rubenstein notes, more cautiously, "We cannot say that excessive partisanship for Bohemond drove all of the authorial decisions behind the text."[12]

It is important to note that the Normans did not necessarily see "opportunism" as negative, even if the author of the *Gesta Francorum* indeed meant to paint Bohemond with that brush. As we will see below, the "desire for profit and domination" was considered typical of the Normans and made them especially dangerous. In the Norman chronicles, a ready acknowledgment of this desire goes hand in hand with the celebration of the Normans as God's chosen people. By plotting to take control of Antioch, and at some other ethically troubling moments (ethically troubling not just from the modern but also from the medieval perspective), Bohemond was merely behaving in a characteristic Norman fashion, which did not disqualify him from being loved by God "more than the others."[13] He was a prisoner of his origins: he could not have behaved in any other way without ceasing to be a Norman. In any case, the Norman background of the author of the *Gesta Francorum* is crucial to the present argument, while the extent of his support for Bohemond is of secondary importance. What matters is that the cultural roots of both Geoffrey Malaterra and the author of the *Gesta* were located in southern Italy.

There is, of course, the question of the originality of the accounts of the battles of Cerami and Antioch. *De rebus gestis Rogerii* and the *Gesta Francorum* present very different cases. Thirty years passed after the battle of Cerami before Malaterra recorded it. Malaterra's is the only extant narrative of the battle, and we know nothing about his sources.[14] In contrast, according to the traditional interpretation, the author of the *Gesta* wrote about the battle of Antioch months if not weeks after it took place, possibly while he was still in Antioch (and definitely still in the East), so he must have relied heavily on the oral accounts of his fellow crusaders. In fact, in his account of the battle, the author refers to the authority of eyewitnesses, alleging that "many" saw the saints.[15] But regardless of the sources of both Geoffrey Malaterra and the author of the *Gesta*, their goals went far beyond a desire to collect information and sew it together in a coherent narrative. They wanted to convey an idiosyncratic version of events, and in pursuit of this goal they made meaningful, yet virtually untraceable, decisions about which testimonies, whether written or oral, to include, which to omit, and which to transform in one way or another. Specifically, both had to decide whether to include or omit the miracle of the intervention of saints.

Malaterra's description of the battle of Cerami and the accompanying miracle occupies a prominent place in the debates among modern historians regarding the possible southern Italian and Sicilian roots of the crusades. John France has interpreted it in the context of the First Crusade: "Geoffrey was projecting contemporary fervor for the crusade back onto Count Roger's conquest of Sicily and portraying the Normans as the chosen of the Lord."[16]

Indeed, although Malaterra was unlikely to have known about the crusaders' successes before finishing his chronicle, he was aware of the preparations for and the earliest stages of the enterprise while he was writing it. Other scholars, however, minimize the importance of the crusading context and, to the contrary, frequently adduce Malaterra's narrative, alongside other evidence, to assert that the Norman conquest of Sicily was a forerunner of the First Crusade. Carl Erdmann offers an early example. "The Norman war in Sicily," he writes, "resembled a crusade to a degree unprecedented by any earlier aggression upon heathens that we know of."[17] Along the same lines, Huguette Taviani-Carozzi argues that "the vision [of Saint George] makes the Battle of Cerami a prefiguration of the crusade."[18] Graham Loud has attempted to establish a middle ground between these two positions, asserting that "while Malaterra . . . may have transferred something of the ethos of the later Crusade to Sicily, we cannot dismiss the Holy War component to the Sicilian conquest as an entirely later construct."[19] Although the importance of Sicily and southern Italy in the history of the sacralization of warfare seems almost universally acknowledged, there has been no attempt to explain why this particular region was the origin of one of the crucial narratives that made the First Crusade into a holy war.

To find an answer to this question, one must turn to direct precedents for this narrative. Erdmann remarks that although saints had used violence from the beginning of the Middle Ages, with the invasions of the ninth and tenth centuries, "the church felt bound to strengthen the laity's powers of resistance by moral support." As a consequence, accounts of saints' interventions in warfare multiplied.[20] Erdmann does not, however, explain the connection between the two clusters of narratives of saints intervening in warfare: those dealing with the invasions (particularly of the Vikings) and those dealing with the First Crusade. But Latin Christianity changed dramatically between these two peaks of saintly belligerence. Embattled in the ninth and tenth centuries, Christians mounted several offensives in the late eleventh century. Whereas saints intervened to preserve their monasteries or towns in the earlier sources, in the later sources they helped armies bent on conquest. It was no accident that this new adaptation of an old narrative took place largely—though not exclusively—in the cultural sphere of the Normans of the South. The Normans and their supporters were interested in the memory of the raiding past of the Vikings, since they considered themselves their descendants. Despite (and to some extent because of) its violence, the Normans found this past a useful element in the construction and celebration of their identity and in the legitimization of their new conquests. The miracle of saintly intervention, a key element in narratives of the Normans' supposed past, became, after undergoing a radical transformation, a major element in the accounts of their recent triumphs.

Although in western Europe the invasions of the Vikings gave rise to the largest group of narratives of supernatural intervention on the battlefield, there are even earlier accounts of the same type of miracle. Several of these accounts originated in southern Italy, so they were likely to be familiar both to the Normans of the South and to their historians. Two such narratives can be found in the works of Paul the Deacon, a monk at Montecassino in the late eighth century: *Historia Romana* and *Historia Langobardorum*.[21] Paul was both read and revered for centuries after his death. Amatus, his successor as a monk of Montecassino and the author of *The History of the Normans*, written around 1080, referred to Paul's work as the reason for his own composition: "Know that I hope to disprove the words of those brothers who say, 'It is not proper for a monk to write of the battles of laymen.' Still, on this matter I remembered that Paul, a deacon and monk of this same monastery [of Montecassino], wrote of the deeds of the Lombards and how they came and remained in Italy. He was a man distinguished in life, knowledge and doctrine."[22]

In his *Historia Romana*, Paul narrates the encounter between Pope Leo the Great and Attila the Hun at the walls of Rome, as a consequence of which Attila withdrew from the city without making an attempt to take it. Paul attributes Attila's decision to his vision of a venerable old man who accompanied Leo and threatened the leader of the Huns with his sword; Paul expected the reader to realize that the "old man" was Saint Peter himself.[23]

In *Historia Langobardorum,* Paul the Deacon describes Saint Sabinus (a sixth-century bishop of Bari and a friend of Saint Benedict's) intervening in the battle of Camerino, fought in the early seventh century between the Lombard duke Ariulf of Spoleto and the Byzantines.[24] This seems to be the first instance in the West of a saint visibly appearing in the context of a pitched battle. After winning a victory over the Byzantines, Ariulf asks his followers about the man who fought with such courage. The followers reply that no one fought with more valiance than Ariulf himself. Ariulf, however, says that he is sure that he saw a man who was stronger than himself and who, each time an enemy tried to strike him, protected him with his shield.

Arriving at the church of Saint Sabinus at Spoleto, Ariulf asks whose house it is. Local Christians tell him that it is the martyr's and that it is their custom to ask him for help before each battle. Ariulf, still a pagan at the time, asks, "Is it possible for someone who is dead to help someone who is living?" He enters the church and, while others pray, examines the paintings. As soon as he sees a painting of Sabinus, he recognizes the man who protected him in battle, thereby learning the answer to his question, and he eventually converts to Christianity. Significantly, in this account, Sabinus performs an exclusively defensive function, apparently wielding a shield but not a sword. Also, while he is visible to Ariulf, he remains invisible to Ariulf's followers. Both episodes in the works of Paul the Deacon, especially the second one, bear some resemblance to the narratives of the victories of Antioch and Cerami in the *Gesta Francorum* and *De rebus gestis Rogerii*. Yet the obvious differences exclude the possibility of imitation.

The cult of Saint Michael at Monte Gargano in northern Apulia generated a narrative that was more likely to have influenced the two eleventh-century chroniclers. Monte Gargano was a popular pilgrimage site from the early sixth century, when Saint Michael was reported to have appeared there.[25] The Normans were in the habit of visiting it, and the foundation myth of Monte Gargano influenced that of the monastery of Mont-Saint-Michel in Normandy.[26] According to William of Apulia, who wrote *Gesta Roberti Wiscardi* (*The Deeds of Robert Guiscard*) in the late 1090s, the Normans first got involved in Italian affairs in 1016 while on a pilgrimage to Monte Gargano. There they met Melo, the leader of the Lombard insurgents against the Byzantines, who appealed to them for help.[27] Already before 1078, a half Norman by the name of Henry founded the County of Monte Sant'Angelo, which incorporated Gargano.[28]

The cult of Saint Michael must have had special appeal to the bellicose Normans. If Michael was credited primarily with healing powers in Byzantium, in the West he "preserved those traits associated with war."[29] There, Michael received the most attention for his role in fighting the dragon, as described in the book of Revelation (12:7–9). It was thus logical that Michael came to be venerated as a patron of war against the heathen. The armies of the emperors Henry I and Otto I carried a banner adorned with his likeness while fighting against the Hungarians.[30] The Norman Count Roger I of Sicily was probably aware of Michael the Archangel's association with warfare when he founded a monastery dedicated to the Holy Trinity and to Saint Michael in the vicinity of Mileto.[31]

The Normans of the South and the authors writing about them were likely to be familiar with the stories that Saint Michael had decided the outcome of a battle found in the *Liber de apparitione Sancti Michaelis*, produced in southern Italy at an uncertain date (perhaps as early as the late seventh century or as late as the early ninth).[32] According to the text, the Archangel Michael appeared in a vision to the bishop of Siponto—a town located in the immediate vicinity of Monte Gargano—when the Sipontans and their neighbors the Beneventans were besieged by pagan Neapolitans. Saint Michael promised his aid and told the bishop that the Sipontans should engage the enemy in battle at the fourth hour of the day. Michael was as good as his word, and the surviving Neapolitans testified that nearly six hundred of their companions had been killed by lightning.[33] So, although Michael did not make a visible appearance, his active participation in the battle—ascertained by hostile, and thus particularly reliable, witnesses—was beyond any doubt.[34]

The reputation of Michael as a saint who was ready to interfere in warfare survived until the late eleventh century. The *Carmen in victoriam Pisanorum*, a vernacular poem dedicated to the attack by the Pisans and the Genoese on the Muslim stronghold of Mahdia in North Africa in 1087, describes two saints appearing on the battlefield and leading the troops into battle. According to the poem, Saint Michael blew the trumpet, "as he did when he was combating the dragon." The author of the *Carmen* seems to have had a faulty recollection of the passage in the book of Revelation in which Michael fought the dragon; he does not blow a trumpet, an attribute of the Archangel Gabriel. According to the *Carmen*, Saint Michael was not alone but was accompanied by Saint Peter, who, bearing a cross and sword, "comforted the Pisans and the Genoese."[35] In the poem, then, in contrast to the *Liber de apparitione Sancti Michaelis*, the saints visibly appear on the battlefield (in the *Liber de apparitione*, Michael appears only in a vision after the battle), but they do not kill any of the enemy (in the *Liber de apparitione*, as noted above, Michael kills six hundred Neapolitans with lightning). The differences and similarities point to the longevity of the tradition associated with Saint Michael and also to its adaptability and flexibility.

The oldest manuscript of the *Carmen* dates from around 1118–19, but, following Carl Erdmann, H. E. J. Cowdrey argues that the poem was composed soon after the battle, that is, circa 1087. According to Cowdrey, "for the date and authorship of the *Carmen* there is no direct evidence whatsoever, either internal or external."[36] The indirect evidence that he adduces for an early date is not conclusive. Cowdrey merely points out that the work does not allude at all to the First Crusade and has a "ring of triumphant immediacy" similar to three other poems dating from the late eleventh and early twelfth centuries and written soon after the victories that they celebrate.[37]

Whatever the date of the *Carmen*, however, the traditions associated with Saint Michael and Monte Gargano were not sufficient precedents for the accounts of the miracles of saintly intervention in the battles of Cerami and Antioch. Another factor that made the two accounts in the *Gesta Francorum* and *De rebus gestis Rogerii* possible was the relatively widespread tradition of representing the Vikings—the "relatives" of the Normans—as objects of saintly vengeance.

There is a cluster of evidence concerning supernatural help against the Vikings in their attacks on both England and the Continent in the mid- and late ninth century. The sources describe Saint Benedict protecting the abbey of Saint-Benoît-sur-Loire at Fleury in Burgundy; Saint Germain giving aid to the defenders of Saint-Germain-des-Prés (and hence of Paris, in the vicinity of which the abbey was located); and Saint Cuthbert prophesying the victory over the Vikings of King Alfred of Wessex. The first two incidents were recorded shortly after the events in question, in the late ninth century, while the story of Saint Cuthbert seems to have originated in the middle of the tenth century.

Adelarius, a monk of the abbey at Fleury, mentions Saint Benedict participating in the battle between Hugh the Abbot and the Vikings—specifically his defense of the monks fleeing the abbey at the news of an impending attack. Adelarius's discussion is to be found in one of the two chapters that he appended to *Miracula sancti Benedicti* (*The Miracles of Saint Benedict*), composed slightly earlier by Adrevald of Fleury.[38] The abbey of Fleury was located on the Loire, upstream from Orléans. The Vikings used the river as one of their chief routes to the wealthy monasteries and towns in the hinterland, attacking Fleury probably in 854 and again in 865. Each time, the monks fled the monastery, taking the relics of Saint Benedict with them, but each time they returned, and the community was able to recover. In 879 the Vikings attacked Fleury once more and again the monks were forced to flee, with their foes in close pursuit. Luckily for the monks, Hugh the Abbot intervened and defeated the Norse.[39]

Hugh the Abbot was a cousin of the king and then emperor Charles the Bald (Hugh's father, Conrad, was a brother of Charles's mother, Judith) and served as the abbot, in succession, of Saint-Germain d'Auxerre and Saint-Martin de Tours.[40] Despite being an abbot, Hugh was the chief strongman in the Loire Valley, defending it as best he could against the Norse. According to Adelarius, when Hugh learned about the plight of the monks of Fleury, he realized that the Vikings far outnumbered his forces, and he hesitated to intervene until his companion told him that a defender of the monks was sure to enjoy the aid of Saint Benedict. After the battle, Hugh inquired about a valiant monk who had fought alongside him. Nobody understood what Hugh was talking about, so he solved the mystery himself: "Certainly St. Benedict protected me through the whole battle, for he held the reins of my horse in his left hand and, holding a staff in his right hand, he sent many of the enemy falling to their death."[41] As far as we can tell from extant sources, this was the last attack on Fleury by the Vikings.

Hugh the Abbot died in 886, during the Viking siege of Paris. His death received brief mention in the *Bella parisiacae urbis* (*Battles of the City of Paris*), an epic poem dedicated to the attack and written by Abbo, a monk of Saint-Germain-des-Prés and an eyewitness of the events.[42] This was not the first Viking attack on Paris. According to the *translatio* of Saint Germain, the Vikings had already made an appearance in 845, but they were paid off. Back in Denmark, the leader of the expedition, Ragnar, bragged that no one had the courage to face him, with one exception: "The only one who resisted was an old man called Germain," meaning, of course, Saint Germain, the protector of Paris.[43]

Similarly, in his *Bella parisiacae urbis*, Abbo presented Saint Germain—whom he called "our firm bulwark, our shield, our two-edged sword . . . our strongest bow and our keenest arrow"—as the key defender of the city against the Normans.[44] Although Abbo credits the saint with many a lucky break during the siege, there are also several instances of his making a visible appearance. Germain appeared to both the attackers and the defenders of the city, both in a vision and in reality, both giving reassurance and actively participating in battle.

In the first instance, "the bright-shining figure of Germain" became visible to the Viking sentries, walking about as if surveying his domain, carrying the same lamp that shone near the tomb where his relics were preserved.[45] In the second, Germain appeared in a vision to a certain Frankish nobleman suffering from gangrene, who was fearful that the defense of the city would be abandoned and that he would be left behind. Germain reassured him by showing him an army ready for combat: "Then that noble arose and saw the ramparts / All bristling with countless young men, each one girt in his bright helm."[46] It is possible to interpret this vision as a prophecy of the reinforcements to be brought by Odo, a future king of western Francia, although Abbo describes the fresh troops emerging "on the heights of Montmartre" and not having anything to do with the ramparts. The two episodes are best understood within the tradition of reports of miraculous appearances on the ramparts of besieged cities, going back to Saint Felix's making himself visible on the walls of Nola as it was besieged by the Visigoths.[47] Finally, Abbo represented Saint Germain actively participating in the fighting: "Then behold— Germain, worthy of praise by the world, showed himself / In body, to bring aid, in answer to our pleas. He showed / himself on the field of Mars, where hardest raged the battle, / Drove the standard-bearers of the Danes into death's embrace, / Along with many more."[48]

It is impossible to know exactly what texts might have influenced Abbo's narrative of Saint Germain's visible appearances in battle. There is an indication, however, that Abbo may have known the story of Castor and Pollux's posthumous participation in battle. Abbo describes twin brothers, Segebert and Segevert (not mentioned in any other document), who slew innumerable Normans before being killed themselves. In his description of the death of Segebert and Segevert, Abbo appears to be drawing a parallel with Castor and Pollux, who became the brightest stars of the constellation Gemini: "Then, these twins of ours met a great and honorable death, / In this way, they set their feet on the path above the stars."[49]

In a third example from the Viking age, before the decisive battle at Edington fought against the Normans in 878, Saint Cuthbert visited King Alfred's retreat disguised as a pilgrim and received a warm welcome. The same night, he appeared to King Alfred and promised him victory as well as dominion over all of Britain to him and his descendants.[50] Alfred, of course, won an overwhelming victory. Recent scholarship attributes the original story of Saint Cuthbert and King Alfred to the middle of the tenth century.[51]

The story of Alfred grew out of an early Anglo-Saxon—more specifically, Northumbrian—tradition of the eighth century. Given that Saint Cuthbert was a quintessentially Northumbrian saint, this was probably a case of direct borrowing. In the first case, recorded by Adomnán of Iona, Saint Columba appeared in a dream to King Oswald of Northumbria before the battle at Heavenfield, fought against the Briton Cædwalla in 633 or 634.[52] Oswald triumphed, and his followers converted to Christianity (the king and his twelve companions were already Christians). In the second case, recorded by Bede, Saint Peter, disguised as a simple traveler, appeared to King Edwin of Northumbria, then a fugitive, before the battle by the river Idle in 616.[53] Edwin won the battle and eventually converted to Christianity.

These two accounts follow the same pattern as that of Constantine's vision before the battle of Milvian Bridge. In the case of Oswald and Edwin, as in that of Constantine, there is a vision or a visit before the decisive battle, a military victory, and an eventual conversion of the protagonist or his followers to Christianity. The story of King Alfred is slightly different: there is both a vision before the battle and a victory, but at this later date the emphasis is on resistance to an invader rather than conversion. This group of texts provides yet another example of the miracle's migration from one source (or group of sources) to another written decades later.

To sum up, in the ninth and tenth centuries we have a series of accounts of saints intervening against the Vikings—to save their monasteries, in the case of Saint Benedict and Saint Germain, or to support a king, in the case of Saint Cuthbert. Despite precedents like those involving Edwin and Oswald, there can be no doubt that saints were becoming increasingly involved in human warfare in response to the Viking invasions, as Carl Erdmann has shown. This tradition of crediting victory to saints who appeared before, during, or after a battle did not disappear with the end of the invasions, but it faded, gaining prominence again during the First Crusade.

The Vikings/Normans—who bore the brunt of saints' violence in the ninth and tenth centuries but became the beneficiaries of saints' help in the late eleventh—form the missing link between the two spikes in saintly military intervention. This hypothesis can be viable only if it can be determined that there was an awareness, in the late eleventh century, that the Vikings who attacked France and England and the Normans who conquered Sicily and parts of southern Italy and the Middle East were somehow related. In order to establish this connection, two gaps need to be bridged: one across space (between Normandy and Italy) and one across time (between the ninth and tenth centuries and the late eleventh century).

If one takes into account merely the place of origin, the ties that united the Normans of the South with the Normans of Normandy are undeniable. In the late eleventh century, many of the Normans of the South were first-generation immigrants from the North, including the three strongmen: Robert Guiscard (the father of Bohemond of Hauteville), his brother Roger I of Sicily, and their brother-in-law Richard of Capua. Orderic Vitalis, the chronicler working in the monastery of Saint-Evroul-sur-Ouche in Normandy, recorded a flow of Normans going south, including the abbot of his monastery, Robert de Grandmesnil, to whom Robert Guiscard gave the church of Saint Eufemia in Calabria.[54] Orderic mentioned another monk at the monastery of Saint

Evroul in Normandy, Reginald, who "was twice sent to Apulia" by his abbot and who found there "his brother William and many other kinsmen who were prospering in this foreign land."[55] Although non-Norman Frenchmen traveled south alongside the Normans, as did immigrants from northern Italy, Castile, and Navarre, "the Norman invasion of Italy was fundamentally, though not exclusively, Norman," as Graham Loud points out.[56] But the question of identity—the perceptions and self-perceptions of the Normans—is more important than that of origin.

There is no evidence that during the First Crusade the Normans of Normandy and the Normans of the South felt a special affinity with each other or that there was any particular cooperation between the contingents of Bohemond of Hauteville and those of Robert of Normandy.[57] As becomes evident from other contemporary sources, however, the Normans of Normandy clearly perceived the Normans of Italy as belonging to the same gens and celebrated the conquest of southern Italy and Sicily as their own.[58] William of Poitiers, writing in 1073–74, commented in his eulogy of William the Conqueror, "His [William's] Norman knights possess Apulia, have conquered Sicily, defend Constantinople and strike fear into Babylon."[59] Baldric of Bourgueil, in a poem written around 1099–1102, claimed that William the Conqueror, in a speech intended to persuade his followers to embark for England, referred to southern Italy among other Norman conquests: "Your [Norman] virtue also rules and restrains the laws of Apulia."[60] This tradition of remembering southern Italy in the series of Norman conquests survived until the middle of the twelfth century, when Aelred of Rievaulx imagined what Walter Espic might have said before the battle of the Standard against the Scots in 1138: "Did not our ancestors invade a very large part of Gaul . . . and erase its very name along with the people? . . . Indeed we and our fathers in a short time mastered this island [Britain]. . . . Who subdued Apulia, Sicily and Calabria if not your Normans?"[61]

While there is little doubt that the Normans of Normandy felt a connection with the Normans of the South, the question of whether these feelings were reciprocal has been debated for more than a century. In 1915, Charles Homer Haskins emphasized the ability of the Normans, especially the Normans of the South, to amalgamate with the local population: "Wherever they went, they showed a marvelous power of initiative and of assimilation; if the initiative is more evident in England, the assimilation is more manifest in Sicily. The penalty for such activity is rapid loss of identity; the reward is a large share in the general development of civilization."[62] Evelyn Jamison, writing in 1938, however, was more skeptical regarding the Normans' "loss of identity." She compared the Norman-held lands to the British Empire: "[In the Middle Ages,] the kinship of Normans all over the world is accepted in the same sense that the kinship of British people is thought of in the Empire today, as an underlying, ever-present fact, but without making a song about it."[63] In contrast, R. H. C. Davis argued in 1976 that if the Normans of Normandy had a "sense of kinship" with the Normans of the South, it was not reciprocal. Perhaps in a polite challenge to Jamison, Davis wondered, "Were the Normans of Normandy behaving like those nineteenth-century Englishmen who insisted that all Americans were really British?"[64] Davis's answer clearly was "yes." The Normans of Normandy were happy to take the credit for the achievements of the Normans of the South, while the Normans of the South were eager to break away from the metanarrative of the mother country.

Recent studies, however, challenge Davis's view and tend to come down on the side of Jamison. The very fact that the Normans persisted in calling themselves "Normans" well into the twelfth century is in itself significant.[65] As Nick Webber puts it, "to call oneself a Norman was to make oneself heir of the culture surrounding the name." According to Webber, after settling in southern Italy, the Normans "were able to maintain their concepts of unity, both among themselves and with their homeland, for some eighty years," till the end of the eleventh century.[66] Ewan Johnson continues the tradition of drawing parallels with the Old World and the New when he compares the two Norman groups to the Irish of Dublin and the Irish of Brooklyn. In the case of the Normans of the South, much like that of the Irish of Brooklyn, "the origin is acknowledged," even though it "is no longer a primary factor in determining political loyalty."[67] Finally, Graham Loud asserts, "That in reality the Normans were not a people with a unified descent, but a hybrid of French thinly overlaid with Scandinavians, was unimportant compared with the conceptions of a separate people enunciated by Norman intellectuals (and echoed by those in southern Italy, whether Norman or not, who wrote about the Normans)."[68] The actual ties between the Normans of Normandy and the Normans of the South are secondary to the fact that the latter adhered to the myth of *Normanitas* ("Normanness"), of being a "distinct people with their own character."[69] This myth was perpetuated, in varying degrees, both by pro-Norman authors, whether or not they were Normans themselves, and by outsiders.

Although there are fewer references to Normandy in southern Italian sources than there are to southern Italy in Norman ones, they are not entirely absent. Amatus of Montecassino, for example, begins his work with a description of Normandy as "a plain filled with woods and fruit trees." When the region became overpopulated, the Normans "took up arms, breaking the bond of peace, and created a great army of foot soldiers and horsemen." Amatus continues, "Now we shall tell you how they scattered throughout the world and made their way."[70] The pages that follow address a variety of Norman enterprises—in England, Spain, and the Holy Land—before Amatus comes to his main subject, southern Italy.

In both Normandy and southern Italy, there were distinct similarities in the descriptions of the Normans (and of the Vikings) as a people characterized and distinguished from others by their warlike nature and shrewdness.[71] Geoffrey Malaterra paid tribute to a long tradition when he described the Normans as a "very shrewd people indeed, quick to avenge injury, scorning the fields of their homeland in hope of acquiring more, avid for profit and domination, ready to feign or conceal anything, maintaining a certain balance between avarice and largesse."[72] These characteristics were an integral part of the Norman myth and can be found in the sources written by both authors favorable to the Normans and authors hostile to them.

Tracing the instances of what is perhaps the more surprising of the two key characteristics—shrewdness—is particularly revealing. As Emily Albu puts it, shrewdness "seems part of the Norman pathology from the very beginning, featured in virtually all Norman histories from the first . . . to the last."[73] Dudo of Saint-Quentin, who wrote *History of the Normans* in the first half of the eleventh century, describes Hastings (a Viking chief and a contemporary of Rollo, the conqueror of the region that was to become Normandy) as a "double-dyed dissimulator" (*duplex simulator*) and a "deceiver" (*deceptor*). At another point, Dudo has a Frank admit that "the Normans are more shrewd than other peoples."[74] William of Apulia never tires of describing the guile of Robert Guiscard, whom he considers more cunning than Cicero and craftier than Ulysses. In fact, guile was part of what made Robert a successful conqueror: "If victory's palm befell him by guile or by arms, he thought it equally fine, because often what force cannot achieve, the mind's adroitness can."[75] Both the Norse and the Normans specialized in feigning death so as to enter a stronghold for burial and then take it over. In different versions of this medieval take on the story of the Trojan horse, we find three

Norsemen (the mythical Danish king Frotho, Hastings, and Harald Hardrada, king of Norway) and three Normans of the South (Robert Guiscard, Roger II of Sicily, and Roger's grandson, Emperor Frederick II).[76] In a variation on this ruse, before sailing from Antioch to Italy in 1104 or 1105, Bohemond, in order to avoid capture by the Byzantines, spread the news of his death. Each time his ship approached shore, he hid in a coffin in which he had also placed a dead rooster that gave off the stench of a rotting body. According to Anna Comnena, "Bohemond himself derived more pleasure than anyone from his imaginary misfortune."[77]

The list of leaders who played dead suggests a sense of shared identity between Normans and Scandinavians. As Nick Webber has argued, from the Franks' perspective, the Normans and the Vikings were largely one and the same (modern French, in which the term *Norman* is often used for both, reflects this fact).[78] The Normans themselves, however, viewed their past in terms of a radical break and at the same time continuity. On the one hand, they represented Rollo's conversion to Christianity and his foundation of Normandy as turning a new page. Dudo of Saint-Quentin and William of Jumièges reveal the Normans' awareness of their mixed descent and their beginnings as a gens only upon conversion to Christianity and settlement in Normandy. On the other hand, both authors attempt to trace the origins of the future Normans to Scandinavia, from which they were driven off by a combination of overpopulation and internal strife. In other words, on the one hand, the Normans celebrated the beginnings of their gens, made up *ex diversis gentibus*, who came together at the time of Rollo. On the one hand, however, they made an effort to represent themselves as heirs to the Vikings. In this way, they could take pride in both their newfound piety and their long-standing military ability.[79]

Dudo of Saint-Quentin located the origins of the Normans in Denmark (Dacia), where people, "by mingling together in illicit couplings... generate innumerable children." The superfluous progeny are then "sent away without wealth from their own people, that they may enrich themselves out of the plenty of foreigners."[80] William of Jumièges similarly claimed that the population of Denmark (Datia or Danamarcha) "grew so rapidly that soon the islands were overrun by people and many men were forced... to migrate from their homes."[81]

In recounting the story of the origins of Normandy, the chroniclers did not attempt to conceal—and sometimes even drew attention to—the misery that the Vikings brought upon the continent. Dudo of Saint-Quentin describes

Francia being "desolated, almost emptied of people."[82] William lamented the Vikings' burning his own monastery, Jumièges, to the ground, so that "the site, which for so long had shown its strength in honorable splendor, became a nesting place for wild animals and birds." William also described the early career of Rollo, plotting "with his men to demolish Paris, scheming in his sly heart and thirsting with a pagan instinct for the blood of the Christians the way a wolf does." More important for the present inquiry, William inserted into his work several passages from Adrevald of Fleury's *Miracula sancti Benedicti* that depict the Vikings at their worst: "It is shameful to repeat the destruction of the most noble communities of monks and nuns . . . the massacre of other folk by no means ignoble, the captivity of matrons, the rape of virgins, and other unspeakable kinds of suffering inflicted upon the conquered by their conquerors."[83] So we know that at least one eleventh-century chronicler read Adrevald's work (and probably the appendix by Adelarius, relating the intervention of Saint Benedict in the battle between Hugh the Great against the Norse, discussed above) in order to learn about the Normans' past.

The chroniclers do, however, provide an excuse—or at least an explanation—for the atrocities committed by the Norse. According to Dudo of Saint-Quentin, the Vikings were a divine instrument, and their ill treatment of the Franks was "not for their destruction, but for their correction."[84] William of Jumièges ventured, more conservatively, that the suffering of the Vikings' victims was "not in every case unmerited."[85] This image of the Vikings/Normans as doing God's work even in their violent acts can be found in southern Italy as well. Geoffrey Malaterra describes the disasters that befell southern Italy in 1058—disease, famine, and the Norman attacks—as "a heaven-sent scourge from an angry God, made necessary—or so we believe—by our sins."[86]

Apparently, some memory of the Normans' Scandinavian roots survived not only in Normandy but also in southern Italy. Geoffrey Malaterra, influenced by Dudo of Saint-Quentin, wrote in the first chapter of his chronicle that Normandy belonged to the kings of the Franks until Rollo, "a most valiant leader from Norway" (Geoffrey departs here from both Dudo and William, who called him a Dane), "took note of the pleasantness of this region and chose to embrace it with his love."[87] Also, according to Graham Loud, some aspects of Scandinavian mythology can be found in the writings of the Normans of the South. Amatus of Montecassino describes a vision in which Robert Guiscard drank up three rivers as an omen of conquest.[88] According to Loud, a Norse saga attributed a similar deed to Thor. For Loud, this was more than a coincidence; "the survival of a Scandinavian element in the legends of the Norman expansion," he writes, "can only have reinforced consciousness of the distinctiveness of the Norman people."[89]

The Normans accepted and, surprisingly, even celebrated their brutal history. The exceptional moments when saints—whether Benedict, Germain, or Cuthbert—curbed their violence were part and parcel of this history. Two sources indicate that the tradition of attributing their setbacks to saintly interventions accompanied the Normans to Italy in the eleventh century. The first of these interventions against the Normans was reported during the so-called Cadalan schism that pitted antipope Honorius II (Bishop Peter Cadalus of Parma) against Pope Alexander II (Bishop Anselm of Lucca).[90] Cadalus had the backing of the Holy Roman Empire, while Alexander II enjoyed the support of the Normans and of Duke Godfrey of Lorraine. It was under the protection of the Norman Richard of Capua that Alexander II was enthroned in Rome on October 1, 1061. In 1062, however, the supporters of Cadalus succeeded in occupying Rome. Duke Godfrey was primarily responsible for the return of Alexander II to Rome in 1063, while the Normans, busy fighting elsewhere, played only a secondary role. As H. E. J. Cowdrey has written, "It was already becoming clear that the Normans would put their own interests first and that . . . they could not be counted upon to promote papal interests unless it suited them to do so."[91] In 1064, the Synod of Mantua confirmed Alexander II as the rightful pope, ending the schism.

Bishop Benzo of Alba was one of the key actors in the Cadalan schism on the side of Cadalus.[92] He tried to negotiate, without success, with Emperor Constantine X Ducas of Byzantium for an alliance against the Normans. In the third book of *Seven Books for Emperor Henry IV*, probably completed between 1064 and 1065, Benzo claimed that in 1063 the apostles, Saint Maurice, and Saint Carpophorus had been at the head of the army of supporters of Cadalus in Rome in a skirmish against the Normans hired by Hildebrand (future Pope Gregory VII and an ally of Pope Alexander II).[93] So, according to Benzo, the Normans, just like the Vikings, were suffering from celestial interventions on behalf of their enemies.

If one is to believe both Benzo of Alba and Geoffrey Malaterra, in 1063 saints intervened in battle both on the side of the Normans (at Cerami) and against them (in Rome). Geoffrey wrote more than two decades after Benzo, but the coincidence of date is indicative of the ongoing transformation of the

Normans in the late eleventh century from persecutors into defenders of Christianity, and of saints from their enemies to their helpers. Benzo's work shows the long tradition in decline, while Geoffrey Malaterra stands for a new one, which built upon but also radically reinterpreted the old.

In another example of the transformation of the centuries-old narrative into its opposite, the chronicle of Amatus of Montecassino contains two references to saintly interventions, one against and one in favor of the Normans. According to Amatus, sometime around 1045, Abbot Richer of Montecassino broke sacred vessels in order to pay mercenaries to protect the monastery from the Normans. "God appeared in the midst of battle," says Amatus, "as did St. Benedict, who showed himself as [his] standard bearer."[94] It is unclear from the wording of the sentence whether Saint Benedict was actually seen on the battlefield, but the narrative resembles those of the battles of Cerami and Antioch, which feature standards of unambiguously supernatural origin. There is also an obvious similarity between this account and that written by Adelarius, who described Saint Benedict protecting the monastery of Fleury in the late ninth century.

It is significant that Amatus chose to include the episode in his chronicle, which implies that he did not deem it disparaging enough of the Normans to omit from his generally laudatory representation of them. Although the Normans lost the battle, Amatus makes sure to mention that they did not suffer significant losses: "To prevent the shedding of too much blood, all the Normans were bound with strips of rope."[95] According to Amatus, the Normans had made a mistake and had learned their lesson. An instrument of correction, the Normans sometimes needed to be corrected. Amatus notes that after the battle, the monastery was safe from any future attacks: "Then the abbot held the land securely, and from this hour on they [the monks] knew no enemy in their land."[96]

The chronicle of Amatus contains another episode in which a saint makes a visible appearance, this time on behalf of the Normans. Amatus describes Saint Matthew appearing to Bishop John of Salerno on the eve of the battle of Civitate, fought between the Normans and the troops assembled by Pope Leo IX in June 1053. John, who fell asleep in the crypt of the cathedral of Salerno, where the relics of Saint Matthew were kept, saw a vision of the apostle explaining to him the things to come: "The pope is coming with base knights to drive out [the Normans], but his men will be defeated, scattered, imprisoned, and killed. Afterwards the pope will return to Rome where he will die, for after his arrival [there] he will only live a short time. This is ordained before the presence of God, for whoever will attempt to drive out the Normans will either die presently or know a great affliction. This land was given to the Normans by God."[97]

Here, then, Saint Matthew's goal is to demonstrate that the Normans' victory is predestined and sanctioned from above. This account belongs to the group of visions before battle in which a supernatural agent prophesies victory. The two episodes in Amatus's chronicle reveal a vision of the history of the Normans of the South, in which they begin by attacking a monastery but, after a hard but necessary lesson at the hands of God and Saint Benedict, become a chosen people, to whom God grants victory over the pope himself. Thus the chronicle contains at once a traditional narrative in which a saint protects a monastery against the Normans, and the same narrative turned on its head, with another saint championing the Normans before a major battle.

Another eleventh-century account of saintly intervention on the battlefield reveals the ways in which various strands of the tradition could come together, despite the difference in time and place. Between 1041 and 1043, Andrew of Fleury composed a continuation of *Miracula sancti Benedicti* in which he dealt primarily with the dependencies of the monastery, arranging the stories of miracles geographically.[98] When it came to Catalonia, he relied on the accounts of two monks, John of Ripoll and his brother, Bernard.[99] According to Andrew, in 1003 Christian Catalans profited from a celestial intervention in a battle that they fought against Muslims. This is the earliest case to feature Muslims in the body of narratives of saintly intervention in battle. A Catalan leader urged his followers not to fear the numerically superior enemy, because the Virgin, the Archangel Michael, and Saint Peter would, "with their own hands," slay five thousand enemy soldiers each. Saints do not appear on the battlefield in this case, but the Virgin makes herself visible when she announces the outcome of the encounter. Before the news of the victory over Muslims in Spain could spread widely, the Virgin appeared to a cleric on Monte Gargano and informed him of it.[100] The miraculous appearance of the Virgin proved that the Catalan leader was speaking the truth and that the three saints had indeed taken part in the battle.

Several traditions come together in Andrew's account. The narrative appears to have originated in Catalonia itself and was perhaps preserved at the monastery of Ripoll. Thanks to chance (and to Andrew's fastidiousness in acknowledging his sources), we know the names of the two monks who brought this story with them from Catalonia to Fleury. At the same time, Andrew of Fleury must have found this narrative credible at least in part because of the existence of a similar one in his own monastery, in which Saint Benedict intervened in battle on behalf of the monks of Fleury when they were attacked by the Vikings. In addition, Andrew's narrative explicitly pays tribute to the tradition that grew up around the cult site of Saint Michael at Monte Gargano, as recorded in the *Liber de apparitione Sancti Michaelis*. There are no references to any monks from Monte Gargano at Fleury, so the exact lines of transmission of this narrative from southern Italy to the region of the Loire are difficult to trace. The accounts of supernatural interventions in battle found in the chronicles of Geoffrey Malaterra and the anonymous author of the *Gesta Francorum* present a similar case. Although we know little about the exact sources of these accounts, both authors (or their sources) must have been no less able than Andrew of Fleury to engage with traditions far removed from them both chronologically and geographically.

Another piece of evidence suggests that contemporaries perceived a connection between the invasions of the Vikings and the wars against Muslims. The *Bella parisiacae urbis* refers to the Vikings desecrating a church by turning it into stable: "Since the Danes could not pen all the beasts in the fields and meadow, / They turned the sacred hall of Saint Germain into a stable."[101] During the crusading period, the very same accusation would be leveled against Muslims.[102] It is, of course, possible that churches, as relatively large structures, easy to secure, were indeed sometimes converted into stables. Whatever reality lies behind it, however, the theme of churches being converted into stables became central to the narratives of battles against those perceived as enemies of the faith. If, to the minds of those living in the ninth and tenth centuries (especially north of the Alps), the Vikings represented absolute evil, from the eleventh century on this role was filled by Muslims. It made sense that the most powerful miracle possible on a battlefield, formerly used against the Vikings, would now be directed against Muslims.

The stakes involved in claiming that victory was due to supernatural intervention were high. The accounts by Geoffrey Malaterra and the author of the *Gesta Francorum* are best understood in the context of the Normans' striving to represent their conquest of southern Italy and Sicily—and of Antioch—not as a land grab but as divinely sanctioned conquest. The agenda of sacralizing the Normans' offensive wars is prevalent in southern Italian chronicles. According to Kenneth Wolf, "the Normans of the *Historia Normannorum* [by Amatus of Montecassino] knew better than to place their trust solely in their martial abilities. They understood that they could win nothing without the help of God."[103] As Graham Loud notes, William of Apulia "undoubtedly felt that God had ordained their [the Normans'] conquest."[104] This was the same message that Geoffrey Malaterra and the author of *Gesta Francorum* tried to convey in representing saints taking an active part in the wars of the Normans against Muslims, whether in Sicily or in the East. According to them, the Normans were the new chosen people. That God had used the same miracle against them in the past did not undermine this claim but, paradoxically, confirmed it.

Carl Erdmann has argued that the invasions of the Vikings gave an important impetus to the development of the idea of "holy war" in Christianity. Many monastic writers believed that the Vikings were such a terrible threat that God and his saints had to oppose them. The supposed descendants of the Vikings, the Normans of the South, also made an important contribution to the idea of holy war. They and their allies were aware—more so than an "average" Western Christian—of narratives involving saints who took an active part in warfare. They used these narratives to remind readers that the Norman *gens* had a long history, predating the occupation of either southern Italy or Normandy and going back to Scandinavia. This *gens* had a set of characteristics that did not correspond very closely to the Christian virtues but did render the Normans particularly effective in warfare. At the same time, the Normans and their supporters recalled the Vikings in order to underscore the differences between the supposed "ancestors" and their "heirs." The pagan Vikings, who attacked monasteries and against whom saints intervened, became the Christian Normans, who were *milites Christi* and enjoyed saintly protection. In short, the presence of virtually the same miracle in stories of the battles of Antioch and Cerami found, respectively, in *De rebus gestis Rogerii* and the *Gesta Francorum* is no coincidence. Rather, it demonstrates that one crucial strategy of sacralizing warfare during the early crusading period grew out of the myth of *Normanitas* as it developed among the Normans of the South.

JUDAS MACCABEUS: A JEWISH WARRIOR, A CHRISTIAN PATRIARCH, AND A MUSLIM GENERAL

The miracle of saintly intervention in the battle of Antioch has its roots not only in the Christian and, indirectly, Greco-Roman traditions, as demonstrated in the previous three chapters, but also in the Old Testament, particularly in the second book of the Maccabees.[1] This precedent is unique in that it is the only one that at least three medieval authors acknowledged. Two chroniclers, Guibert of Nogent and William of Malmesbury, noted that the account of saints helping crusaders in the battle of Antioch was credible, as angels had also helped the Maccabees in similar circumstances. The poet Gilo of Paris was less explicit, but he also referred to divine aid to the Maccabees in his account of the battle. At first glance, this and numerous other comparisons between crusaders and Maccabees in the sources of the First Crusade are easily explicable. Already in the course of the First Crusade, the participants seem to have imagined that they were reliving the events described in the Bible. In crusading sources, the proliferation of imagery, especially that having to do with warfare and rulership, from the historical books of the Old Testament legitimized both crusaders' conquest and the establishment of the kingdom of Jerusalem.

On closer inspection, however, it appears that the representations of crusaders and settlers in the Holy Land as the "new Jews" were not acceptable to everyone, at least not in the form in which they appeared in the late eleventh and early twelfth centuries. In the eyes of several authors, such representations broke radically from established tradition. That tradition developed in response to the anxiety that Jewish heritage provoked in many Christian theologians from the apostolic era on. One could neither be rid of this heritage nor embrace it; either choice would be heretical. The dichotomy between the Jewish past and the Christian present and future, which revolved around the incarnation that closed the old era and inaugurated the new one, provided a solution of sorts. David Nirenberg has established, for example, that the author of the Gospel of John viewed history "through a polarizing lens of a dualist cosmology." He divided "the cosmos into world and word, into a realm of flesh, falseness, and death, and one of spirit, truth and immortality." The first realm was associated with the Jews and the second with the Christians.[2]

This dichotomy, which was implied even when it was not clearly stated, made it safe, from a theological standpoint, to refer to the historical books of the Old Testament in discussions of current affairs. Literal comparisons between Christians and Jews were never a problem, as long as they did not touch upon higher matters such as salvation. For example, the valor of a Christian warrior could be compared to that of a Maccabean warrior, in that military courage was of little importance in the Christian hierarchy of virtues. The dichotomy made it possible to make comparisons between Christians and Jews on a metaphorical level. Certain rules had to be followed: Christians had to be associated with spirituality and Jews with carnality, and Christianity's supersession of and superiority to Judaism had to be apparent. Thus a Christian monk could be compared to a Maccabean warrior, since the reader would know that spiritual battles waged by the monk had superseded the physical ones waged by the Maccabees as the best way to serve God. Already in the third century, Origen made it clear that the possibility of reading them metaphorically was the only reason why the historical books of the Old Testament had any value for Christians: "unless these carnal wars were meant as types of spiritual warfare, the books of Jewish history . . . would never have been handed down by the Apostles to be read in their churches by the disciples of Christ, Who has come, after all, on order to teach peace."[3] Katherine Smith has demonstrated that the divide between physical and spiritual warfare and, by extension, between knights and monks was not as radical as Origen and his successor theologians sometimes made it appear. For instance, a knight who had become a monk merely had to transfer his "desire for battle" from the physical to the spiritual realm.[4] Still, until the second half of the eleventh century, battles could be either physical or spiritual, not both at the same time.

Although not every use of Israelites as a metaphor for Christians was strictly typological, typology was a crucial mechanism underpinning the use of Jewish heritage to explore and explain the Christian present. Originally, typology related the Old to the New Testament, so that an element (a type) in the former adumbrated another element (an antitype) in the latter. From early on, however, typology evolved beyond this schema to apply to events not necessarily described in either the Old or the New Testament.[5] Erich Auerbach has defined typology broadly as an "interpretation of one worldly event through another," where the first event signifies the second and the second fulfills the first.[6] David Berkeley has refined Auerbach's definition by adding new characteristics, the most important of which for the present discussion is that the antitype has to be *forma perfectior* of the type.[7]

During the investiture controversy and, to a much greater extent, during and after the First Crusade, the rules governing the uses of the historical books of the Old Testament, outlined above, appear to have ceased functioning. Comparisons between Christians and Israelites became both literal *and* related to higher matters. The most crucial parallel had to do with the fact that engaging the enemy—whether of the papacy or of Christianity writ large—on the battlefield became one of the highest forms of expressing piety, as it had been in the Old Testament. The First Crusade signaled a dramatic—in fact, from the point of view of at least some contemporaries, miraculous—change in the paradigm: warriors became equal to monks. Guibert stated very clearly that knights now earned a "measure of God's grace" without choosing a monastic life.[8] The First Crusade was a gift from God, which made it possible for knights to wage physical and spiritual war simultaneously. In his youth, Guibert himself had to choose between joining the ranks of the *oratores* or the *bellatores*. His younger contemporaries, by contrast, could become *oratores* without ever ceasing to be *bellatores*.

Since Christians now also served God by fighting, their superiority to the Israelites, who had done exactly the same thing, was no longer apparent. The case of the Maccabees was especially problematic, if only because their status in Christianity was not clear. They did not belong to the pantheon of Old Testament heroes who had become an integral part of the Christian tradition from early on. Moreover, there was the possibility of confusion between Maccabean martyrs (who resisted without recourse to physical violence) and Maccabean warriors (who fought the enemy with arms). Almost always considered separately until the middle of the eleventh century, it appears that during the investiture controversy Maccabean warriors began to acquire the aura of Maccabean martyrs. Some of the sources of the First Crusade—particularly the chronicles of Caffaro and Fulcher of Chartres—went a step further, so that the reader has difficulty deciding whether references to "Maccabees" imply the warriors, the martyrs, or both. Such references call into question the boundaries between Jews and Christians and between physical fighting and martyrdom.

Comparisons between crusaders and the Israelites did not just bring together two peoples that had triumphed, at different times, in the same region. They also closely associated two peoples seen as God's chosen ones. As in the past, some theologians deemed this real or perceived challenge to the boundary between Judaism and Christianity a threat. Several chroniclers of the First Crusade were alarmed that the notion of Christianity's supersession of Judaism—and thus of the centrality of the incarnation—was, as they saw it, being pushed into the background. They did not oppose comparisons between Christians and Israelites as such, but they hoped to reestablish the relationship along more traditional lines. Although these chroniclers had the same program and a similar general approach, revolving around the deprecation of Jews, their techniques were different. Guibert of Nogent, the key figure, developed a particularly sophisticated approach to the problem, stressing that any similarities between Christians and Jews were superficial and concealed profound differences. To prove his point, Guibert recalled the old dichotomy between the flesh and the spirit. On the one hand, he reminded the reader of the supposed carnality of the Jews; on the other, he argued that crusading warfare, despite all the blood and gore, was inherently spiritual. In order to distinguish between the two types of warfare more clearly, Guibert had little choice but to present a caricature of both Jewish carnality and Christian spirituality.

Although Guibert provided a uniquely articulate solution to the perceived danger of Christians coming to resemble Jews, his dualist approach can be found in a variety of sources, both Latin and vernacular. This approach could have dramatic, though probably not always intended, consequences. In a world that was increasingly seen as bipolar, some Christians began to group Jews together with Muslims. From their point of view, both Jews and Muslims were associated with the flesh, and both had lost Jerusalem at one point in history. The two emerged as diametrical opposites of Christians, who were associated with the spirit and who had conquered Jerusalem. In many of these sources, the capture of Jerusalem *by* the Jewish Maccabees was no longer the most fitting precedent for the capture of Jerusalem by crusaders. Rather, Titus's capture of Jerusalem *from* the Jews was the pertinent parallel.

Anti-Jewish rhetoric did not always accompany the sacralization of crusading warfare, but it helped to counterbalance the threat of Judaizing that at least some observers perceived in the representation of physical warfare as "holy." The First Crusade thus led to a new manifestation of and further elaboration on the exegetical Jew. One consequence of this was greater and more hostile attention to living Jews.[9]

As recorded in the first and second books of the Maccabees, the Maccabees were a priestly family that, under the leadership of the priest Mattathias, initiated the revolt against King Antiochus IV Epiphanes of Syria, who tried to force paganism upon his Jewish subjects in the second century B.C.[10] The name Maccabee, which literally means "hammer," was originally the surname of Judas, Mattathias's ablest son. Angels assisted Judas Maccabeus in two of his battles. In one of them, "five resplendent men on horses with golden bridles" surrounded Judas, protected him with their armor, and "showered arrows and thunderbolts upon the enemy" (2 Macc. 10:29–30). In the second battle, just one celestial horseman appeared, this time "clothed in white and brandishing weapons of gold," and instilled courage in the fighters (11:8–9).

Eventually, Judas's surname, "Maccabee," came to be applied to the so-called Maccabean martyrs—seven brothers, their mother, and the priest Eleazar—who refused to renounce their faith and whom King Antiochus tortured and executed in a gruesome manner. While patristic authors virtually ignored Maccabean warriors, they found the execution of Maccabean martyrs very useful in constructing the concept of Christian martyrdom.[11] Many of the early hagiographers used the martyrdom of the seven brothers, their mother, and Eleazar as a template for the *Vitae* they were writing. Moreover, from early on, the church adopted the Maccabees not merely as prototypes of Christian martyrs but as Christian martyrs in their own right, despite the fact that they had lived long before Christ. Jerome claimed that the Maccabean martyrs had suffered *pro Christo*.[12] Augustine mentioned Maccabean martyrs several times in his writings and even dedicated a sermon to them, in which he argued unambiguously, "So the first thing I must impress . . . is that when you are admiring these martyrs, you should not think they were not Christians. They were Christians."[13]

Although Maccabean warriors had no connection to Antioch, Maccabean martyrs did. The location of the execution of the martyrs and their initial burial (the remains eventually found their way to Constantinople and Rome) is uncertain, but a number of patristic sources designate Antioch, at one point the center of the Christian cult of the Maccabees. In a sermon in which he argues vehemently that the Maccabean martyrs belong not to the Jewish but to the Christian tradition, Augustine refers to a church dedicated to the Maccabees in Antioch. Augustine found it at once ironic and fitting that the city bearing nearly the same name as Antiochus, the persecutor of the Maccabean martyrs, would celebrate those whom he persecuted.[14]

Although the majority of patristic authors kept silent about the Maccabees, there was one notable exception. In his *De officiis* (*On Duties*), Ambrose of Milan used Maccabean warriors as an example of courage in adversity. While the story of the Maccabees is above all a story of victories, Ambrose chose to emphasize the deaths of two of the warriors, Eleazar and Judas. Ambrose considered at length the battle of Beth-Zechariah, in which Antiochus employed elephants made drunk with juice of grapes and mulberries. During the battle, one of the Jews, Eleazar, stabbed the largest elephant, thinking, erroneously, that the king was riding upon it. The animal fell and crushed Eleazar, who was thus "buried under his own triumph" (1 Macc. 6:43–46). Although Eleazar did not attain his immediate objective, his courage "so terrified King Antiochus . . . that he treated for peace." Next, Ambrose addressed the death of Judas Maccabeus, who engaged an army of twenty thousand with a mere nine hundred warriors. Judas's followers were "desperate to retreat," but he persuaded them "to fight and die with glory rather than flee and bring shame on themselves." Judas was killed in the fighting but, like Eleazar, "found in death a place of greater glory than his triumphs had afforded." From Maccabean warriors Ambrose moved on to Maccabean martyrs, which allowed a seamless transition from a literal military vocabulary to a metaphorical one. According to Ambrose, "when the children fought their own battle they conquered without arms." Subsequent examples include the innocents killed by Herod and two early Christian martyrs, Saint Agnes and Saint Lawrence.[15]

The series of examples Ambrose offered constructs a hierarchy of sanctity in which Maccabean warriors who died in battle occupy the lowest rank, Maccabean martyrs the intermediate one, and Christian martyrs the highest. These ranks are on the same scale; the difference between them is one of degree. In other words, dying for one's faith on the battlefield, like Eleazar and Judas, emerges as similar to dying for one's faith without offering any physical resistance, like the Maccabean martyrs, the innocents, and the saints. In Ambrose's picture, there is more to unite Jews and Christians, namely, their glorious death, than to separate them. It might appear that the incarnation no longer occupies the central position. While this treatment of the Maccabees was unique at the time, the idea that the two groups of Maccabees, the warriors and the martyrs, were essentially similar reemerged in the eleventh century.

Between the fourth century, when Ambrose was writing, and the eleventh century, there was little interest in the Maccabean warriors. Only two authors proposed an extended reading of the books of the Maccabees. They did so in the traditional manner, with the incarnation clearly central to their interpretations. In the first half of the ninth century, Rabanus Maurus examined the books on the literal, typological, and allegorical levels. On the typological level, he argued that Mattathias was a type of Christ, that his sons signified the community of saints, and that Antiochus stood for the Antichrist. On the allegorical level, Rabanus considered the Maccabees' wars parallel to the struggles of the church against its enemies. Jean Dunbabin has commented on Rabanus's allegorical interpretation of the Maccabees, "He was apparently unconscious of any irony in paralleling the Maccabees' wars on behalf of the integrity of Judaism with those of the Church against, among others, the Jews."[16] Yet the exegetes using the tools of typology and allegory took delight in this type of irony. From their perspective, the superficial similarities between the Maccabees and the church—both struggled against apparently superior forces—were useful in highlighting substantial differences. The former fought for the law, while the latter struggled for Christ; the Maccabees' struggles were physical, while those of the church were spiritual.

A century and a half later, Aelfric, abbot of the Anglo-Saxon monastery of Eynsham, also became interested in the Maccabees and also åinterpreted them in the traditional manner, with its emphasis on the incarnation. If Judas Maccabeus, living before Christ, had no choice but to fight physical battles, Christians now could choose between physical and spiritual battles. The *bellatores* (the lower order) could still use Judas Maccabeus as a fitting model of literal imitation. The *oratores* (the higher order), however, could use Judas only as an inspiration in their spiritual struggles. This scheme endured throughout the Middle Ages and beyond. For example, in his *Deeds of William*, written between 1071 and 1077, William of Poitiers provided a metaphorical comparison between two *oratores*, who were in turn monks and hermits, and the Maccabees: "Thus, with their soul victorious, they fought with energy rivaling the Maccabees, now under the yoke of monks, now in the wrestling-ring of a hermit's life, to win everlasting freedom of spirit and peace, seeking no preferment, but the humblest place in the exile of this transitory world."[17]

In the two centuries before the First Crusade, several authors also used the Maccabees as literal prototypes of the *bellatores*. From a theological perspective, this use could become problematic when such literal comparisons between Jews and Christians appeared to involve the issue of salvation. For instance, the anonymous author of the *Annals of Fulda* compared Count Robert, who was killed in 866, to Judas Maccabeus: "Robert . . . was killed at the River Loire fighting bravely against the Northmen. He was, so to speak, a second Macchabeus in our times, and if all his battles which he fought with the Bretons and Northmen were fully described they would be on the same level as the deeds of Macchabeus."[18] A comparison between Robert and Judas is apt, since both died in battle against enemies of the faith. However, it is possible that this was more than an innocuous historical parallel. The comparison with Judas elevated Robert to the status of a biblical hero. More important, it also hinted that his death was glorious not only in secular terms but perhaps in God's eyes as well. This implied that his death might not have been much different from the type of death that merited the greatest divine approval in the period after the incarnation, namely, martyrdom.

Papal reforms, particularly those associated with the pontificate of Gregory VII, presented a serious challenge to traditional divisions, not only between death on the battlefield and martyrdom but also between spiritual and physical battles and, by extension, between monks and knights.[19] Some of the key examples of this trend feature references to the Maccabees, who emerge as prototypes of warriors whose physical battles attained the status usually reserved for spiritual battles. For example, Bernold of St. Blasien designated the anti-king Rudolph of Swabia, who died of a wound received on the battlefield, "another Maccabaeus," who "deserved to fall in the service of St. Peter."[20] This case is similar to the previous one, for Bernold, like the anonymous author of the *Annals of Fulda*, appears to hint that his hero's death might have been similar, or perhaps even equal, to martyrdom.

The narratives associated with Erlembald, the military leader of the Gregorian faction in Milan, provide the most revealing examples of the sacralization of warfare in the decades before the First Crusade. Abbot Andreas of Strumi recorded that Erlembald had considered becoming a monk, but the holy deacon Ariald managed to dissuade him by arguing that he would gain greater merit with God by remaining a knight and fighting for the church. However, as Carl Erdmann has observed, "What Bernard of Clairvaux would celebrate two generations later under the name of 'new knighthood [*nova militia*]' was still very novel in the time of Alexander II." So Erlembald sought further advice in Rome, where the pope confirmed what Ariald had said.[21] Bonizo of Sutri called Erlembald "the mighty soldier of God" (*miles Dei*), who "stood, like Judas Maccabeus, unperturbed" in the face of grave danger.[22] Eventually, "a host of conspirators" attacked Erlembald, who fought back but was overwhelmed. Bonizo stated unambiguously that Erlembald was martyred and that God performed miracles at his tomb.[23] In 1078, Pope Gregory VII announced the miracles to the Roman synod, thereby officially declaring Erlembald a saint.[24] Although Judas Maccabeus makes only a brief appearance in the narratives concerning Erlembald, the very fact of his association with a knight who became a saint not in spite but because of his military valor is significant.

Although he also took the side of Gregory VII, Manegold of Lautenbach adopted a different approach in his comparison of the Maccabees and papal supporters from the one employed by Bernold and Bonizo. Manegold's tactic reveals that even at this early date there was some concern about the assimilation of Christian fighters to Jewish heroes of the Old Testament. In his list of precedents for the legitimate exercise of violence, Manegold referred to the episode of Mattathias, the father of Judas Maccabeus, who killed a Jew about to offer a pagan sacrifice and the official who forced the Jew to do so. Manegold then recalled Saint Oswald, who fought "for country and for faith," died in battle, and was deemed a martyr.[25] At first glance, the reference to Mattathias is surprising. It would have been more fitting for Manegold to refer to Judas Maccabeus, who was also killed in battle. Manegold's choice of Mattathias over Judas might be due to his reluctance to equate the deaths of an Israelite and a Christian in battle. But Manegold's attempt to make theologically acceptable a comparison between Maccabees and Christian knights fighting in defense of the papacy could not be entirely satisfactory. It hinged on "forgetting" a well-known story in which Judas got himself killed and "remembering" one in which Mattathias killed an enemy.

The investiture controversy merely announced the popularity that the Maccabees were to enjoy in the wake of the First Crusade. Many of the trends that were nascent at the time became much more pronounced. For example, although Maccabean warriors might have acquired some traits of their martyred brethren in the sources dealing with warfare between the papacy and the empire, the two groups became indistinguishable in at least two accounts of the First Crusade. Caffaro describes angels in heaven receiving some of his compatriots who died during the siege of Antioch and giving them a place next to the Maccabees.[26] It is impossible to tell whether Caffaro means the warriors or the martyrs. On the one hand, crusaders obviously resembled the former more closely than the latter. On the other hand, as discussed above, in Christian tradition it was only the martyrs, not the warriors, who were granted a place in paradise. It seems most likely that Caffaro meant a collective image, which included both Maccabean martyrs and Maccabean warriors.

This erosion of the boundary between Maccabean martyrs and Maccabean warriors is even more pronounced in the writings of Fulcher of Chartres. In the prologue to his chronicle, Fulcher asks, "in what ways do the Franks differ from the Israelites or Maccabees?" He answers that the similarities are numerous and profound. "In the same regions" as the Israelites or Maccabees, the Franks had suffered "dismemberment, crucifixion, flaying, death by arrows or by being rent apart, or other kinds of martyrdom, all for the love of Christ."[27] Once again, it is not clear whether Fulcher means Maccabean warriors or Maccabean martyrs. Dismemberment and death by arrows could refer to death on the battlefield, but the list taken as a whole suggests methods of execution. In fact, Fulcher borrows here from stock descriptions of early Christian martyrs, who, according to an eleventh-century text, "met death through various tortures, some were decapitated, some flayed alive, some burned, some drowned in rivers, some pierced by spikes, some deprived of their eyes, some maimed in their limbs, some sawn in two, some stoned."[28]

Even if we take the chronicles of the First Crusade at face value, few crusaders suffered martyrdom in its traditional definition of execution as punishment for refusal to abandon one's faith.[29] Fulcher does mention that crusaders were ready for martyrdom. He writes that they "could not be overcome by threats or temptations" and that "if the butcher's sword had been at hand, they would not have refused martyrdom for the love of Christ."[30] But he does not describe a single instance of a crusader being executed after refusing to deny Christ. In this he differs from other chroniclers, several of whom include one or two episodes of captives being killed for refusing to convert to Islam in the course of the First Crusade.[31] Fulcher was well aware that there were no mass martyrdoms, in the traditional sense, during the First Crusade. Thus his graphic description of crusaders' "dismemberment, crucifixion, flaying, death by arrows or by being rent apart" cannot be understood literally. It seems that Fulcher used the vocabulary of martyrdom to describe the general suffering of crusaders, including their death on the battlefield. At least in this instance, his definition of "martyrdom" was so broad that it undermined the traditional dichotomy between resistance with and without arms. Fulcher's intentionally ambiguous reference to "Maccabees" supported his aims. Fulcher brought Maccabean warriors and Maccabean martyrs together here as those willing to die for their faith. At the same time, he brushed aside what had always been the crucial difference between the two: the manner of death. Thus Fulcher's comparison of crusaders to "Maccabees" allowed him to close the gap between traditional martyrdom and death in battle, and thereby to come a step closer to the sacralization of crusading warfare.

Fulcher's reference to the Maccabees gives no indication as to when crusaders began identifying themselves with the Jewish warriors. The location of such references in Caffaro's text—in connection with the siege of Antioch—is more revealing. It is highly probable that crusaders learned about the longstanding association of Antioch with the Maccabean martyrs while encamped outside the city, possibly from native Christians.[32] Even if they were unaware of the tradition designating Antioch the original burial site of the martyrs, they were capable of constructing an associative link between Antioch the city and Antiochus the king. The anonymous author of the *Gesta Francorum* claimed that Antioch got its name from King Antiochus.[33] Two other chroniclers of the First Crusade, Robert the Monk and Albert of Aachen, erroneously attributed the foundation of Antioch to Antiochus.[34]

It is difficult to explain the existence of a cluster of at least five references (four in addition to Caffaro's) to the Maccabees in crusading sources that mention Antioch unless they all sprang from a common, probably oral, tradition, the roots of which must go back to the siege of 1097–98. As noted above, two chroniclers of the First Crusade drew a parallel between the miracles on behalf of the Maccabees and that of the intervention of saints in the battle of Antioch. They did so in order to demonstrate that the accounts of saintly intervention on the side of Christians had to be true. According to Guibert of Nogent, crusaders were much more deserving of "celestial help" than the Maccabees. Crusaders "poured out their blood for Christ, purifying the churches and propagating the faith," while the Jews were "fighting for circumcision and the meat of swine."[35] William of Malmesbury, writing two decades later, made his comparison in a more neutral tone. He wrote that it was undeniable that saints had aided crusaders, "just as angels once gave help to the Maccabees."[36]

The third reference to supernatural help offered to the Maccabees is found in Gilo of Paris's epic poem, probably written after Guibert's chronicle but before William's. Gilo begins the book dedicated to the capture and battle of Antioch with the following words: "Come, Christ the King, reveal now the accustomed prowess which neither the strength of men nor many weapons give to you. Come O Christ, grant now that divine gift often granted to your Maccabeans, that one may trounce thousands upon thousands."[37] Finally, the so-called Charleville poet also mentions the Maccabees in connection with Antioch. He claims that the city is very ancient and recalls the death of the priest Onias, described in the second book of the Maccabees (2 Macc. 4:34), in the vicinity of the city, near Daphne.[38]

While crusaders must already have begun imagining themselves as marching in the footsteps of the Maccabees at Antioch, the process was likely to have intensified when they reached and eventually took Jerusalem. The probable identification of crusaders with the Maccabees would have been part of a broader trend in which they consciously imitated the heroes and reenacted some of the key moments of the Old Testament, as described in a number of sources. According to Ralph of Caen, for example, before marching on Jerusalem, the crusaders "proposed that an image of the savior be molded from the purest gold in the model of the Israelite tabernacle."[39] During the siege of Jerusalem, the bishops and priests accompanying the army commanded the crusaders to march in procession around the city, which is what Joshua's army did before the capture of Jericho (Josh. 6).

In Jerusalem, the crusaders had several opportunities to remember the Maccabees. About fifteen miles from the city, at Emmaus, Judas had fought an important battle against the forces of Antiochus. After the battle, the surviving Jews, on examining the corpses of their fallen comrades, discovered that they had kept "sacred tokens of the idols of Jamnia, which the law forbids the Jews to wear" (2 Macc. 12:40). Judas prayed for them, "beseeching that the sin which had been committed might be wholly blotted out" (12:42). Judas's prayer revealed his belief in the resurrection of the dead; otherwise "it would have been superfluous and foolish to pray for the dead" (12:44–45). This is the only passage in the Bible concerning prayer for the dead, and from the seventh century on, it was integrated into the liturgy.[40] At least one twelfth-century pilgrim thought it worthwhile to include a reference to this episode in connection with Jerusalem.[41]

More significantly, Jerusalem was of course the location of the Temple, which the Maccabees restored after its desecration. Although the Temple had been destroyed, the crusaders sometimes identified it with the Dome of the Rock (As-Sakhrah, a mosque built in the seventh century by the Umayyad caliph Abd al-Malik).[42] As Sylvia Schein has demonstrated, the Temple Mount was largely and deliberately ignored by Christians until the First Crusade. Once again, the dichotomy between the flesh and the spirit, and the anxiety about "Judaizing" that could threaten it, was at play. According to the Apostle Paul, there was no longer any need for the physical Temple in Jerusalem, because, metaphorically, each individual Christian was a temple, as was the entire community of Christians. Paul wrote to the Corinthians, "Do you not know that you are God's temple and that God's Spirit dwells in you?" (1 Cor. 3:16). In the centuries that followed, pilgrims shunned the Temple Mount as if it were literally, to quote Jerome, the "dung heap" of Christian Jerusalem.[43]

From the start, crusaders had a radically different attitude toward the Temple Mount and thus broke away from a tradition that went back to the apostolic era. Ralph of Caen narrates an episode in which Arnulf, the future Latin patriarch of Jerusalem, disagreed with Tancred on the meaning of the "Temple of the Lord" (by which Ralph means the Dome of the Rock) in the aftermath of the capture of the city. According to Ralph of Caen, Arnulf objected to Tancred's appropriating some of the riches found there. In defense of the integrity of the building, Arnulf referred to a series of passages from both the Old and New Testaments referring to the Temple: "This is the house of the Lord. The Lord himself founded it. This is the place, which is called the gate of heaven, where the patriarch Jacob learned truly that there was a God. It was here that he saw the ladder touching the heavens with angels climbing up and down. As an infant, the Lord Christ illuminated this place with his words. As an adolescent, after driving out the money changers with his holy zeal, he said, 'it is written that this house is called a house of prayer.'" Tancred claimed that he put the wealth to good use, namely, for the defense of the realm: he "crushed the enemy with gems," Ralph wrote, and "created soldiers from silver."[44] Tancred also argued that he was the first to enter the "Temple" during the capture of Jerusalem and thus had a right to it. The dispute between Tancred and Arnulf reveals two different understandings of the Temple Mount. Tancred acknowledged the significance of the

"Temple" by promising to repay what he took from it, but it was not as sacred to him (or, one assumes, to other crusaders) as it was to Arnulf.

Godfrey of Bouillon, the first ruler of the kingdom, hardly considered the Temple Mount a "dung heap." He chose the al-Aqsa mosque, also on the mount, as the location for his palace. This former mosque became known as the "Temple of Solomon" (Templum Solomonis) or "Palace of Solomon" (Palatium Solomonis) in the sources. King Baldwin II let a recently established military order—which, as a consequence, would become known as the Order of the Temple—reside in the palace. Even after the kings of Jerusalem moved their residence elsewhere, they did not sever ties with the Mount, which played an important part in coronation ceremonies. Upon being crowned at the Holy Sepulcher, a new king would go to the "Temple of the Lord," where, in imitation of Christ's presentation to the Temple, he offered his crown and then bought it back. Then he held a banquet at the "Temple of Solomon."[45] The revalorization of the Temple Mount went hand in hand with a revalorization of the Maccabees. Several of the kings of Jerusalem, beginning with Baldwin I, were called "second Maccabees."[46] The unqualified willingness of Fulcher of Chartres, a chaplain to Baldwin I from 1097 to 1115, to assimilate crusaders to Maccabees, as discussed above, fits into this pattern.

According to Sylvia Schein, "the transformation of the status of the Temple Mount produced, it seems, some confusion among twelfth-century writers" in the West, who, "influenced by the exegetical tradition, were used to perceiving the Temple as a metaphor, a symbol or *typus*."[47] As a consequence, she argues, the vast majority of writers (with the notable exception of Bernard of Clairvaux) ignored the Temple Mount. It seems that the new prominence of the Maccabees, concomitant with the renewed prominence of the "Temple," similarly resulted in confusion and perhaps even alarm. Orderic Vitalis was one of the few to respond to the perceived threat. He included three references to the Maccabees in his *Ecclesiastical History*, two of them in connection with the First Crusade; unlike those of Caffaro or Fulcher of Chartres, both references are unambiguously to the warriors. According to Orderic, King Baldwin of Jerusalem addressed his troops before the battle of Jaffa in 1102: "Remember David, bravest of kings, and his soldiers Joab and Abishai, remember Banaiah and Uriah and Ethite and Jonathan and Judas Maccabaeus and many other memorable champions of your people.... May the mighty Emmanuel, son of the blessed Virgin Mary, who is your King and the leader and invincible defender of his Church, be with you."[48] Orderic's choice of military models for emulation is rather unusual, as he puts David and Judas Maccabeus, two major heroes, on a par with minor figures of the Old Testament. Joab, Abishai, Banaiah, and Uriah were David's military commanders, and their respective fates were remarkably different. Joab, for instance, ended up murdering David's son Absalom. Uriah, by contrast, was a victim himself, whom David sent to certain death in order to carry on an affair with his wife, Bathsheba. The Ethites were one of the gentile peoples mentioned in the book of Ezra.[49] No miracles are associated with the battles of any of the people in Orderic's list. For King Baldwin, as recalled by Orderic, the warriors of the Old Testament are simply examples of military prowess. The king is different from all of them because he can hope to receive help from "the mighty Emmanuel" (Christ) himself.

Orderic also mentions the Maccabees in his account of the battle of the Field of Blood, fought in 1119, which ended in the death of Prince Roger of Antioch and the annihilation of his entire army. According to Orderic, just before the battle began, Bernard of Valence, the patriarch of Antioch, warned Roger against engaging the enemy, begging him to wait for reinforcements. Abandoning the discourse of divinely sponsored victory of the few over the many, the patriarch gave Roger very practical advice: "Temper your zeal with prudence, valiant duke, and wait for King Baldwin and Joscelin and the other loyal lords who are coming early to our assistance. Rash haste has brought many men to ruin and deprived great princes of life and victory." Citing historical precedent, the patriarch told Prince Roger, "Study ancient and modern histories, and ponder seriously over the fates of some remarkable kings. Call to mind Saul and Josiah and Judas Maccabeus, and the Romans who were defeated by Hannibal at Cannae, and take great care not to drag your subjects with yourself into a disaster of the same kind. Wait for your worthy allies."[50] Orderic's narrative of the battle of the Field of Blood seems to be a reaction to frequent references to the Maccabees' triumphs despite their numerical inferiority.[51] More specifically, it seems to be a response to Fulcher's narrative of an earlier battle, fought and won by Roger of Antioch in 1115, that of Tall Danith. In his description of the battle, Fulcher reminds the reader of the Maccabees' victories against all odds: "For when did the victory of fighters ever depend upon the number of men? Remember the Maccabees, Gideon, and many others who confided not in their strength but in that of God and in that way overcame many thousands."[52] At Tall Danith, Roger managed to prevail against a numerically superior opponent. At the battle of the Field of Blood, his rash decision to engage another numerically superior enemy cost him his army and his life. Fulcher describes a battle in which faith in God is sufficient for victory, while Orderic stresses the danger of foolhardiness. In support of their diametrically opposite messages, both cite the Maccabees, but in strikingly different ways: as divinely inspired victors and as the vanquished.

In this second reference, Orderic compares Judas Maccabeus to Saul and Josiah, once again two relatively obscure Old Testament figures, neither of whom ever profited from any miracles or enjoyed special status in Christianity. In contrast to Fulcher's pairing of the Maccabees with Gideon, this is a demotion. The common denominator for these three figures is that they were all defeated and killed in battle.[53] That Orderic also mentions pagan Romans, defeated in the battle of Cannae, further underscores his desire to present the Maccabees as merely historical figures. This is a literal comparison devoid of any reference to higher matters.

Orderic's secularization of the Maccabees was not unique. Like Orderic, an anonymous participant in the Third Crusade, who wrote or compiled a popular account of the enterprise entitled *Itinerarium Peregrinorum et Gesta Regis Ricardi*, also remembered Judas's death on the battlefield. He also found nothing particularly glorious about it but rather used it as a foil to the apparent invincibility of King Richard the Lionheart:

> All people tell of the battles of the mighty Judas Maccabeus. He fought many remarkable battles which should be admired forever; but when his people had deserted him in battle, he engaged many thousands of foreigners in battle with a small company and he fell nearby with his brothers and died. However, King Richard had been hardened to battle from his tender years. In comparison to his strength, Roland would be reckoned weak. I do not know how he remained invincible and invulnerable among all the enemies; perhaps by divine protection. His body was like brass, unyielding to any sort of weapon.[54]

Like Ambrose centuries earlier, the anonymous chronicler chose to mention not Judas's victories but his death. Unlike Ambrose, however, he did not consider that death in any way similar to martyrdom. On the contrary, he argued that Richard was superior to Judas because, unlike the Jewish hero, he remained alive through all of the battles that he fought in the Holy Land. The chronicler suggests that Richard's survival was a miracle, a consequence of "divine protection." In mentioning Roland in the same breath with Judas and Richard, the chronicler provides an early example of constructing a pantheon of heroes who have fought against the "infidels," a pantheon that was to become famous under the name the Nine Worthies.[55]

Orderic was not the only chronicler of the First Crusade to resist the new trend of assimilating crusaders to either Maccabean warriors or the hybrid Maccabean warrior-martyrs. Raymond of Aguilers argued that the crusaders were worthier than the Maccabees because they won their victories against greater odds: "I daresay, if I were not modest, I would rate this battle before the Maccabean war, because Maccabeus with three thousand struck down forty-eight thousand of his foes while here four hundred knights routed sixty thousand pagans. But we neither disparage the courage of Maccabeus nor boast of the bravery of our knights; however, we proclaim God, once wonderful to Maccabeus, was even more so to our army."[56] In another passage, Raymond returned once again to the juxtaposition between the past, when God assisted the Maccabees, and the present, when God came to the aid of the crusaders. Raymond's discussion of Peter Bartholomew's vision of Christ reveals the chronicler's anxiety about the crusaders being too closely associated with the Jews. In the vision, Christ asks Peter, "By the way, do you know what race I especially esteem?" Peter Bartholomew responds, "The Jewish race." Christ corrects Peter: "I entertain hatred against them as unbelievers and rank them the lowest of all races. Therefore, be sure you are not unbelievers, or else you will be with the Jews, and I shall choose other people and carry to fulfillment for them my promises which I made to you."[57] Raymond tacitly acknowledges the similarities between Jews and crusaders. The Jews are the chosen people before the incarnation, and the crusaders, afterward. According to Raymond, however, no two groups could be more different in the present. Quite the opposite; Raymond places the Jews below "all races," presumably including Muslim enemies of crusaders.

Guibert of Nogent's reaction to the attempts to assimilate crusaders to the Israelites is as visceral as Raymond's, but also much more sophisticated. Guibert felt an urgency to reinstate what he considered the correct way of using typology to compare recent events to those described in the Old Testament. He wanted to demonstrate that crusaders were similar to monks and thus qualitatively different from and far superior to the Jews of the Old Testament. In arguing that appearances concealed a different reality, Guibert could rely on a centuries-long tradition of pegging the opposition between spirit and flesh to that between Christians and Jews. According to Saint Paul, "the real Jew is one who is inwardly a Jew, and real circumcision is in the heart, a thing not of the letter but of the spirit" (Rom. 2:25). Along these lines,

Guibert set out to prove that crusaders were, in contrast to the Jews themselves, the "real" Jews.

On the surface, Guibert's commentary on the miracle of the intervention of saints in the battle of Antioch is very similar to that of William of Malmesbury. Like William, Guibert refers to the Maccabees in order to demonstrate that the miracle of divine aid in battle was credible. In contrast to William, however, Guibert makes evident the superiority of the crusaders to the Maccabees. While the Maccabees fought for material things, "circumcision and the meat of swine," crusaders struggled "for Christ." In order to convey his point more forcefully, Guibert offers a highly inaccurate summary of the goals of the Maccabean revolt. According to the biblical text, Antiochus tried to ban circumcision and desecrated altars by sacrificing pigs. Guibert's statement belongs to the line of anti-Jewish, usually highly derogatory rhetoric revolving around the interdiction of pork.[58]

Guibert repeats the same idea—that the Jews of the Old Testament waged their wars for material benefits, while crusaders sought spiritual ones—several times in his chronicle. In a preface to book 7, Guibert urges his readers to celebrate the Crusades but not the wars of the ancient Jews: "Let us rejoice then in the battles they won, undertaken purely out of spiritual desire, granted by a divine power, which had never before appeared, but was made manifest in modern times; and let us not admire the fleshly wars of Israel, which were waged merely to fill the belly."[59] Later in the same book, Guibert repeats the same idea, writing that God "granted glory to our own times, so that modern men seem to have undergone pain and suffering greater than that of the Jews of old, who, in the company of their wives and sons, and with full bellies, were led by angels who made themselves visible to them" (143/305). Once again, Guibert juxtaposes the crusaders, who had to endure great privations, and the Jews, who fought in relative comfort, accompanied by "wives and sons" and with "full bellies." Guibert seems to imply that the only reason why the Jews won was that angels led them.

From early on in the enterprise, "the grain and other food for the body began to diminish severely" (76/172). Guibert describes how while the crusaders were besieging Antioch, "famine, like madness, plagued them" (82/184). When they in turn were besieged within the city, "the suffering of our men was so great that they were compelled to eat the foulest food, the flesh of horses and donkeys" (99/218). Guibert describes in detail the "dangers of famine," during which "the poor prepared the dried skins of . . . animals, cut them into slices, boiled them and then ate them" (103/225). He emphasizes that crusaders "suffered from great hunger" (117/254), were "weakened by long hunger" (140/299), and experienced "steady, destructive starvation" (145/308). Often, they had to make do with the coarsest food: "How many jaws and throats of noble men were eaten away by the roughness of this bread?" (128/274). Guibert depicts one crusader—Peter the Hermit, who attempted to escape during the siege of Antioch but was brought back—as a foil for the rest. Guibert mocks him for his inability to withstand hunger, which is particularly unseemly for a hermit: "Stay your steps and recollect your old hermitage, your earlier fasting. . . . Why do you remember immoderate eating?" (81/180). Clearly, Guibert equates the crusaders' privations with voluntary moderation in food, something that Christian theologians eagerly advocated; Isidore of Seville, for example, declared that "fast is a holy thing, a heavenly work, the doorway to the kingdom, the form of the future, for he who carries it out in a holy way is united to God, exiled from the world, and made spiritual."[60]

According to Guibert, the crusaders also exercised sexual abstinence. In contrast to the Jews, who were accompanied by their families, they did not hesitate to abandon their wives and children upon taking up the cross: "The most beautiful women were treated as though they were worthless dirt; pledges of domestic love [children], once more precious than any gem, were scorned" (29/87–88).[61] Later, they missed the families that they had left behind, but they resisted the temptation to turn back: "Although the hearts of the pilgrims burned for the dear, distant pledges of their affections, for their sweet wives and for the dignity of their possessions, nevertheless they remained steadfastly in place" (128/275). According to Guibert, the crusading army as a whole strove to maintain a purity worthy of their enterprise: "Sexual crimes were punished with particular severity" (87/196). Even speech was subject to correction: "so it happened that merely speaking of a prostitute or of a brothel was considered intolerable" (88/196). Crusaders' privations when it came to food had a positive effect on their morality. Their "bodies were so weak" that "none of them had the ability to perform sexually." In all cases, they "restrained themselves from all the foulness of carnality" (151/332). In sum, according to Guibert, there were, of course, superficial similarities between the wars of crusaders and the wars of the Jews. However, the differences between the two types of warfare—the meaning behind the appearances—were much more important.

According to Guibert, if we look beyond appearances, then crusaders were similar not to the Israelites but to early Christian martyrs. He wrote that God, who "strengthened the minds of the martyrs to undergo torture out of love for invisible things, again in our own times, in an entirely unexpected way... placed in the hearts of our men... contempt for the things of this world" (124/266). One description of crusaders pursuing the "infidels" is particularly revealing of the unlikely meaning that Guibert saw behind appearances: "Prodigious was the slaughter of the fleeing army; we hardly had enough swords to do all the killing. Swords became dull with cutting so many limbs.... Here they cut a head, here a nose, here a throat, here a pair of ears; a belly is sliced open; everyone in their path dies." However, Guibert made it clear that there was another reality behind the visible one: "I do not say they were as brave as lions, but, what is more fitting, brave as martyrs" (67/157). So, according to Guibert, those who appear to be bloodthirsty warriors are in fact similar to martyrs, who accept death without physical resistance.

The aims of Fulcher of Chartres and Guibert, to use the most extreme examples, were similar: both wanted to sacralize crusading warfare by associating crusaders with martyrs. However, they assigned diametrically opposite roles to the Israelites. Fulcher argued that crusading warfare was sacred because it was similar to the struggles of the Maccabees, whereas Guibert claimed that crusading warfare was sacred because it was different.

Although Guibert's treatment of the Israelites was unique among the chroniclers of the First Crusade, his ideas, coincidentally or not, found an echo in the writings of Bernard of Clairvaux.[62] Like Guibert, Bernard also believed in the possibility of physical and spiritual warfare coinciding in space and time. In his *Liber ad Milites Templi*, Bernard also displayed a yearning for the correct use of typology when it came to the Temple. According to the first book of the Maccabees, Judas decorated the Temple of Jerusalem "with golden crowns and small shields" (1 Macc. 4:57). The Templars' temple—presumably the al-Aqsa mosque, converted into the Templars' headquarters—was very different: "Sanctity befits the house of God as He is pleased by beautiful morals and not by polished marble. He prefers pure minds to golden walls. The façade of this temple is also decorated, but by arms not by jewels; its walls are covered with hanging shields, not with ancient golden crowns. Instead of candelabra, incense burners and spice jars the house is protected on all sides by bridles, saddles, and lances."[63] Bernard creates a picture of two buildings. The first is adorned with "polished marble," "golden walls," "jewels," "golden crowns," and "candelabra." The second has only military accoutrements, "bridles, saddles, and lances," on its walls. Its beauty is hidden and has to do with the Templars' "beautiful morals" and "pure minds." The physical beauty of the first (Jewish) Temple is worthless. The physical barrenness of the second (Templars') temple conceals its spiritual wealth. The spiritual reality is the exact opposite of outward appearances. Bernard's contrasting of the two temples corresponds to one of the overarching goals of the treatise: to describe how the physical presence of the Templars in the Holy Land and their physical battles in its defense were both spiritual exercises.[64]

Guibert of Nogent's juxtaposition of the spirit, associated with Christians, and the flesh, associated with Jews, involves a third party: Muslims. Like Jews, Muslims were keen to pursue the pleasures of the flesh, although, in contrast to Jews, these pleasures are almost exclusively of a sexual nature and are characterized by greater excesses.[65] Guibert followed the *Gesta Francorum* closely in his rendition of the letter purportedly written by Kerbogha to be sent "throughout the provinces of Persia," which contains the following advice to fellow Muslims: "give yourselves up to pleasure, eat the finest foods, lie with the multitude of wives and concubines to propagate the race" (96/212). However, in contrast to the *Gesta Francorum*, Guibert developed the theme of Muslims' sexuality on two other occasions. First, he supplemented his source by paraphrasing the letter in which Emperor Alexius asks Count Robert of Flanders for help. In this letter, sexual crimes dominate the list of offenses committed by Muslims against Christians. "Mahometries," according to the letter, are places where "all kinds of filthy activity" is carried out, so that they are more like "brothels and theatres" than like "cathedrals" (37/101). Second, Guibert added an original discussion of Islam in which he claimed that Muhammad contracted epilepsy because of excessive sexual intercourse with his wife (33/96). According to Guibert, Muhammad later wrote a book of law that gave his followers "license for random copulation": "the greater opportunity to fulfill lust, and, going beyond the appetites of beasts, by resorting to multiple whores, was cloaked by the excuse of procreating children. However, while the flow of nature was unrestrained in these normal acts, at the same time they engaged in abnormal acts, which we should not even name, and which were unknown even to animals" (34–35/98).

Guibert did not compare Jews and Muslims explicitly. Rather, the two groups logically ended up resembling each other because of the dualism of his vision. Other authors, however, went a step further as they developed a parallel between the Muslims' defeat at the hands of crusaders and the Jews' defeat at the hands of the Romans in A.D. 70. Ekkehard of Aura recorded a vision that preceded the First Crusade: "Not many years before, a priest of venerable life by the name of Siger one day at about three in the afternoon saw two knights charging against each other in the sky and fighting for a long time. The one who was carrying a good-sized cross with which he struck the other turned out the victor."[66] The meaning of this vision is obvious; the knight carrying the cross stands for crusaders and his victim represents their enemies, i.e., Muslims.

One of two texts describing celestial battles is probably behind Ekkehard's narrative. The second book of the Maccabees records an apparition that took place in Jerusalem when Antiochus was on a campaign to Egypt: "And it happened that over all the city, for almost forty days, there appeared golden-clad horsemen charging through the air, in companies fully armed with lances and drawn swords—troops of horsemen drawn up, attacks and counterattacks made on this side and on that, brandishing of shields, massing of spears, hurling of missiles, the flash of golden trappings, and armor of all sorts. Therefore all men prayed that the apparition might prove to have been a good omen" (2 Macc. 5:2–4). The apparition did not prove to be a good omen. During the absence of Antiochus, the Jews killed Jason, the corrupted high priest. Antiochus interpreted this as a revolt against his authority, took Jerusalem by storm, massacred the inhabitants, and plundered the holy vessels in the Temple.

In his *Jewish War*, Flavius Josephus echoed the account in the second book of the Maccabees in his description of another apparition. In this case, the event was not a battle between two forces but an invading army: "before sunset throughout all parts of the country chariots were seen in the air and armed battalions hurtling through the clouds and encompassing the cities."[67] In this case, the omen proved to be even worse, foreshadowing not a mere plundering of the Temple but its utter destruction by Titus in A.D. 70.

The vision of battle in the skies is a rare one. That all three accounts involve the conquest of Jerusalem further supports the hypothesis that, despite numerous differences in detail, they are related. There is evidence that other contemporaries of the First Crusade used Josephus's work to understand the events in the East.[68] However, Ekkehard significantly altered the emphasis by relating the vision of celestial battle from the point of view of the victors rather than the vanquished. Both the author of the second book of the Maccabees and Flavius Josephus were on the side of the Jews, who were about to endure an assault upon and a sack of Jerusalem. For them, the vision presaging the capture of the city was ominous. Ekkehard was on the side of the crusaders who captured Jerusalem, and in his account the vision was supposed to be a good omen.

In Ekkehard's chronicle, identification between the crusaders and past conquerors of Jerusalem, particularly the Romans, is only implicit. Other sources, however, represent Vespasian, who began the suppression of the Great Revolt before passing the command to his son, Titus, as a protocrusader.[69] The vernacular *Song of Antioch* claims that Judas Maccabeus possessed a sword that had belonged to Alexander the Great and that passed on to Vespasian, who "took vengeance" on the Jews for the Crucifixion, and offered it to the Holy Sepulcher. The sword then passed on to the Saracens. The *Song* seems to be suggesting that the possession of the sword alternates between legitimate owners (Alexander the Great, Vespasian) and illegitimate ones (Judas Maccabeus, Saracens).[70] In the *Song*, Vespasian is not just an unwitting instrument of God exacting vengeance on the Jews for the death of Christ, but a patron of the Holy Sepulcher.[71] The *Song* implies that his conquest of Jerusalem from the Jews in A.D. 70 resembled the conquest of Jerusalem from the Muslims during the First Crusade.[72]

Another reference to Judas Maccabeus found in the *Song of Antioch* is even more disparaging. In fact, the *Song* claims that Judas was one of the generals in Kerbogha's army, fighting against crusaders in the battle of Antioch. Other generals included the heroes of the Old Testament (Samson, David, and Solomon), the rogues of the New Testament (Herod and Pilate), and, ironically, Antiochus, the Maccabees' archenemy. Thus, instead of following in the footsteps of Judas Maccabeus, crusaders, quite literally, fought against him.[73]

Similarly, Peter Tudebode includes Iudas Machabeus in the list of seventy-five kings who ruled in Antioch.[74] The list clearly resembles the list of infidel kings opposing crusaders in the *Song of Antioch*. Samson, Solomon, Pilate, and Herod figure in both cases. In Peter Tudebode's chronicle, in addition to these biblical figures, Judas Maccabeus shares the honor of having presided over Antioch with, among others, David hereticus, Garbandus impius de Samardandum, Satanus, Drahonus, and Impius Telandus. By associating him with such unsavory characters, Peter clearly undermined the worthiness of Judas. Of course, in both cases we are dealing with a farrago drawn from a variety of sources. However, in the context of the celebration of the Romans' conquest of Jerusalem in the *Song*, the placement of Judas Maccabeus among the "bad guys" does not appear to have been entirely fortuitous.

The two lists mentioned above come into stark contrast with another, found in the chronicle written by William of Malmesbury. William includes a Maccabee in the fictional list of the patriarchs of Jerusalem, beginning with James, "the Lord's brother," and ending with Simeon, during whose tenure the Franks delivered the city "from the hand of the Turks and of the king of Babylonia."[75] Here, William of Malmesbury Christianizes the Maccabees not only by having them live after Christ but also by making one of them into a patriarch. These two references to Maccabees—one as an "infidel" ruler of Antioch and the other as a patriarch of Jerusalem—are located on opposite sides of the spectrum. Both were attempts to inscribe the First Crusade into the narrative of sacred history. However, while one of them signaled continuity, the other emphasized a radical break with the Jewish past.

Although the sources displaying more or less pronounced anti-Jewish rhetoric were written years or even decades after the massacres of the Jews in northern France and the Rhineland that took place during the early stages of the First Crusade, it is difficult to argue that such rhetoric was utterly unrelated to anti-Jewish violence that became closely associated with crusading activity.[76] The attitudes of some of the perpetrators of the massacres of living Jews, as described by Guibert of Nogent and other sources, are similar to that of Guibert himself toward the Jews as exegetical creations. In both cases, there is a more or less explicit attempt to "reclassify" the Jews and to make them "a small subset of a much larger class" to which Muslims also belong.[77] In both cases, Jews and Muslims are diametrically opposed to Christians. According to Guibert, crusaders embarking on their journey to the Holy Land began to complain to one another: "Do we need to travel to distant lands in the East to attack the enemies of God, when there are Jews right before our eyes, a race that is the greatest enemy of God? We've got it all backwards!"[78] Guibert does not give his opinion of the massacre that ensued. The Augustinian doctrine of witness would not allow him to approve of it.[79] However, a possible clue about his attitude emerges from the fact that Guibert claims that something good came out of the massacres: one of the Jewish infants survived, was brought up as a Christian, and later became a monk at the monastery of Fly.

Many participants and contemporaries alike believed that the First Crusade was a "holy war." The Jewish wars of the Old Testament were not just the most obvious but the only universally accepted models of sacred warfare. Some Christian authors embraced the similarities between the biblical and the recent past. Other Christian observers, however, perceived that sacralizing crusading violence carried the danger of transforming crusaders into Jews, and they felt the need to draw a clear distinction between Jewish and Christian fighters. Later comparisons between Jews and Christians adhere, implicitly or explicitly, to a more theologically sound use of typology, with its emphasis on the incarnation and the superiority of spiritual to physical warfare (including and especially when the two coincided). They signal a reinstatement of the traditional formula, according to which the Maccabees were a fitting model for literal imitation by the *bellatores* and for metaphorical imitation by the *oratores*. Crusaders, who were supposed to be both *bellatores* and *oratores* at once, imitated the Maccabees literally as warriors and metaphorically as quasi-monks. This solution allowed the celebration of similarities between the crusaders and the Old Testament Jews to continue until the very end of the crusading era.[80] Thus comparisons between crusaders and the Old Testament Jews developed along the lines suggested by some of the chronicles of the First Crusade, especially Guibert of Nogent's. Judging from the number of surviving manuscripts, Guibert's chronicle was not particularly popular. The resemblances between his thinking and that of Bernard of Clairvaux, however, might not be fortuitous. One of the manuscripts of Guibert's chronicle was originally located in the monastic library of Clairvaux.[81] Although Guibert wrote about crusaders in general and Bernard about the Templars, both of them accepted similarities between the Christian fighters of their own time and the Jewish warriors of the Old Testament. At the same time, both were eager to emphasize the key difference, namely, the spiritual nature of the former and the carnal nature of the latter. Although one cannot exclude the possibility of coincidence, it seems probable that Guibert inspired the one person who mattered.

SIX

"THE WEST PREPARES TO ILLUMINATE THE EAST"

According to the *Gesta Francorum*, only a fraction of those present witnessed the intervention of saints in the battle of Antioch. However, it seems that everyone who was at Antioch at the time got a chance to observe another unusual occurrence shortly before the battle: "there appeared a fire in the sky, coming from the West, and it approached and fell upon the Turkish army, to the great astonishment of our men and of the Turks also."[1] Although descriptions vary, other chroniclers also describe unusual happenings in the skies either during or, in one case, just before the two sieges of Antioch, which together covered the period from October 1097 through June 28, 1098.

Modern historians have virtually ignored these references to unusual celestial phenomena. This silence is understandable, since medieval historical writings are full of references to similar occurrences.[2] A particularly large number of sources mention Halley's Comet, which passed through the sky shortly before the Norman invasion of 1066. Writing within five years after the event, William of Jumièges gave the following account in his *Gesta Normannorum Ducum*: "At that time a star appeared in the north-west, its three-forked tail stretched far into the southern sky remaining visible for fifteen days."[3] Other descriptions are more difficult to match with specific astronomical phenomena. The *Gesta Stephani*, an anonymous chronicle written in the middle of the twelfth century, described a different phenomenon, when "no small part of the sky" sent out "a cloud of fiery sparks like coals of living fire, moving nimbly and closely massed together."[4] Chronicles sometimes describe the unusual occurrence in the skies without providing any explanation. Often, however, they either state or imply a connection between it and subsequent turmoil of some kind. According to William of Jumièges, the comet portended "a change in some kingdom."[5] The "fireworks" described in the *Gesta Stephani* foretold "either the great bloodshed that was to be, or the unspeakable burning of villages and towns that followed."[6]

Jay Rubenstein is a rare scholar who has discussed specifically the *signa* observed during the First Crusade. Referring to a sign that Fulcher of Chartres reported seeing in September 1097—"a brilliant whiteness in the shape of a sword" pointing toward the east—he argues that the crusaders must have interpreted it as a warning for having "abandoned the road to Jerusalem in the name of some vaguely defined goals in Syria."[7] Rubenstein also notes that they were likely to have considered the apocalyptic analogues, namely, the breaking of the sixth seal, after which "the sun became black as sackcloth, and the moon became as blood" (Rev. 6:12).

It is impossible to know how crusaders interpreted the phenomena they might have seen. It is likely that several interpretations competed against one another in each case. Those chroniclers who did offer an explanation tended to explain the signs as portents of victory. In their works celestial phenomena functioned like Halley's Comet did in Norman narratives. In the latter case, to quote Carl Watkins, the comet "set a divine seal on the Conqueror's seizure of the crown, victory on the field being inscribed in the heavens."[8] Strange occurrences in the skies in the months before the battle of Antioch similarly "set a divine seal" on the victory of crusaders.

While descriptions of celestial phenomena reported to have occurred in 1097 and 1098 are not unique, there is one characteristic, already noted by Rubenstein, that attracts attention: the fact that many chroniclers specified the direction in which they moved, namely from west (or, in one case, north) to east. It is true that other medieval chroniclers sometimes, although by no means systematically, recorded the direction of celestial objects. William of Jumièges, for example, noted that Halley's Comet appeared in the northwest and that its tail stretched into the southern sky. However, viewed in the context of other references to cardinal points, especially west and east, in several chronicles of the First Crusade, such precision acquires considerable significance. Some chroniclers, such as Raymond of Aguilers, mention cardinal points only when describing local geography (such as, for example, the fact that the River Orontes flowed to the west of Antioch).[9] Other chroniclers, however, use west and east not as mere indicators of direction but as cultural constructions. In their works, references to cardinal points are not there to add greater precision to the basic storyline of the First Crusade but are an integral part of the interpretation of the events. Moreover, they conceal a complex argument regarding not only the fates of the "West" and the "East" but the logic of sacred history in its entirety, stretching from the Fall to the second coming. Many of the chroniclers of the First Crusade assumed that at least some of their readers would have an education similar to theirs or, in other words, that they would have a similarly thorough grounding in both the Bible and patristic writings. As a consequence, they presented their argument regarding the "West" and the "East" in the form of passing allusions. It is possible to ascertain the argument's existence and, eventually, to appreciate its originality only through an analysis of interpretative traditions of cardinal points going back centuries before the First Crusade.

The cardinal points—east, west, north, and south—provide a relatively complex way of ordering the world. Cecil Brown, in his comparative study of words signifying directions in more than a hundred languages, argues that "for much of human history cardinal points have been of little interest to people."[10] It was only when members of a particular linguistic group begin to venture beyond their familiar environment, for which specific terms such as "toward the mountain" or "on the other side of the river" suffice, that the need for pan-geographic terms arises.[11] Also, the four cardinal points are not created equal. Brown's study reveals that in languages that have terms for only some of the four cardinal points, the east-west axis occurs much more frequently than the north-south one. With rare exceptions, the encoding of east and west tends to appear before, and to bring about, that of north and south. Moreover, the term for east is more common than the term for west, from which Brown concludes that east is "greater in natural salience" than west.[12] It is not by accident that, in English, the meaning of the expression "to orient oneself" literally means to find which way is east.

At some point in history, however, the geographical pair of east and west, intended simply to order the world, began to acquire a multitude of additional meanings. In his influential study published in 1978, Edward Said discussed "Orientalism" as "an elaboration not only of a basic geographical distinction (the world is made up of two unequal halves, the Orient and Occident) but also of a series of 'interests' which . . . it not only creates but maintains."[13] According to Said, "a very large mass of writers, among whom are poets, novelists, philosophers, political theorists, economists, and imperial administrators, have accepted the basic distinction between East and West as the starting point for elaborate theories, epics, novels, social descriptions, and political accounts concerning the Orient, its peoples, customs, 'mind,' destiny, and so on. *This* Orientalism can accommodate Aeschylus, say, and Victor Hugo, Dante and Karl Marx." This discourse, which, according to Said, is twenty-five centuries old, was used for "dominating, restructuring, and having authority over the Orient."[14]

Said focused on the nineteenth and twentieth centuries and made only passing references to earlier periods. A number of medievalists and early modernists, expressly acknowledging their debt to Said, tested the usefulness of his theories in their respective fields. In his *Saracens: Islam in the Medieval European Imagination,* John Tolan traced the roots of the Orientalist discourse Said describes to the early centuries of Islam and the crusading era: "from the 7th century to the 13th, anti-Muslim discourse by Christian authors is used to authorize and justify military action, legal segregation, and social repression of Muslims."[15]

While Tolan uses Said's theories to explain the denigration of Muslims in medieval Christian sources, he barely mentions "the basic distinction between East and West," which, as the very term suggests, is fundamental to Orientalist discourse. Indeed, cardinal points would have been out of place in his discussion, which touches upon both the Christians of the "East" (in the chapter on early interfaith encounters taking place in the Middle East) and the Muslims of the "West" (in the chapter on the Spanish Reconquista). In this, Tolan's work owes as much to Said's *Orientalism* as it does to earlier studies of anti-Muslim rhetoric in Latin Christian sources, such as Norman Daniel's *Islam and the West* or Richard Southern's *Western Views of Islam.*

Sharon Kinoshita has attempted to correct the slant of earlier scholarship, which tended to focus on the negative representation of Islam. She has analyzed "medieval Christians' lived reactions and interactions with Muslims and the Islamic world-interactions much more complex and multifaceted than implied in the demonizing depictions by Norman Daniel or Edward Said himself."[16] Similarly, albeit focusing on a later period, Margaret Meserve underscores a plurality of discourses and the importance of disagreements between them: "At different times and in different places, European writers can be found saying radically different things about the Islamic East."[17]

Suzanne Conklin Akbari has identified another major problem in applying Said's theory to the Middle Ages, which earlier scholars tended to ignore and which is crucial for the present discussion: the "easy conflation of Islam and the Orient."[18] In order to rectify this problem, Akbari analyzes the "geographical discourse of the Orient"—as opposed to that of the Muslim Other—in the Middle Ages. She argues that if the "East," as a cultural category, existed from time immemorial, the "West" as its opposite emerged not at the time of Aeschylus, as Said claims, but only in the fourteenth century. According to Akbari, the dichotomy between the North and the South was much more important in the Middle Ages. If those living in western Europe before the fourteenth century ever identified themselves with a particular cardinal point, it was north. It was only during the early Renaissance that western Europeans began to identify themselves with the West, which has acquired some of the characteristics previously proper to the North, while the East began to be perceived in the same way as the South had been before:

> It is only in the fourteenth century . . . that the Orient comes to be known as a place of overwhelming heat, understood in both a literal and a moral sense. By characterizing the Orient in terms of (formerly southern) heat, it becomes possible to characterize its opposite, the Occident, in terms of (formerly northern) cold. It is thus only during the late fourteenth century that something like our modern notion of a European "West" appears in literature: an Occident characterized by cold, and the external whiteness and internal fortitude born of it.[19]

Akbari brings a necessary correction to Said's argument in separating, as much as possible, the stereotypes regarding Muslims from those regarding the East proper. Also, her claim that a juxtaposition of the East and the West in terms of climate appeared relatively late is entirely convincing. Yet this does not mean that the binary between the East and the West appeared only in the early modern period.

In the Middle Ages, one way of constructing the dichotomy between the East and the West was through the theory of the westward progression of history, which appears in the writings of three twelfth-century authors: Hugh of Saint Victor, Otto of Freising, and Gerald of Wales. Hugh of Saint Victor, who wrote in the second quarter of the twelfth century, argued that "at the beginning of time" everything of importance took place in the East, but "as the time moved on towards the end," it was now taking place in the West, which was proof that the end of the world was near.[20] According to Otto of Freising, who was directly influenced by Hugh, "all human power or wisdom" originated "in the East," but during his time this power or wisdom "began to reach its limit in the West." Like Hugh, Otto interpreted this process within an eschatological framework: "Men divinely inspired were able to foresee and as it were to have a vision of these things. But we are in position not merely to believe but also actually to see the things which were predicted, since we behold the world . . . already failing and, so to speak, drawing the last breath of extremest old age."[21]

But Otto incorporated another system of understanding universal history in his chronicle, without reconciling it with that of the westward progression of history: he represented the course of history in terms of four empires (Babylon, Persia, Greece, and Rome).[22] The origins of this quadripartite division of history, corresponding to the four cardinal points, go back to the Old Testament. A famous passage in the book of Daniel describes the dream of Nebuchadnezzar II, in which the ruler of Babylon saw a statue with a head of gold, a body of silver, and legs of clay. At Nebuchadnezzar's request, the prophet Daniel interpreted this dream to represent a succession of four empires (Dan. 2:31–45).[23] In the early fifth century, Saint Jerome identified these empires as Babylon, Media and Persia, Macedonia, and Rome, the theory that Otto incorporated into his work.[24]

In his *Conquest of Ireland*, concluded in 1189, Gerald of Wales, the third author, explored the idea of the westward progression of history using solar imagery. Gerald cited an ancient prophecy: "The West will enjoy what was formerly the prerogative of the East, and at the setting of the sun, while the sun rises in its setting, while its light seems to be quenched and extinguished, the daylight illuminates with a new brightness the mists of the western land and of the closing age of the world."[25] According to Gerald, at the time when he was writing, the sun rose not in the east but in the west. In describing the light of the east as "quenched and extinguished," it is probable that Gerald had the fate of Jerusalem, captured by Saladin in 1187, in mind. Gerald demonstrated his preoccupation with the events in the Holy Land when he lamented bitterly that King Henry II sent his son John "not to the East, but to the West, not against Saracens, but against Christians."[26] Like Hugh and Otto, Gerald speculated that the sun's rising in the west meant that the setting of the sun—the end of the world—must be near.

Earlier scholarship considered the ideas of these three twelfth-century authors representative of their time period. John Kirtland Wright, for example, claimed that in the Middle Ages the idea of the westward progression of history was raised "to a position of theological doctrine and philosophical principle."[27] In a correction—or perhaps an overcorrection—of this view,

Stephen McKenzie has argued that "some scholars placed an undue emphasis" on an idea to be found in the work of a restricted circle of thinkers.[28]

McKenzie sees Severian, bishop of Gabala in Syria, active at the end of the fourth century, as a rare precedent for Hugh's and Otto's writings. According to Severian, the creation of Adam in the East was God's way of telling humankind "that, just as the light of heaven [the sun] moves towards the West, so the human race hastens towards death."[29] In other words, Severian associated the East with the beginning and the West with the end of the world. In McKenzie's view, "A passage from a fourth-century apologist [Severian], combined with rather different ideas from two twelfth-century writers [Hugh and Otto] . . . cannot be said to form a long-lived and well-known idea." McKenzie also rejects the idea of grouping the "theme of westward progression . . . with other medieval theories concerning the properties of the cardinal directions," such as that of the four empires.[30]

Yet McKenzie, like Akbari, in order to rectify previous oversimplifications, goes too far in the opposite direction. The dichotomy between East and West was relatively common, while the theory of the westward progression of history was held by more than a small circle of intellectuals. Also, although it is indeed important, as McKenzie suggests, to distinguish between the themes of westward progression and the periodization of history corresponding to the four empires, the two were not always entirely distinct (for example, both appear in the work of Otto of Freising).

Although Severian was one of the first to associate the West with the death of the human race, it had been used as shorthand for death before. In fact, already in ancient Egypt the realm of the dead was located in the West. On one Egyptian tomb, pallbearers carrying a coffin proclaim, "May the goddess of the West open her arms to you, / may she extend her arms to you! / The goddess of the West rejoices at you. / To the West, to the West!"[31] In a curious parallel, the expression "to go west" means to die or to break in modern British slang.[32]

In Christianity, the West came to be associated with an end of a different kind, namely, damnation, which Augustine described as the death of both the body and the soul.[33] In the fourth century, Cyril of Jerusalem described the initial stage of the ritual of baptism, in which catechumens enter the antechamber of the baptistery and there stretch forth their hands westward. Cyril explained to the catechumens the meaning of this gesture: "Since the West is the region of sensible darkness, and he [Satan] being darkness, has his dominion also in darkness, ye therefore, looking with a symbolical meaning towards the West, renounce that dark and gloomy potentate."[34] In other words, according to Cyril, the West is the location of hell, Satan's dark abode.

In locating the beginning of human history (the creation of Adam and Eve and their subsequent expulsion from paradise) in the East, Severian also drew on a venerable tradition. Although Jerome translated the term *miquedem*, used in the book of Genesis to describe paradise, as "in the beginning," the Old Latin translation rendered it as "in the East."[35] "Apostolic constitutions," probably dating to the late third century, followed the latter interpretation: "let all rise up with one consent, and looking towards the East . . . pray to God eastward, who ascended up to the heaven of heavens to the east; remembering also the ancient situation of paradise in the East."[36] As a physical embodiment of this command, most Italian churches had their choirs in the east from the fifth century onward, and by the eighth century this custom had become nearly universal.[37]

If the ascension of Christ took place "to the East," as the Apostolic Constitutions make clear, the second coming of Christ was supposed to take place in the East as well. The association of Christ with the sun (based on the prophecy of Malachi, in which God promised the faithful, "for you who fear my name, the sun of righteousness shall rise with healing in its wings") reinforced this belief.[38] The Gospel of Matthew unambiguously compares the second coming of Christ to the light of the sun, which "comes from the East" but "is visible even in the West" (Matt. 24:27).

These examples, which could easily be multiplied, demonstrate that during the early Christian era, the "East" and the "West" have very distinct and often opposing characteristics, east tending to be a positive direction and west a negative one, primarily because of their association with the path of the sun in the sky.[39] In the languages surveyed by Brown, the terms for east and west are correlated just less than half the time with the rising and setting of the sun. With some exceptions, the rising of the sun designates east as the direction of beginnings, light, and life, while the setting of the sun associates west with endings, darkness, and death. Other dichotomies equally privilege east over west (origin/destination; active/passive; subject/object). In those cases when east and west do not have to do with the rising and the setting of the sun, east still usually retains its privileged position. East is associated with the front of a human being (in Hebrew, there is one word for both), while west is, by extension, associated with the back.[40] The associations of Christ with the sun logically extended the series of dichotomies, which reinforced the positive nature of the East and the negative nature of the West

(Christ/Satan; virtue/sin; salvation/damnation). Lactantius, writing in the early fourth century, gives a telling example of the grouping together of several dichotomies associated with the East and the West: "[God] made two parts contrary to and different from one another, the Orient and the Occident. Of these, the Orient is ascribed to God, because he himself is the fount of light and illuminator of things, and because he causes us to arise to everlasting life; while the Occident is ascribed to that twisted and depraved mind, because it takes away the light, always induces darkness, and because it makes men fall and perish in sins."[41]

In these early sources, the juxtaposition between east and west was a cosmological and theological construct and had nothing to do with the political ordering of the world. Augustine was one of the earliest writers to introduce, in passing, a historical element into the east/west dichotomy. If we search for the first appearance of the concept of "Orientalism"—in other words, to recall Said, the first time that someone "accepted the basic distinction between East and West as the starting point for elaborate theories"—this is probably it. Augustine compared the fates of Babylon and Rome, arguing that Rome rose in the West at the same time that Babylon declined in the East (in passing, this comparison demonstrates that the East/West binary could grow out of the theory of the four empires when the two intermediate ones are ignored). Still, although Rome was supposed to play a crucial role in sacred history, Augustine's main concern remained for the otherworldly city of God.

Paulus Orosius elaborated upon Augustine's juxtaposition and underscored the temporal coincidence of King Cyrus of Persia taking over Babylon in the East and the Romans overthrowing the monarchy in the West. "Indeed," says Orosius, "at one and the same accord of time, the one fell, the other arose; the one, at the time, first endured the domination of foreigners; the other, at that time, also rejected the haughtiness of her own princes; the one, at that time like a person at the door of death, left an inheritance; but the other, then attaining maturity recognized itself as the heir; at that time the power of the East fell, that of the West arose."[42] While Orosius emphasizes the importance of this temporal coincidence, his theory incorporates two other empires, which coincide with the remaining cardinal points. After the fall of Babylon in the East, Macedonia arose in the North, succeeded by Carthage in the South, over which Rome, in the West, triumphed.[43] Like Augustine, Orosius thus manages to reconcile an East/West dichotomy with a quadripartite vision of the world.

Augustine and Orosius were among the earliest authors to historicize the East and the West. These crucial new dichotomies—past/present or past/future—complicated the Manichean vision of east and west outlined above. They introduced another parallel that represented the West in a distinctly positive light (as young and strong) and the East in a negative one (as old and weak). After all, few could have questioned the superiority of Rome in the West over Babylon in the East.

Perhaps the earliest expression of the idea of the westward progression of history, which had more to do with history than with eschatology, was the product of a political and ideological vacuum caused by the disappearance of the Roman Empire in the West. Avitus, a sixth-century bishop of Vienne, drew upon the East/West dichotomy in order to understand the relations between barbarian kingdoms in the West and the Roman Empire in the East. In addition to being a bishop, Avitus was a secretary to King Sigismund of Burgundy, who acted as an independent ruler but formally drew his legitimacy from the emperor Anastasius. In a letter written in Sigismund's name, Avitus compares Anastasius to the sun: "the light of the East touches Gaul and Scythia, and the ray of light that is believed to rise there, shines here. We do not take in the brilliance of your [Anastasius's] countenance with our own eyes, but in our longing we possess the light of serenity that you radiate in every direction."[44] Avitus uses the centuries-old ploy of transferring solar imagery associated with Christ to a Roman or Byzantine emperor; here, he depicts Anastasius, in the East, as the sun, while Sigismund, implicitly in the West, benefits from the rays of the sun.

When writing to a Byzantine emperor, Avitus acknowledged the superiority of the East over the West. However, in another letter that he composed in Sigismund's name, to Clovis, congratulating him on his conversion to Christianity, Avitus represents the West as appropriating some of the characteristics of the East. In this letter, Avitus once again uses the imagery of light, although in a strikingly different manner: "let Greece . . . rejoice in having an orthodox ruler but she is no longer the only one to deserve so great a gift. Now her bright glory adorns your [Clovis's] part of the world also, and in the West, in the person of a new king, the ray of an age-old light shines forth."[45] What exactly the "age-old light" signifies is open to debate, but it is likely that Avitus had in mind the eastern star that pointed the way for the magi, which makes sense given that Clovis was baptized on Christmas day. According to Avitus, with Clovis's conversion to Christianity, the West, no longer a passive receiver of light from the East, was in full possession of its own source of light. No less important, this implied a usurpation of one of the characteristics of the East, with the star of the East literally becoming the star of the West.

If King Sigismund of Burgundy still looked for legitimacy to Constantinople, Charlemagne and his successors searched for and found it in Rome. As a result, they had little use for the idea of the westward progression of history. The notions of a *translatio* or of the *renovatio* of the Roman Empire were much more fitting.[46] So it is not surprising that during the Carolingian era the idea of westward progression, albeit once again in embryonic form, is to be found at the papal court rather than the imperial one.

The rule of Pope Nicholas I coincided with intense competition between the papacy and the patriarchs of Constantinople, notably over the conversion of barbarian peoples in eastern Europe, which surfaced most spectacularly during the Photian Schism. The pope attempted to undermine the prestige of Byzantium by writing that, thanks to the apostles Peter and Paul, the West was "transformed" into the East.[47] Thus, as they physically traveled to the West, the two apostles metaphorically took the East with them. While Avitus found some characteristics of the East in the West, Nicholas argued that such characteristics were sufficiently important to claim that the East was actually to be found in the West.

The new reassertion of the West (and also of the North) at the expense of the East (and also of the South) is found in the *Histories* of Raoul Glaber, written in the first half of the eleventh century. Glaber noted that conversions to Christianity tended to take place in the West and North rather than in the East and South, and he explains this phenomenon by recalling Christ's crucifixion: "When he was hung on the cross the immature people of the East were hidden behind His head, but the West was before His eyes, ready to be filled with the light of the faith. So too His almighty right arm, extended for the works of mercy, pointed to the North, which was to be mellowed by the holy word of faith, while His left was the lot of the South, which swarmed with barbaric peoples."[48] This image reverses the conception of the East as the front and the West as the back found in the Hebrew language. For Glaber, then, the West and North are the blessed lands, while the East and South belong to "immature" and "barbaric" peoples. In Glaber's work, east has become a negative cardinal point, while west has turned into a positive one, the exact opposite of what they had been in the patristic era.

In the early twelfth century, several chroniclers of the First Crusade expanded upon the idea of the superiority of the West over the East. Guibert of Nogent built on the tradition found in the writings of Avitus of Vienne and Pope Nicholas, and his attack on the East was also an attack on Byzantium. Guibert's position is best understood in comparison with that of Robert the Monk. Although Robert was generally highly critical of Emperor Alexius, he still acknowledged Constantinople as a worthy, albeit inferior, counterpart to Rome. For example, he wrote that Constantine the Great, inspired from above, "made it [Constantinople] equal to Rome in the height of its walls and the noble structure of the buildings, making it sublime in equal glory and earthly distinction: just as Rome is the capital of the West, thus Constantinople should be the capital of the Orient. This city is richer than all others through its fertile land and all the trade of mercantile riches." According to Robert, Constantinople continued to play an important role in the history of salvation, as a bulwark against the Muslim world: "Let none doubt that it was founded on divine will—God saw what was to come, which we now see come pass. For if such a city had not been founded, where would the Christianity of the East have found refuge?" Robert then paid tribute to the city as a repository of relics from across "Asia and Africa," finally concluding that Rome and Constantinople were equals in all respects but one: Rome, "elevated by the presence of the Pope," was "head and chief of all Christendom."[49]

Guibert of Nogent, by contrast, described the situation in the East is if there was no Christian state there anymore. If Robert represented Constantinople as a place of refuge for the "Christianity of the East," Guibert disregarded it completely when he described the Muslim conquest: "the obscurity of this nefarious sect [Islam] . . . has wiped out Christ's name from the furthest corners of the entire East."[50] For Guibert, it was crusaders who reintroduced Christianity to the East: "the Eastern Church was restored by the labor of the Western faithful" (124/266).

Guibert argued that there was a link between the religion of Byzantium (no longer Christianity, from his perspective) and Islam, and that both revealed a typical Eastern inconsistency with regard to matters of faith. According to Guibert, "the faith of the Easterners" "has always been variable and unsteady, searching for novelty, always exceeding the bounds of true belief" (30/89). The first example of this fickleness was the fact that the majority of heresies, with one exception, had their origin "in the East and Africa." From early on, "the Eastern regions were lands cursed on earth in the works of its teachers, bringing forth thorns and prickly weeds for those working it" (30/90). In talking about "cursed lands" (*terra maledicta*), Guibert refers to a passage from Genesis, in which God addresses Adam after the Fall with the following words: "Cursed is the ground for thy sake; in sorrow shalt thou eat of it all the days of thy life" (Gen. 3:17). Guibert undermined the importance of the East as the location of paradise by noting that the Fall, the loss of paradise, must have taken place in the East as well. Whereas, for Robert, a Christian Constantinople was a bulwark against the Muslim East before the First Crusade, for Guibert, there was a close connection between a "heretical" Constantinople and the "infidel" East.[51]

At the same time, Guibert remembered the importance of the East as the origin of Christianity. He described its decline as a temporary situation to be rectified by immigrants from the West: "The most splendidly noble cities, Antioch, Jerusalem, and Nicea, and the provinces, Syria, Palestine, and Greece, the seed-beds of the new grace, have lost their initial strength at the roots, while the Italians, French, and English, who migrated there, have flourished" (31/92). Pope Nicholas I argued in the ninth century that the West became the East when the apostles Peter and Paul came to Rome. Guibert went a step further, claiming that the East was no longer the East of the past, the seedbed "of the new grace," but a land devoid of "strength." It was the people of the West who, by settling there, could make the East resemble the East of the apostolic era.

Although in this instance Guibert did not refer to the apostles explicitly, he seems to have been developing the theme of crusaders imitating the apostles, which, as William Purkis has demonstrated, is common in the sources of the First Crusade.[52] If we are to believe the *Gesta Francorum*, Urban II had already made a comparison between the future crusaders and the apostles when he preached at Clermont.[53] According to Raymond of Aguilers, the capture of Jerusalem on July 15 was tantamount to the apostles' return: "It is also noteworthy that on that day the apostles were thrown out of Jerusalem and dispersed throughout all the world. On that day the children of the apostles freed the city for God and the Fathers."[54]

Like Guibert, Fulcher of Chartres also noted the success of Latin migration, which had transformed the region: "Consider, I pray, and reflect how in our time God has transformed the Occident into the Orient. For we who were Occidentals have now become Orientals. He who was a Roman or a Frank has in this land been made into a Galilean or a Palestinian. He who was of Rheims or Chartres has now become citizen of Tyre or Antioch."[55] Fulcher described a seemingly trivial situation (which was his own) of crusaders settling in the East and thus becoming "easterners." However, like

Guibert, he seems to have participated in the theme of the First Crusade as a reverse apostolic mission. While in the apostolic era the East was the origin of Christian settlers, such as the apostles Peter and Paul, the West was now playing that role.

In a further elaboration of this theme, Robert the Monk and Guibert of Nogent introduced the theme of "debt," arguing that the West "owed" the East for the introduction of Christianity during the apostolic era. The Crusades were a form of repayment of this debt. In his rendition of Urban II's speech at Clermont, Guibert used aquatic metaphors to describe this idea: "If all Christian preaching flows from the fountain of Jerusalem, then let the rivulets, wherever they flow over the face of the earth, flow into the hearts of the Catholic multitude, so that they may take heed of what they owe to this overflowing fountain" (43/113). According to Guibert, Urban then quoted King Solomon, who remarks in Ecclesiastes, "All the rivers run into the sea; yet the sea is not full; unto the place whence the rivers come, thither they return again" (Eccles. 1:7). Guibert did not attend the Council of Clermont, and it is most likely that this biblical allusion in Urban's sermon is Guibert's own. So, according to Guibert, the "rivulets" (i.e., common Christian faith) were supposed to remind "the Catholic multitude" of the fate of the "fountain of Jerusalem," from which the "rivulets" had originated, and to incite them to rescue it. Although Guibert did not include an East/West dichotomy in this case (as we shall see, he did so later in Urban's speech), his imagery of the brimming fountain is similar to the imagery of the sun in his own and other chronicles. Also, the episode contains some of the same ideas that Guibert put forward in his explicit discussions of opposition between the East and the West. According to Guibert, while Jerusalem was the source of water in the beginning, the First Crusade reversed the direction of giving/receiving: it was "glorious" for Western Christians to "purify the place whence" they "received the cleansing of baptism and the proof of faith" (43/113). Thus, during the apostolic era, the West received Christianity from the East. Now, in the course of the First Crusade, the East renewed its Christian faith thanks to the West. Before, the East was a "purifier"; now it became "purified." Before, the East was the source; now it became the destination.

Both Guibert of Nogent and Robert the Monk found a prophecy of Isaiah even more appropriate than the passage from Ecclesiastes to describe what they saw as the recent takeover of the East by the West. In this prophecy, God addresses Israel, "Fear not: for I am with thee: I will bring thy seed from the East, and gather you from the West. I will say to the North, Give up; and to the South, Keep not back" (Isa. 43:5–6). In this passage, the four cardinal points play an equal role, a situation that did not satisfy the two chroniclers. According to Guibert, Urban II transformed the passage and introduced the East/West dichotomy when preaching at Clermont: "The Lord has led our seed from the East, in that he brought forth for us in a double manner out of the Eastern land the early progeny of the Church. But out of the West he assembled us, for through those who last began the proof of faith, that is the westerners (we think that, God willing, this will come about through your deeds), Jerusalem's losses will be restored" (44/115-16). Here, using Urban as his mouthpiece, Guibert ignores Isaiah's references to the North and South and concentrates his attention on the East and West. Guibert acknowledged that the East was the place of origin of Christianity. He reiterated that the apostles Peter and Paul, "in a double manner," brought the faith from the East to the West. However, the movement was now reversed. It was up to the West to restore "Jerusalem's losses."

Later in his chronicle, in his overview of biblical passages relevant to the enterprise of the First Crusade, Guibert recalled the passage of Isaiah once again: "He [God] stretches the skies who spread [the influence of] the church, as he propagated his seed from the East, according to Isaiah, by means of the apostles, even as he had to gather the church through them from the West." Here, once again, Guibert acknowledged the role of the East as the origin of Christianity, but, in an obvious allusion to the papacy, celebrated the West as the place of the "gathering" of the church (141/301). It appears that Guibert also had an answer to the question concerning what would happen after the West rescued the East, which, once again, he put into the mouth of Urban II. Guibert believed that the Antichrist could not come "unless Christianity is established where paganism now rules." Shortly after the restoration of the East to Christianity, the end of the world was supposed to ensue (43–44/113–14).

Like Guibert, Robert also referred to the prophecy of Isaiah. Although the letter of his exegesis is considerably different from Guibert's, the gist is the same: Isaiah predicts the takeover of the East. This time, however, not merely the West but the combined forces of the West, North, and South oppose the East. Robert divided the leaders of the First Crusade into two groups. Robert of Normandy, Robert of Flanders, and Hugh of Vermandois came "from remote parts of the West towards the North." Bishop Adhémar of Le Puy and Raymond IV, Count of St. Gilles, came "from the South." Robert explained the meaning of this assembly: "now we see demonstrated in actual fact what

God promised through the mouth of the Prophet Isaiah: 'Fear not, for I am with thee: I will bring thy seed from the North, and gather thee from the West; I will say to the North, Give up; and to the South, Keep not back: bring my sons from far, and my daughters from the ends of the earth.'"[56] In freely paraphrasing Isaiah's prophecy, Robert omitted the "East" entirely from the list of four cardinal points. This new version fit the situation described in the chronicle much better than the original. The South, North, and West are the crusaders' places of origin. The East is, implicitly, the destination of their journey.

In a subsequent passage, Robert reintroduced the East/West dichotomy: "Now we see the sons and daughters of God making for Jerusalem from the ends of the earth.... In very truth God now rises above the West, resting as he does in the spirit of the Westerners. The West prepares to illuminate the East, rousing new stars to dispel the blindness which oppresses it."[57] Robert returns here to the traditional analogy between Christianity and the sun or, by association, light in general. At the same time, he innovates in claiming that the West is now the source of Christianity. The West literally becomes the East, while the East in its "blindness" (an image akin to "darkness") becomes the West. Here, then, the West is the subject, the source of light, while the East is the object, waiting to be "illuminated."

It is worth noting in passing, however, that Robert demonstrates a good deal of freedom in dealing with cardinal points, as he is attempting to pay tribute to several different traditions at once. At times, as in the example above, Robert turns to the East/West dichotomy. At other times, supporting Akbari's argument, he refers to the North as the origin of crusaders.[58] Finally, on other occasions, he mentions the four cardinal points together in order to emphasize the universality of Christendom restored by the labors of crusaders.[59]

While the West could become the source of light metaphorically, the sun continued to rise in the East. However, in several chronicles, other celestial phenomena involving light took the place of the sun as sources of light and were reported to have appeared in the West or to have moved toward the East in the course of the First Crusade. It is, of course, difficult to know the extent to which the narratives correspond to the empirical experience of crusaders. It is likely that at some point crusaders saw a comet: Chinese, Japanese, and Korean sources include observation of one in the fall of 1097.[60] If a comet was seen in the Far East, it was surely visible in the Middle East at the same time. Still, none of the chroniclers offered a mere report of the sighting but interpreted it as a prophecy of or a commentary on Muslim-Christian warfare. Some claimed that a supernatural phenomenon (which might or might not be related to the actual comet) appeared at a later date, closer to the fateful weeks of June 1098. Others described the phenomenon using imagery that makes sense only in the context of crusading. Finally, still others related the movement of the phenomenon through the skies to the idea of domination of the East by the West.

On several occasions these phenomena did not merely illuminate but mimicked a violent subjection of the East. Fulcher of Chartres recorded a curious sight observed by crusaders in Heraclea in September 1097: "When we reached the city of Heraclea, we beheld a certain sign in the sky which appeared in brilliant whiteness in the shape of a sword with the point towards the East. What it portended for the future we did not know, but we left the present and the future to God."[61] If, before the capture of Jerusalem, crusaders "did not know" what the celestial display signified, the reader would have no trouble understanding that a sword pointing toward the East had to mean divine sanction for crusaders' warfare in the region.[62] In Fulcher's account, the West did not merely acquire its own source of light that would "illuminate" the "blindness" of the East, as it did in the passage by Robert the Monk discussed above. Rather, a "brilliant whiteness" moving toward the East stood for the military conquest of the East. The relationship between the two cardinal points reached its highest degree of polarization here. If, in previous examples, the East lost its role as the giver and turned into the receiver, now the opposition was that of the victor versus the vanquished.

Fulcher reported another celestial sign in late December 1097, when crusaders were besieging Antioch: "At that time we saw a remarkable reddish glow in the sky and besides felt a great quake in the earth, which rendered us all fearful. In addition many saw a certain sign in the shape of a cross, whitish in color, moving in a straight path toward the East."[63] Both moving toward the East, the sword at Heraclea and the cross at Antioch performed the same function. They announced the immediate future (the victory of Christians over "infidels"), but they also explained the grand scheme of things (the West subjugating the East).

Ralph of Caen claimed to have seen something similar to Fulcher's description in the sky at about the same time, in February 1098, in his native Normandy: "The following night brought a horrible redness to the sky positioned so that those in the west could see it. They shouted, 'The East fights.' I myself saw this same sign when in my father's home at Caen where I spent my youth.... Many people marveled at this vision, and they all said with one voice that it indicated war and blood."[64] Although in this case there is no movement, Ralph still conceived of the phenomenon in terms of an East/West dichotomy. The strange coloring reminded people in the West of the fighting in the East.

Fulcher was not the only one to read a deeper meaning into reports of strange occurrences in the skies. Robert the Monk recorded a comet on the night of June 2–3, 1098, when Antioch was taken by crusaders: "It is worth remembering that on that night a comet blazed amongst the other stars in the heavens, giving off rays of light and foretelling a change in the kingdom; the sky glowed fiery red from North to East. It was with these portents shining prominently in the heavens and as dawn began to bring light to the earth that the army of God entered Antioch."[65] In this case, references to the North (here, once again, used interchangeably with the West) and East are hardly accidental; the two cardinal points symbolize, respectively, the origin and the destination of crusaders. By insisting that crusaders entered Antioch at dawn, Robert also developed the same parallel as in his exegesis of Isaiah, discussed above, between "the army of God" conquering the Holy Land and the sun illuminating the world.

As mentioned at the beginning of this chapter, the anonymous author of the *Gesta Francorum* reported another sighting in June 1098, when Muslims led by Kerbogha besieged the crusaders at Antioch. Then, the fire "coming from the West" fell on the Turkish camp. This is a rare use of the East/West dichotomy in the *Gesta*, and it is possible that the author merely recorded what he saw. Robert the Monk, however, reworking the passage, unambiguously interpreted it in terms of the opposition between the East and the West as cultural constructs. According to Robert, "a flame appeared in the sky coming from the West and fell onto the Turkish army." The flame caused a stir in both camps: "This sign deeply impressed everyone, particularly the Turks amongst whose tents it fell. They began to see glimmerings of what would come to pass: that the fire descending from heaven represented the anger of God; because it had come from the West it symbolizes the armies of the Franks through whom he would make his anger manifest."[66] Here, there is a near coincidence between prophecy and the actual event it prophesies. The "flame" symbolizes crusaders' armies, but it actually falls upon the Turks.

This and other narratives continue the discussion concerning the East and the West that had begun in late antiquity. A comet from the West that fell on the East was a new response to the sun's rising in the East and setting in the West; to Christianity's spreading from east to west; and to the Roman Empire's surviving in the East but not in the West. It served as visible proof that the tables had turned.

In his narrative of the battle of Antioch, Ralph of Caen emphasized a natural incident of a different type, but he also interpreted it to signify divine support for the conquest of the East by the West. According to several authors, a propitious wind contributed to the crusaders' victory. Ralph claimed that at the beginning of the battle the crusaders had suffered greatly because of the east wind: "The East Wind came to battle from the kingdom of Nabatea in support of the Persians who were its neighbors. It overcame horses, bows and quivers. It hurled back spears against those who cast them. Attacks were turned back on the attackers. The Frankish sword was hardly able to stand against the javelins of the East Wind." At first, the west wind, which was supposed to help the crusaders against the east wind, did nothing: "The now languid West Wind lazed in its Aeolian grotto. It had been a faithful companion to the Franks. . . . It now betrayed them. The West Wind gives no aid while Francia fights in the East."[67]

The "infidels" set the grass on fire, and the east wind blew clouds of smoke into the crusaders' faces. Ralph closed the chapter with a direct address to the west wind: "Rush to our aid O West Wind, rise up sluggish one, the East Wind rages on behalf of the Turks, rise up on our behalf."[68] God "took pity" on the crusaders and "opened his treasures": "He sent forth the favorable North-west Wind which struck the East wind and forced the defeated one to return to its vaults. Freed from its western prison, the North Wind tormented the eyes of the Turks with their own smoke." Finally, Ralph addressed the east wind directly: "Behold the East Wind, you flee and you are overcome by your own smoke." Ralph concluded the discussion with a dichotomy that no longer had to do with the wind: "The West then carried on and the East pitied those who were carried off."[69]

The role of wind from the east in bringing various forms of discomfort corresponds, generally speaking, to natural patterns observed in the Middle East.[70] However, it is impossible to explain Ralph's account of the battle of Antioch as a battle between winds from the east and west (and northwest) as merely a faithful rendition of crusaders' experience. The narrative can be understood best within the context of an East/West dichotomy. Ralph implicitly introduces into his discussion the body of biblical references to east and west winds. There are numerous examples in the Old Testament of God taking the wind "out of his treasures" and using it as a vehicle of divine arbitration. Much of the time, the east wind is nocuous, while the west wind is beneficial. A prophecy of Jeremiah mentions wind in a military context, when the lord threatens to scatter the Jews "as with an East wind before the enemy" (Jer. 18.17). The book of Exodus juxtaposes an east wind that brings locusts to a West wind that blows them away (Exod. 10:13, 19).[71] Thus, according to Ralph, west was and had been since biblical times a "positive" cardinal point, while east was a "negative" one. The amusing story of the west wind trouncing the east wind was another way of narrating the crusaders' defeat of "infidels" but also, more generally, of the West prevailing over the East, or good over evil.

To summarize, in the patristic era the East represented positive concepts (Christ, light, life, virtue), while the West came to symbolize negative ones (Satan, darkness, death, sin). This characterization of the two cardinal points, however, did not apply to any specific regions. Augustine and Orosius began to introduce geography into the equation, emphasizing that Babylon, where history apparently began, was located in the East and that Rome, where history was supposed to end, was located in the West. But such references were rare and hesitant. When a new geopolitical reality emerged, pitting the former territories of the western Roman Empire against Byzantium, some thinkers, such as Avitus of Vienne and Pope Nicholas I, began to update the patristic authors, arguing that if the East had once been a positive cardinal point, the West had now taken its place. The negative view of the East was a reaction to (in a way, a compensation for) a negative view of the West.

The Crusades led to renewed interest in the idea of an East/West dichotomy, in that warfare in the Holy Land appeared to demonstrate that the East was now what the West had been in the past (a dark place, awaiting illumination) and, vice versa, that the West was the new East (a source of light, ready to illuminate). As cultural constructs, the West became the East, while the East became the West. Robert the Monk and Guibert of Nogent especially believed that it was the moral obligation and a providential necessity of the West to do what the East had done for it in the past and to transfer sanctity from the West back to the East. Thus the idea of the debt incurred during the early Christian era provided a powerful justification for crusading. It is possible that the chroniclers suspected that this spread of Christianity from west to east was to bring about the end of time, which the spread of Christianity from east to west a thousand years earlier had failed to do.

The chroniclers of the First Crusade elaborated a tripartite program in support of their interpretation of the East/West dichotomy. They stressed both the utter desolation of the East and the disappearance of Christianity from the region.[72] They also discovered biblical prophecies that were supposed to have predicted the West's taking on the traditional role of the East as the source of Christianity. Finally, they framed miracles involving celestial phenomena that occurred, or purportedly occurred, in the course of the First Crusade in terms of an East/West dichotomy, with the West usurping the traditional function of the East as the source of light.

Rubenstein demonstrates that "apocalypticism was fundamental to crusade thought."[73] Indeed, an analysis of the East/West dichotomy makes it apparent that several authors represented the First Crusade as a miraculous event that literally changed the course of history like no other. Before, history moved westward; now it began to move eastward. One possible implication was that, with the move completed, history would end.

As the reality of the beleaguered Latin states became increasingly difficult to ignore, the theory of the progression of history held by some chroniclers of the First Crusade, according to which the West "illuminated" the East, could no longer be sustained. Hugh of Saint Victor and especially Otto of Freising and Gerald of Wales must have been aware of this. There is ample evidence that the latter two were preoccupied with the fate of the Latin states: Otto chronicled the failure of the Second Crusade, while Gerald was actively involved in a preaching campaign to liberate Jerusalem after the Muslims recaptured the city in 1187. Possibly inspired by the vision laid out in some chronicles of the First Crusade, these three authors produced a more pessimistic and also more overtly eschatological version of the East/West binary. According to this version, the East was engulfed by darkness, while the last rays of light still illuminated the West before the sunset of history and the new sunrise of the second coming.

CONCLUSION

Many contemporaries of the First Crusade, awestruck by the apparent immensity of the accomplishment, wondered about the meaning and implications of the event and struggled to find it a worthy place in the continuum of sacred history. To them, the crusade was not just unlike other wars; it was entirely unprecedented. Although, true to their habits, chroniclers looked to the past for helpful clues, their explanations of the crusade tended to be more original than most contemporary accounts of conflicts perceived as more ordinary. The chroniclers disagreed with one another on many aspects, but together they came up with a series of ideas that were either brand new or freshly reformulated regarding warfare, the relations between Western Christianity and other faiths, and, more broadly, the mechanisms governing the course of history. At least some of these ideas had (and, to a limited extent, still have) a significant influence on subsequent interpretations of both the past and the present.

The greatest achievement of the chroniclers was to demonstrate that contemporary wars, and not just biblical ones, could also be "holy." Although attempts have been made to justify and even sacralize warfare in the past, especially during the period of the invasions, these precedents cannot compare in their number, spread, intensity, or impact. The present book has analyzed four of the devices that the chroniclers used to depict the First Crusade as a "holy war." Of course, there were others, most notably the representation of Muslims as idol-worshipping pagans, but these four seem to be at once understudied and consequential.

First, several chroniclers argued that the First Crusade was, in an extraordinarily literal sense, the work of God. They presented accounts of miracles—especially of the intervention of saints in the battle of Antioch—as proof of this. The claim that saints appeared in what was normally an inherently sinful occupation was radical to the point of straining the reader's or listener's credulity. At first, it appears that it was primarily the Normans of the South who were willing to take this risk. Because of their unique position, they were aware of two distinct strands of precedent involving saints intervening in warfare. First, they maintained that they were the descendants and heirs of the Vikings, who were supposed to have frequently borne the brunt of saintly violence. Second, they had intimate knowledge of Byzantines insisting on the close connection between imperial forces and military saints. Their acquaintance with these two traditions put the Normans of the South in the best position to transform them to their own advantage.

Second, some chroniclers perceived that God's backing was not sufficient for a Christian war to deserve the title of "holy." If it were, Christian warfare would have been no different from the Jewish warfare described in the Old Testament, in which God took a close interest. In order for a Christian war to be "holy," it had to be spiritual. So the chroniclers worked hard to emphasize the difference between crusaders and the Jewish warriors of the Old Testament, particularly the Maccabees, and also to demonstrate the spiritual nature of crusading warfare. The two tasks were closely related, and one solution sufficed for both. While acknowledging superficial resemblances, the chroniclers strove to define the crusaders as the exact opposites of the Jews. In doing so, they recalled and gave new force to the old tradition of using the Jews as shorthand for carnality.

Third, the chroniclers allotted a central place to the First Crusade within the larger narrative of sacred history. At least one of them, Robert the Monk, claimed that nothing of comparable importance had happened in more than a millennium, since the incarnation and the subsequent conversion of the Gentiles. Moreover, they perceived symmetry between their own time and the apostolic era. They conceived this symmetry in terms of cardinal directions: if the apostles went from east to west to spread Christianity there, the crusaders went from west to east to do the same. This symmetry worked to justify the crusade as a necessary step in the history of the world and as an integral part of the divine plan for humankind.

Fourth, although history and theology were often closely linked in the Middle Ages, this connection reached a new intensity in the chronicles of the First Crusade. Several authors argued that someone who had not taken part in the enterprise and who had never set foot in the Holy Land could know more about it than any crusader, simply because of his experience with exegesis and his knowledge of theology. In other words, they claimed that contemporary history could call for the same approach and necessitate the same skills as biblical exegesis.

In many crucial ways, the chroniclers of the First Crusade succeeded not only in transforming the heritage they had received (or had actively sought) from the past but also in passing the result on to subsequent generations. Crusades continued to evoke wide interest for centuries after Jerusalem had been won and lost. As evidence of this, the most successful chronicle, written by Robert the Monk, survives in more than eighty manuscripts of impressive chronological and geographical scope: they date from the twelfth through the seventeenth centuries and are preserved in libraries all over Europe, from Vienna to Uppsala, indicating their wide circulation. The first printed edition of the chronicle appeared in Cologne in 1472, just a couple of decades after the invention of the printing press. By the end of the sixteenth century, it had undergone five independent translations into German.[1] Although, in terms of popularity, other chronicles trail far behind, twelfth-century interpretations of the First Crusade clearly enjoyed wide currency for many centuries after they had been written down. Although a discussion of the influence of the chronicles of the First Crusade is well beyond the scope of the present book, I would like to recall three examples from the early modern and modern periods that reveal the impact of this vision.

In the thirteenth century, Kamal ad-Din, the author of a work titled *Everything Desirable About the History of Aleppo*, wrote an account of the battle of the Field of Blood, fought in 1119. This was one of the greatest military disasters in the history of the Latin states, and Prince Roger of Antioch was killed in it. Upon examining the prisoners, Ilghazi, the ruler of Aleppo and the leader of the Muslim troops, noticed a soldier "of magnificent physique who had been captured by a small, thin, ill-armed Muslim." Ilghazi's warriors mocked him, saying, "Aren't you ashamed to have been captured by this little man, with a physique like yours?" He replied, "By God, this man did not capture me; he is not my conqueror. The man who captured me was a great man, greater and stronger than I, and he handed me over to this fellow. He wore a green robe and rode a green horse!"²

That the conqueror of the Christian wore green and rode a green horse indicates that the speaker is describing a celestial agent, because green, in Islam, is a heavenly color. More specifically, green is the color of Al Khidr (literally, "the Green One"), a mystical companion of Moses. According to one narrative, Al Khidr had bathed in the well of life, and his skin and clothes had turned green, causing him to leave green footprints wherever he went.³ Thus, describing the man wearing green and riding a green horse, Kamal ad-Din probably meant not just any celestial agent but Al Khidr himself.

In Islamic tradition, there are several key narratives of supernatural intervention in battle. All of them have to do with battles waged by the prophet Muhammad, especially the battle of Badr, fought in 624 against the Meccan clan of Quraysh. One of the Koran's *suras* mentions the battle of Badr by name, and another one obviously refers to it. *Sura* 3, "The House of Imran," describes two companies of Muhammad's army "about to lose heart" on the battlefield. They receive reassurance: "if you are patient and god-fearing, and the foe come against you instantly, your Lord will reinforce you with five thousand swooping angels." Similarly, in *sura* 8, "The Spoils," God promises to reinforce the faithful with "a thousand angels riding behind."⁴

The *Life of Muhammad*, written by Muhammad Ibn Ishaq in the eighth century, adds many new details to the *sura*'s accounts of supernatural intervention in the battle of Badr. Throughout, Ibn Ishaq refers to several witnesses, the first of which, a member of the Quraysh, was following the course of the battle from a nearby hill when he heard a voice saying, "Forward, Hayzum." This made it possible to identify the speaker, as "Hayzum" was the name of the archangel Gabriel's horse. The same eyewitness also claimed that his cousin, who was watching the battle with him, became so overwhelmed, apparently by Gabriel's presence nearby, that his heart burst and he died on the spot.⁵

Another eyewitness, one of the Meccans who survived the battle, reported being overpowered by an irresistible force: "As soon as we met the party we turned our backs and they were killing and capturing us just as they pleased; and by God I don't blame the people for that. We met men in white on piebald horses between heaven and earth, and by God they spared nothing and none could withstand them."⁶ The Meccan was reluctant to believe in supernatural intervention, but after he had spoken, someone in his audience commented, "Those were the angels." In Islamic tradition, the color white is associated above all with the archangel Gabriel.⁷ According to Ibn Ishaq, the battle of Badr was not the only battle in which supernatural intervention took place, although in other battles the angels "did not fight."⁸

Until Kamal ad-Din, Muslim authors did not attribute any victories in battles waged after Muhammad's death to the direct intervention of celestial troops. Kamal ad-Din must have drawn his inspiration from the accounts of celestial intervention in the battle of Badr and other battles fought by the prophet. At the same time, however, it is highly probable that Kamal ad-Din was aware of Christian narratives of celestial intervention, headed by Saint George, in the battle of Antioch. This would explain his choice of Al Khidr, rather than the archangel Gabriel, as the agent intervening on the battlefield. From early on, there emerged an association between Al Khidr and Jirjis (the Arabic name for Saint George), to the point that the two came to be considered one and the same. So it is likely that Kamal ad-Din was referring to this hybrid figure, Al Khidr/Jirjis.

Thus Kamal ad-Din's description of the battle of the Field of Blood was a Muslim's response to the Christians' claim that they profited from divine assistance in general and from that of Saint George in particular. From Kamal ad-Din's perspective, Muslim victory at the battle of the Field of Blood appeared to prove, on the contrary, that both God and Jirjis/Saint George were on their side. Although this seems to be the only Muslim reaction to the narratives of saintly intervention in the battle of Antioch, its significance should not be underestimated. It demonstrates that by at least the thirteenth century, Muslims were aware not just of the gist but also of the details of Christian sacralization of warfare against them, and they strove to respond to this development in kind.⁹

The second example of the far-reaching influence of the narratives of the First Crusade is found in a fourteenth-century chronicle from Aragon, which describes a German knight who rode behind Saint George in the battle of Antioch, unaware of the identity of the rider in front of him. The knight was then transported miraculously to Alcoraz, where Saint George helped King Pedro of Aragon defeat Al-Mustain II of Zaragoza.¹⁰ Ironically, the battle of Alcoraz took place in 1096, two years before that of Antioch. It is possible that the anonymous chronicler, well aware of the failures in the Middle East and the successes in Iberia, wanted to emphasize the transfer of divine patronage for Christian warriors from the Holy Land to Spain.

The chronicler was just one in a series of Spanish authors who rewrote history and added celestial interventions to accounts of battles that had occurred as much as three centuries before the First Crusade. If Saint George was the key crusading saint, Saint James became the main patron of the Reconquista. Richard Fletcher has argued convincingly that the figure of Saint James the Moor-Slayer (Santiago Matamoros) was foreign to Spain before the First Crusade: "the 'crusade-idea' was an alien importation which took root in Spain only in the second quarter of the twelfth century. It further seems to me of significance that the notion of St. James as a patron saint of warfare against Islam emerges clearly for the first time at the same period."[11] In various sources, all of which postdate the First Crusade, Saint James was reported to have intervened in the battles of Clavijo in 844 and Simancas in 939, and to have helped King Ferdinand I of León and Castile capture Coimbra in 1064.[12] Saint James continued to intervene in later battles as well. At Jerez in 1231, "he appeared on a white horse with a white banner in his hand and a sword in the other and there was with him a legion of white knights." At Alange in 1299, he "visibly appeared in this battle with a host of white knights."[13]

With the discovery of the New World, Saint James underwent a new transformation. From a hero of the Reconquista he became a helper of the *conquistadores*. In Latin America, Santiago Matamoros became Santiago Mataindios (the Indian-Slayer).[14] In the nineteenth century, during the wars of independence, he underwent another transformation to become Santiago Mataespañois (the Slayer of Spaniards).[15] Although, from late antiquity on, saints began to take interest in warfare, the First Crusade popularized the image of saints actively engaged in combat. The wide acceptance of this image made it easier to sacralize wars (and also to demonize enemies) in the future.

To give a final, more recent example of the longevity of some of the ideas found in the chronicles of the First Crusade, the authors of a best-selling American evangelical textbook, first published in 1989, describe a movement from east to west: "God's plan for the nations has been unfolding in a specific geographic direction. This geographical march of history is called the Chain of Christianity or the Chain of Liberty. . . . It seems as if God's direction is westward."[16] Although the textbook does not contain an explicit reference to the East/West binary, it participates in the same conglomerate of ideas. Once again, cardinal points become temporal concepts. Once again, the West is associated with a later point in history and a higher point of maturity than the East.

The authors of the textbook, of course, did not get these ideas from Guibert of Nogent or Robert the Monk, but rather inherited them from the Protestant theologians of the sixteenth and seventeenth centuries.[17] During this period, America was at the center of speculation concerning the westward progression of history. For example, William Twisse conjectured in 1634 that America might become the new East: "And then, considering our English Plantations of late, and the opinion of many grave divines concerning the Gospel's fleeing westward, sometimes I have such thoughts—Why may not that be the place of the new Jerusalem?"[18] In 1699, John Edwards argued, by contrast, that the gospel would "be spread even to the utmost parts of this western hemisphere" and from there would "step into the East again," before finally returning "to the Place where it set out first of all," which would signal the end of the world.[19] Thus, according to Twisse, the West was becoming the new East ("the new Jerusalem"), while in John Edwards's view the progress of history would circle the globe and, crossing the Pacific Ocean, end up once again in the East (the actual Jerusalem).

In the eighteenth and nineteenth centuries, the notion of the westward progression of history became part of the discourse of the decline of Europe. The French naturalist Bernard Lacépède wrote to President Thomas Jefferson in 1803, "May your fellow citizens, by the wisdom of their choice, preserve forever their liberty, their government, and the peace! Hitherto, the movement of enlightenment has been from east to west. The inhabitants of the United States, if they do not reject this destiny, will one day halt and reverse this movement."[20] Although Lacépède undoubtedly wished to flatter Jefferson with this observation that the New World might one day become the teacher of the Old, it also reflected an elegiac attitude toward the future of Europe shared by a number of thinkers of the era.

In his *Philosophy of History*, Georg Wilhelm Friedrich Hegel attempted to counter the pessimism inherent in many European discussions of westward progression: "The History of the World travels from East to West, for Europe is absolutely the end of History, Asia the beginning. . . . Here [in the East] rises the outward physical Sun, and in the West it sinks down: here [in the West] consentaneously rises the Sun of self-consciousness, which diffuses a nobler brilliance." For Hegel, the East was the land of beginnings, but this very characteristic made it inferior to the West. Hegel explained that in the beginning (at "sunrise"), one experiences "astonishment" and forgets one's individuality. With the passage of time, however, "this astonishment is diminished," and "the individual proceeds to the contemplation of his own being." By evening, then, "man has erected a building constructed from his own inner Sun; and when in the evening he contemplates this, he esteems it more highly than the original external Sun."[21] For Hegel, then, the sun that mattered—that of "self-consciousness"—rose in the West. As history progressed from east to west, so did freedom. Hegel argued that while the East suffered from despotism, and the Greek and Roman world from democracy and aristocracy, Germany enjoyed the freedom conferred by monarchy.

The chronicles of the First Crusade had an indirect influence on these later representations of the world in terms of an East/West binary. After reconceptualizing it in a new and powerful way, the chronicles transmitted the heritage of late antiquity. The most immediate recipients were Hugh of Saint Victor, Otto of Freising, and Gerald of Wales. Although early modern and modern thinkers found the East/West binary in their study of the church fathers, at least some of them also drew on these late twelfth-century authors (Otto of Freising's work, for example, first appeared in print as early as 1515).

In a recent article, David Nirenberg has examined another binary opposition: that between the West and Islam. It is closely related to the East/West binary, although it focuses on people rather than geography. Nirenberg argues that both ways of conceiving this opposition, in terms of either conflict or complementarity, are faulty. "Despite their seeming political differences," he writes, "to the extent that our two major modes—clash and alliance, opposition and synthesis—for understanding the Christian West's relationship to Islam (or Judaism) are equally dialectical, they are equally fantastic. . . . The more dialectical the model the more studied its lack of consciousness, and the more fantastic the visions of the past, present, and future that it produces."[22] The similarities between the two oppositions—West/Islam and West/East—are numerous. Both are dialectical models and ignore any details that do not fit. Both are equally "fantastic" in that they hinder, rather than help, a mature, sound understanding of the world. Both trace their lineage to the church fathers, and both gained prominence during the era of the Crusades.

The significance of the First Crusade lies less in what it achieved (after all, Jerusalem remained in Christian hands for only eighty-eight years) than in the reactions to this achievement. In response to the crusade, many people, including those who went and those who did not go to the Holy Land, felt an urgent need to rethink their world. Old paradigms no longer sufficed and had to be replaced with new ones. The relationship between present, past, and future had to be conceptualized anew. The intellectual response to the First Crusade is most readily apparent in the chronicles, but this does not mean that it is easily discernable. The chroniclers did not advertise the originality of their vision. Since they all narrated pretty much the same sequence of events, it is necessary to examine carefully the choices they made in order to appreciate the idiosyncrasies of each work. A choice of wording in the narrative of a miracle might be accidental, or it might signal a radical new departure. An inexactness in paraphrasing a biblical passage might be due to a memory lapse, or it might be a way to communicate a provocative idea.

Although each chronicler had his own set of ideas, most of those who decided to write a narrative of the First Crusade believed that they were recording the appearance of a radically new type of warfare. On the one hand, it was similar to the wars of the Israelites in that God directly supported it. On the other hand, it was different in that Christians fought in it and could expect God to reward them for their service both in this life and, more important, in the next. The chronicles of the First Crusade are not just narratives but attempts, disguised as narratives, to prove that this campaign was different from any that had taken place in the past and to understand what this new development meant for the future. Long after the lands conquered by the participants in the First Crusade had been lost, echoes of this intellectual effort continued to be heard.

NOTES

INTRODUCTION

1. Robert the Monk, *History of the First Crusade*, 77; *Historia Iherosolimitana*, 4.
2. Guibert of Nogent, *Deeds of God*, 155, 28; *Dei gesta per Francos*, 328, 87.
3. Peter Damian, *Letters*, 2:307; *Briefe*, 2:513–14.
4. Hamilton, *Practice of Penance*, 194.
5. Spiegel, "History as Enlightenment," 177.
6. Riley-Smith, *First Crusade and the Idea of Crusading*, 135–52.
7. This definition of a miracle is Anselm of Canterbury's; see his *Conception virginale*, 164; translation in Ward, *Miracles and the Medieval Mind*, 4. For discussion, see Watkins, *History and the Supernatural*, 18.
8. See Riley-Smith, "Death on the First Crusade"; Cowdrey, "Martyrdom and the First Crusade"; Flori, "Mort et martyre des guerriers"; Morris, "Martyrs on the Field of Battle."
9. For a similar argument, see Schmitt, *Revenants*.
10. Erdmann, *Origin of the Idea*. See also MacGregor, "Ministry of Gerold d'Avranches"; Holdsworth, "'Airier Aristocracy.'"
11. Erdmann, *Origin of the Idea*, 7.
12. See, among many others, Smith, *War and the Making of Medieval Monastic Culture*; France, "Holy War and Holy Men"; Riley-Smith, "Erdmann and the Historiography"; Bull, "Roots of Lay Enthusiasm."
13. Clarke, *Angels of Mons*.
14. Loud, "'Gens Normannorum.'"
15. For crusaders depicted as apostles, see Purkis, *Crusading Spirituality*. For Muslims portrayed as pagans, see Tolan, *Saracens*, 105–34.
16. Throop, *Crusading as an Act of Vengeance*.
17. For overviews of the sources of the First Crusade, see Flori, *Chroniqueurs et propagandistes*; Bull, "Western Narratives"; Edgington, "First Crusade"; Hiestand, "Cronista medievale."
18. Morris, "*Gesta Francorum* as Narrative History."
19. Rubenstein, "Putting History to Use."
20. Bull, "Relationship Between the *Gesta Francorum*."
21. Flori, *Chroniqueurs et propagandistes*, 177.
22. Ibid., 221.
23. See Biddlecombe's introduction, in Baldric of Bourgueil, *Historia Ierosolimitana*; and Biddlecombe's essay "Baldric of Bourgueil and the *Familia Christi*."
24. Rubenstein, "Guibert of Nogent, Albert of Aachen."
25. Biddlecombe's introduction, in Baldric of Bourgueil, *Historia Ierosolimitana*, lxxv; and Huygens's introduction, in Guibert of Nogent, *Dei gesta per Francos*, 24.
26. Kempf and Bull's introduction, in Robert the Monk's *Historia Iherosolimitana*, ix–lxiv.
27. D'Angelo's introduction, in *Hystoria de via et recuperatione Antiochiae*, xiii–lix.

28. Grocock and Siberry's introduction, in Gilo of Paris, *"Historia vie Hierosolimitane,"* xiii–lxiv.
29. Kempf and Bull's introduction, in Robert the Monk, *Historia Iherosolimitana*, xiii.
30. Chibnall's introduction, in Orderic Vitalis, *Ecclesiastical History*, 5:xi–xix.
31. Thomson, "William of Malmesbury."
32. Greenway's introduction, in Henry of Huntington, *Historia Anglorum*, xxiii–xlxv.
33. D'Angelo's introduction, in Ralph of Caen, *Gesta Tancredi in Expeditione*, v–ci; Bachrach and Bachrach's introduction, in Ralph of Caen, *History of the Normans*, 1–17.
34. McCarthy's introduction, in *Chronicles of the Investiture Contest*, 44–53.
35. Hall and Phillips's introduction, in *Caffaro, Genoa, and the Twelfth-Century Crusades*, 1–48; Bellomo, *A servizio di Dio*.
36. Edgington and Sweetenham's introduction, in *Chanson d'Antioche*, 9.

CHAPTER 1

1. Isidore of Seville, *Etymologies*, 67. For discussion, see Fontaine, *Isidore de Séville*, 1:182; Cizek, "Historia comme témoignage oculaire." For a general discussion of the problem of eyewitnesses from antiquity to modern times, see Hartog, *Evidence de l'histoire*.
2. According to Fontaine, "Le concept païen de l'histoire témoignage oculaire semble avoir pris ici une valeur nouvelle dans le contexte du christianisme." *Isidore de Séville*, 1:181. See Horace, *Satires, Epistles, and Ars Poetica*, 464–66; John 19:35.
3. Guenée, *Histoire et culture*, 77–78, 132.
4. Beer, *Narrative Conventions of Truth*, 10.
5. Damian-Grint, *New Historians*, 68.
6. Ainsworth, "Contemporary and 'Eyewitness' History," 271.
7. Guenée, *Histoire et culture*, 132.
8. Damian-Grint, *New Historians*, 72.
9. Ainsworth, "Contemporary and 'Eyewitness' History," 258.
10. Bull, "Views of Muslims," 15. Similarly, Ainsworth recognizes that the use of the term "eyewitness" "raises a number of awkward questions." "Contemporary and 'Eyewitness' History," 249. Several historians have seen a merely literary topos in the eyewitness claims of some chroniclers of the First Crusade. See Levine, "Pious Traitor"; and Schuster, "Raymond d'Aguilers."
11. Harari, "Eyewitnessing in Accounts of the First Crusade," 98–99.
12. Guenée, *Histoire et culture*, 129.
13. John Scotus Eriugena, *Homélie sur le prologue de Jean*, 168–71. See also Chenu, *Théologie au douzième siècle*, 62–89; Nichols, *Romanesque Signs*; Spiegel, "History as Enlightenment."
14. Chrétien, "Neuf propositions," 76. On the uses of the word μάρτυς in the New Testament, see Spicq, *Léxique théologique du Nouveau Testament*, 969–74. On the use of the term martyr as witness, see Andrew Louth, "Martyre," in Lacoste, *Dictionnaire critique de théologie*, 715. See also Trites, *New Testament Concept of Witness*.
15. "Of course, because he [the Holy Spirit] will give, you also will give: he in your hearts, you in your voices; he by inspiring, you by resounding, so that it can be fulfilled, 'Their sound has gone forth into the earth' (Ps.18.5)." Augustine, Homily 93, *Tractates on the Gospel of John*, 2:175; *Homélies sur l'Évangile de Saint Jean*, 226. See Chrétien, "Neuf propositions," 86; Chrétien, *Saint Augustin*, 137–48; and Joseph Wolinski, "Esprit Saint," in Lacoste, *Dictionnaire critique de théologie*, 404–11.
16. Kierkegaard, *Philosophical Fragments*, 102. "Autopsy" literally means "the personal act of seeing."

17. On the holy lance in the context of the First Crusade, see Asbridge, "Holy Lance of Antioch"; Giese, "'Lancea Domini' von Antiochia"; Morris, "Policy and Visions"; Runciman, "Holy Lance Found at Antioch."

18. Raymond of Aguilers, *Historia Francorum*, 57; *"Liber" de Raymond d'Aguilers*, 75.

19. Ralph of Caen, *History of the Normans*, 119; *Gesta Tancredi in Expeditione*, 86–87.

20. Ralph of Caen, *Gesta Tancredi in Expeditione*, 87.

21. Ralph of Caen, *History of the Normans*, 120; *Gesta Tancredi in Expeditione*, 87.

22. Ralph of Caen, *Gesta Tancredi in Expeditione*, 78.

23. Raymond of Aguilers, *Historia Francorum*, 100; *"Liber" de Raymond d'Aguilers*, 120. The ordeal was an exceptional example of firsthand testimony failing to fulfill its customary function. In medieval jurisprudence, the ordeal was the last resort, used only when there were no witnesses. Yet there must have been witnesses other than Raymond both of the discovery of the holy lance and also of its miraculous power in battle. See Bartlett, *Trial by Fire and Water*, 28–29.

24. Raymond of Aguilers, *Historia Francorum*, 100; *"Liber" de Raymond d'Aguilers*, 121.

25. Raymond of Aguilers, *"Liber" de Raymond d'Aguilers*, 121–22.

26. Raymond of Aguilers, *Historia Francorum*, 101; *"Liber" de Raymond d'Aguilers*, 122.

27. Raymond of Aguilers, *Historia Francorum*, 101; *"Liber" de Raymond d'Aguilers*, 122.

28. A certain priest named Bernard of Puy fell ill, apparently because of his doubts concerning the lance. Raymond of Aguilers, *"Liber" de Raymond d'Aguilers*, 119.

29. Ibid., 84.

30. Ralph of Caen, *History of the Normans*, 126–27; *Gesta Tancredi in Expeditione*, 92–93.

31. Fulcher of Chartres, *History of the Expedition*, 100–101; Fulcher *Historia Hierosolymitana*, 236–37, 241. On reaching consensus concerning the outcome of ordeals, see Brown, "Society and the Supernatural"; Hyams, "Trial by Ordeal"; Bartlett, *Trial by Fire and Water*, 34–42.

32. Raymond of Aguilers, *Historia Francorum*, 15; *"Liber" de Raymond d'Aguilers*, 35.

33. Quoted in Rubenstein, "Putting History to Use," 154.

34. This quotation and those in the following two paragraphs are from Guibert of Nogent, *Deeds of God*, 157; *Dei gesta per Francos*, 333.

35. According to Spiegel, Suger's *Vita Ludovici* presents similar themes: "Ever in flux, Suger's world is one of perennial challenges to order that must be set right.... It is a hierarchically ordered world constantly undergoing deformation and thus continually in need of reformation and reform." "History as Enlightenment," 170.

36. Guibert of Nogent, *Deeds of God*, 157; *Dei gesta per Francos*, 333.

37. Guibert of Nogent, *Deeds of God*, 156; *Dei gesta per Francos*, 330.

38. Guibert of Nogent, *Deeds of God*, 157; *Dei gesta per Francos*, 333.

39. Yuval Harari reaches a similar conclusion, writing, "Guibert offers a division of labor that every modern historian would love to adopt, between the crude uneducated producers of 'bare' facts and the professional scholar who alone knows how to interpret them correctly and to set them into an eloquent narrative. "Eyewitnessing in Accounts of the First Crusade," 93. However, Harari does not sufficiently take into account that, for a twelfth-century medieval monk, a "correct interpretation" of history would be the one most in accord with sacred history.

40. Walter the Chancellor, *Antiochene Wars*, 101; *Bella Antiochena*, 74. As Thomas Asbridge and Susan Edgington have noted, Walter's description of the battle has distinct parallels with accounts of intervention by a celestial army, equally "white-clad," in the course of the First Crusade. See their note in Walter the Chancellor, *Antiochene Wars*, 101n149.

41. Fulcher of Chartres, *History of the Expedition*, 126; *Historia Hierosolymitana*, 312–14.

42. William of Malmesbury, *Gesta regum Anglorum*, 1:653.

43. Raymond of Aguilers, *Historia Francorum*, 135; "Liber" *de Raymond d'Aguilers*, 158.

44. *Chronicle of the Third Crusade*, 26.

45. The device of "hostile witnesses" (those who bear the brunt of divine wrath on the battlefield yet are the ones who testify to the fact) occurs in a wide variety of historiographical traditions. See, for example, Ibn Ishaq, *Life of Muhammad*, 310.

46. *Gesta Francorum*, 69.

47. Baldric of Bourgueil, *Historia Ierosolimitana*, 81.

48. Guibert of Nogent, *Deeds of God*, 110; *Dei gesta per Francos*, 240.

49. William of Malmesbury, *Gesta regum Anglorum*, 1:638–39.

50. Schmitt, *Revenants*, 40.

51. William of Malmesbury, *Gesta regum Anglorum*, 1:638–39.

52. Baldric of Bourgueil, *Historia Ierosolimitana*, 81.

53. Robert the Monk, *History of the First Crusade*, 141–42; *Historia Iherosolimitana*, 51–52.

54. Robert the Monk, *History of the First Crusade*, 171; *Historia Iherosolimitana*, 76. Similarly, the vernacular *Song of Antioch* also presented Adhémar as the first to witness the miracle. When the rest of crusaders perceived the army, they were thunderstruck, but the bishop reassured them by saying that the army, "composed of angels," was coming to their aid. *Chanson d'Antioche*, 920–23.

55. Henry of Huntington, *Historia Anglorum*, 438–39.

56. The anonymous author of the *Gesta Francorum* and Peter Tudebode were more reticent about their participation in the First Crusade. See Harari, "Eyewitnessing in Accounts of the First Crusade," 85–91.

57. Fulcher of Chartres, *History of the Expedition*, 71, 145, 131; *Historia Hierosolymitana*, 153, 377, 330.

58. Walter the Chancellor, *Antiochene Wars*, 109–10; *Bella Antiochena*, 78.

59. Asbridge and Edgington's introduction, in Walter the Chancellor, *Antiochene Wars*, 5.

60. Raymond of Aguilers, *Historia Francorum*, 63; "Liber" *de Raymond d'Aguilers*, 82.

61. Peter Tudebode, *Historia de Hierosolymitano itinere*, 138; English translation in the Hills' 1974 edition, 61.

62. William of Malmesbury, *Gesta regum Anglorum*, 1:654–55.

63. Orderic Vitalis, *Ecclesiastical History*, 1:132–33.

64. Guibert of Nogent, *Liber quo ordine sermo fieri debeat*, 57; English translation in Rubenstein, *Guibert of Nogent*, 96.

65. Guibert of Nogent, *Deeds of God*, 73; *Dei gesta per Francos*, 166.

66. Baldric of Bourgueil, *Historia Ierosolimitana*, 4.

67. Ibid., 4, 81.

68. Fontaine, *Isidore de Séville*, 1:182.

69. Guibert of Nogent, *Deeds of God*, 73; *Dei gesta per Francos*, 166. See, among other passages, Luke 2:20, 7:22; John 3:32; Acts 4:20, 22:14–15.

70. Robert the Monk, *History of the First Crusade*, 75; *Historia Iherosolimitana*, 3.

71. Orderic Vitalis, *Ecclesiastical History*, 5:189.

72. This argument can be found in two of the eyewitness accounts as well: *Gesta Francorum*, 43–44, and Peter Tudebode, *Historia de Hierosolymitano itinere*, 82. For commentary, see Beer, *Narrative Conventions of Truth*, 29.

73. Guibert of Nogent, *Deeds of God*, 90; *Dei gesta per Francos*, 200.

74. Guibert of Nogent, *Deeds of God*, 25–26; *Dei gesta per Francos*, 82.

75. Rubenstein, *Guibert of Nogent*, 100.

76. This complaint contrasts sharply with claims by early Christian authors that form was altogether unimportant. As Tore Janson has observed, "a wealth of prefaces from the

fifth century onwards states that the art of oratory is superfluous for the presentation of the Christian faith and that the reader should attend to the content, not to the very imperfect style." Janson, *Latin Prose Prefaces*, 134–35.

77. Robert the Monk, *History of the First Crusade*, 77; *Historia Iherosolimitana*, 3. According to Kempf and Bull, "Guibert of Nogent's history of the crusade may be his particular target here." See their introduction to *Historia Iherosolimitana*, xi.

78. Baldric of Bourgueil, *Historia Ierosolimitana*, 4; English translation in Riley-Smith, *First Crusade and the Idea of Crusading*, 138.

79. Guibert of Nogent, *Deeds of God*, 24; *Dei gesta per Francos*, 79.

80. Guibert of Nogent, *Deeds of God*, 24; *Dei gesta per Francos*, 80.

81. Guibert of Nogent, *Deeds of God*, 165–66; *Dei gesta per Francos*, 351. According to Robert Levine, Guibert confused Aulus Hirtius, a continuator of Caesar's *Commentaries*, with C. Vibius Pansa; both were nominated for consulship in 43 B.C. See Levine's translation *Deeds of God*, 165n269.

82. Chaurand, "Conception de l'histoire," 382.

83. Guibert of Nogent; *Deeds of God*, 165; *Dei gesta per Francos*, 350–51.

84. Spiegel, "Medieval Historiography," 82.

CHAPTER 2

1. On the battle of Antioch, see France, *Victory in the East*, 269–96.
2. Asbridge, "Holy Lance of Antioch," 15–20.
3. France, *Victory in the East*, 269; *Historia Hierosolymitana*, 249.
4. Fulcher of Chartres, *History of the Expedition*, 103.
5. Smail, *Crusading Warfare*, 174.
6. Rubenstein, *Armies of Heaven*, 226.
7. France, *Victory in the East*, 293, 296.
8. Asbridge, *First Crusade*, 239. See also Rice, "Note on the Battle of Antioch."
9. *Gesta Francorum*, 58, 69.
10. MacGregor, "Negotiating Knightly Piety," 326.
11. "Epistula cleri et populi Luccensis ad omnes fideles," in Hagenmeyer, *Kreuzzugsbriefe*, 165–67.
12. "Epistula II Anselmi de Ribodimonte ad Manassem archiepiscopum Remorum," in Hagenmeyer, *Kreuzzugsbriefe*, 156–60; "Epistula Boemundi, Raimundi comitis S. Aegidii, Godefridi ducis Lotharingiae, Roberti comitis Normanniae, Roberti comitis Flandrensis, Eustachii comitis Boloniae ad Urbanum II papam," ibid., 161–65.
13. Peter Tudebode, *Historia de Hierosolymitano itinere*, 100, 112; English translation in the Hills' 1974 edition, 75, 87–88.
14. Raymond of Aguilers, *Historia Francorum*, 60, 63–64; "*Liber*" *de Raymond d'Aguilers*, 78, 82.
15. In his account of the battle of Dorylaeum, Raymond mentions "two handsome knights in flashing armor" who were "seemingly invulnerable to the thrusts of Turkish lances." *Historia Francorum*, 28; "*Liber*" *de Raymond d'Aguilers*, 46. A later chronicler, Bartolf of Nangis, whose account of the battle of Dorylaeum is similar to Raymond's, identifies the crusaders' helpers as Saints George and Demetrius. Bartolf of Nangis, "Gesta Francorum Iherusalem expugnantium," 496. In his account of the siege of Jerusalem, Raymond describes a knight, whose name was unknown to him and who turned the tide of battle. *Historia Francorum*, 127; "*Liber*" *de Raymond d'Aguilers*, 150. Raymond also describes a vision to an unnamed Syrian Christian reported by a certain priest named Ebrard. Ebrard recounted that he wanted to go to Antioch, but because it was under siege

by Kerbogha, he could not. So he went to the church of the Virgin, where the Syrian approached him and told him about seeing "a clerk in white vestments" who identified himself as Saint Mark. Mark told the Syrian, "Christ now resides in Antioch and commands His disciples to join Him and aid in the battle which the Franks must wage against the Turks." *Historia Francorum*, 97–98; "Liber" de Raymond d'Aguilers, 117.

16. For an overview of later narratives, see MacGregor, "Negotiating Knightly Piety"; Dehoux, "Con avès non, vasal al ceval blanc"; Flori, *Guerre sainte*.

17. Homer, *Iliad*, 89 (hereafter cited parenthetically in the text).

18. Xenophon, *Hellenica*, 56–57.

19. Cicero, *Nature of the Gods*, 3 (hereafter cited parenthetically in the text). On *The Nature of the Gods*, see Hunt, *Humanism of Cicero*, 131–42.

20. On Castor and Pollux, see Allen, *Star Names*, 222–37. See also Walter, "Thracian Horseman."

21. Goar, *Cicero and the State Religion*, 119–20.

22. Dionysius of Halicarnassus, *Roman Antiquities*, 3:276–77; Plutarch, "Aemilius Paulus," in *Lives*, 6:420–23; Valerius Maximus, *Memorable Deeds and Sayings*, 33–34.

23. Plutarch, "Theseus," in *Lives*, 1:82–83. Similarly, Pausanias, a traveler and geographer of the second century A.D., described a painted portico in Athens that contained a representation of Theseus "coming up from the under-world" at Marathon. Pausanias, *Description of Greece*, 1:79.

24. Frontinus, *Strategems*, 74–75.

25. Ibid. See also Polyaenus, *Strategems of War*, 40.

26. Frontinus, *Strategems*, 74–77.

27. Lactantius, *Divine Institutes*, 122.

28. On the adoption of Castor and Pollux in Christian tradition, see Alexander P. Kazhdan and Alice-Mary Talbot, "Dioscouroi," in Kazhdan, *Oxford Dictionary of Byzantium*, 1:633.

29. On the battle, see King, *Emperor Theodosius*, 87–92.

30. Kolbaba, "Fighting for Christianity," 208.

31. On medieval interpretations of this passage, see Christe, *Apocalypse de Jean*, 102–3; McGinn, *Visions of the End*, 114–15.

32. See van Dam, "Many Conversions of the Emperor Constantine."

33. Augustine may be referring to the sack of Nola by the Arian Visigoths led by Alaric in 410. Augustine, "De cura pro mortuis gerenda," 510–11. For discussion of Augustine's attitude toward miracles, see Brown, *Augustine of Hippo*, 413–18; Schmitt, *Revenants*, 31–43.

34. Augustine, "De cura pro mortuis gerenda," 510–13.

35. Ibid., 512–13.

36. Zosimus, *New History*, 101. Zosimus, however, was mistaken; Alaric did manage to capture Athens.

37. For an example of similar competition between pagan and Christian traditions, see Kovács, *Marcus Aurelius' Rain Miracle*, 145–46.

38. Cameron, "Elites and Icons," 5; Jenkins, "Bronze Athena at Byzantium."

39. Pentcheva, *Icons and Power*, 64.

40. *Chronicon Paschale*, 180.

41. Quoted in Pentcheva, *Icons and Power*, 64. On the cult of the Virgin in the context of the siege, see Angelidi and Papamastorakis, "Picturing the Spiritual Protector," 211; Pentcheva, "Supernatural Protector of Constantinople," 15–16; Cameron "Elites and Icons."

42. Constantine Porphyregenitus, *De administrando imperio*, 228–31.

43. *Chronicon Paschale*, 28.

44. On Saint Demetrius, see Russell, *St. Demetrius of Thessalonica*; Tóth, "Sirmische Legende des heiligen Demetrius"; Lapina, "St. Demetrius of Thessaloniki"; Skedros, *Saint*

Demetrios of Thessaloniki; Frendo, "Miracles of St. Demetrius"; Alexander P. Kazhdan and Nancy Patterson Ševčenko, "St. Demetrios of Thessaloniki," in Kazhdan, *Oxford Dictionary of Byzantium*, 1:605–6; Magdalino, "St. Demetrios and Leo VI"; Cormack, "Making of a Patron Saint"; Lemerle, *Plus anciens recueils*; Walter, "St. Demetrius"; Forrai, "Interpreter of the Popes"; and Obolensky, "Cult of St. Demetrios."

45. For a medieval Latin translation, see Anastasius Bibliothecarius, "Passio sancti Demetrii martyris," 720–21.

46. Ibid., 722–23.

47. Ibid., 723.

48. Skylitzes, *Synopsis of Byzantine History*, 388.

49. Ibid., 292; Leo the Deacon, *History*, 80–81.

50. On Saint Theodore and Valens, see Binon, *Essai sur le cycle*, 17; Baynes, "Death of Julian the Apostate," 24; P'awstos Buzand, *Epic Histories*, 130–32.

51. On Saint Mercurius, see Baynes, "Death of Julian the Apostate." On the death of Julian, see Bowersock, *Julian the Apostate*, 116–17; Browning, *Emperor Julian*, 214; Braun and Richer, *Empereur Julien*, 67–87.

52. Socrates Scholasticus, *Ecclesiastical History*, 90. Theodoret also listed a number of hypotheses, including the possibility that Julian "was wounded by an invisible being." Theodoret, *Ecclesiastical History*, 106.

53. Sozomen, *Ecclesiastical History*, 346–47.

54. Delehaye, *Légendes grecques*, 98; Binon, *Essai sur le cycle*, 58; Baynes, "Death of Julian the Apostate."

55. Delehaye, *Légendes grecques*, 98; Binon, *Essai sur le cycle*, 15–16, 23; *Chronicon Paschale*, 42.

56. *History of the Patriarchs*, 2:420. See also Baynes, "Death of Julian the Apostate," 26–27.

CHAPTER 3

1. Peter Tudebode, *Historia de Hierosolymitano itinere*, 100, 112; English translation in the Hills' 1974 edition, 75, 87–88. On the four saints mentioned in the *Gesta Francorum* and the *Historia de Hierosolymitano itinere*, see Immerzeel, "Holy Horsemen and Crusader Banners" and "Divine Cavalry"; White, "Byzantine Tradition Transformed"; Folda, "Mounted Warrior Saints"; MacGregor, "Negotiating Knightly Piety"; MacGregor, "Ministry of Gerold d'Avranches"; Walter, "Thracian Horseman"; Walter, *Warrior Saints in Byzantine Art*; Delehaye, *Légendes grecques*. The literature on Saint George is considerable. Among others, see Dehoux, "Représenter le martyre"; Good, *Cult of Saint George*; MacGregor, "*Salue martir spes anglorum*"; Riches, *St. George*; Bengston, "Saint George"; Laborderie, "Richard the Lionheart"; Didi-Huberman, Garbetta, and Morgaine, *Saint George et le dragon*; Frend, "Martyrdom in East and West"; Alexander P. Kazhdan and Nancy Patterson Ševčenko, "St. George," in Kazhdan, *Oxford Dictionary of Byzantium*, 2:834–35; Ovčarov, "Sur l'iconographie de St. Georges"; Hill, "Aelfric, Gelasius, and St. George"; Cormack and Mihalarias, "Crusader Painting of St. George"; Setton, "Saint George's Head"; Howell, "St. George as Intercessor"; Deschamps, "Légende de Saint George"; Williams, "Mural Paintings of St. George"; and Huber, "Zur Georgslegende." On Theodore, Demetrius, and Mercurius, see the previous chapter.

2. Walter, *Warrior Saints in Byzantine Art*, 292; Walter, "Thracian Horseman," 662. In the West, the matter of defining "warrior-saints" is more complex. To quote Katherine Smith, "Modern scholars have traditionally used the term 'warrior-saints' to describe a handful of martyred Roman soldiers . . . , but medieval Christians would hardly have

defined this category so narrowly; these ancient warrior-martyrs comprised but a small subsection of a much larger, more heterogeneous cohort which included knights who had renounced the world to become monks and even legendary epic heroes who embraced the spiritual warfare of religious life." Smith, *War and the Making of Medieval Monastic Culture*, 157.

3. Delehaye placed five saints in this category: George, Demetrius, Saint Theodore Tiron, Saint Theodore Stratelates, and Saint Procopius. Delehaye, *Légendes grecques*, 2–3.

4. Erdmann, *Origin of the Idea*, 273.

5. Ernst Kantorowicz has remarked that the very character of these *laudes* was "soldier-like" and has suggested the possibility that the *laudes*' ancestors were the "cheers proffered, on the occasion of a triumph, by Roman soldiers." Kantorowicz, *Laudes Regiae*, 29–30. See also Erdmann, *Origin of the Idea*, 276–77; Holdsworth, "'Airier Aristocracy,'" 105–6.

6. Bernard of Angers, *Liber miraculorum sancte fidis*, 68; *Book of Sainte Foy*, 95–96.

7. Erdmann, *Origin of the Idea*, 275.

8. Orderic Vitalis, *Ecclesiastical History*, 3:216–17.

9. Ibid., 5:114–15.

10. MacGregor, "Ministry of Gerold d'Avranches," 235.

11. Erdmann, *Origin of the Idea*, 275.

12. On the relations between the Eastern Christian world and the West at the time of the First Crusade, see, among others, MacEvitt, *Crusades and the Christian World*; France, "Byzantium in Western Chronicles"; Klein, "Eastern Objects and Western Desires"; Laiou and Mottahedeh, *Crusades from the Perspective of Byzantium*; Ciggaar, *Western Travellers to Constantinople*; Lilie, *Byzantium and the Crusader States*; Shepard and Franklin, *Byzantine Diplomacy*; Howard-Johnston, *Byzantium and the West*; Goss and Bornstein, *Meeting of Two Worlds*; Skoulatos, "Auteur anonyme des 'Gesta Francorum'"; Geanakoplos, *Interaction of the "Sibling"*; and Nicol, *Byzantium*.

13. Riley-Smith, "First Crusade and St. Peter," 54. One possible exception is Saint George. En route to Jerusalem, a priest in the army of Count Robert of Flanders, Gerbault of Lille, stole the saint's arm from a Byzantine monastery. Riley-Smith, *First Crusade and the Idea of Crusading*, 93–95.

14. Holdsworth, "'Airier Aristocracy,'" 108.

15. Riley-Smith, "First Crusade and St. Peter," 58. For a similar viewpoint, see MacGregor, "Negotiating Knightly Piety," 323. John France finds it startling that crusaders would want to adopt Byzantine saints if indeed, as modern historians tend to believe, the majority of crusaders shared anti-Byzantine sentiments. France argues that they did not, with some exceptions, such as the anonymous author of the *Gesta* or Raymond of Aguilers. For France, then, the adoption of Byzantine saints implied sympathetic sentiments toward Byzantium. Yet the reports of four Byzantine saints intervening in the battle of Antioch appear in the most anti-Byzantine chronicle, the *Gesta Francorum*, and are absent from those more friendly to Byzantium, including that by Albert of Aachen. France, "Byzantium in Western Chronicles," 6.

16. Asbridge, *Creation of the Principality of Antioch*, 140.

17. Raymond of Aguilers, *Historia Francorum*, 112–13; *"Liber" de Raymond d'Aguilers*, 133–34.

18. According to William of Tyre, after Patriarch Daimbert of Jerusalem "fled to Bohemond," Bohemond granted him "the church of St. George, below the city of Antioch, together with its great estates and rich revenues." William of Tyre, *A History of Deeds*, 1:452; *Chronique*, 1:484.

19. Cheynet, "Culte de saint Théodore." I would like to thank Catherine Holmes for this reference. There are some other circumstantial pieces of evidence of the saints' ties to Antioch. Emperor Julian marched out of Antioch to confront the Persians, the campaign

during which Saint Mercurius was believed to have assassinated him. Apparently, some narratives that have Saint Theodore assassinating Emperor Valens bear "clear traces of... Antiochene origins." Baynes, "Death of Julian the Apostate," 24–25.

20. Walter, *Warrior Saints in Byzantine Art*, 133–34; Festugière, *Vie de Théodore de Sykéôn*, 97; Schlumberger, *Empereur byzantin au dixième siècle*, 74.

21. Hagenmeyer, *Chronologie de la première croisade*, 69; Duncalf, "First Crusade," 274. Adhémar of Le Puy, papal legate during the crusade, halted at the city in order to recover from a wound inflicted on him by the Pechenegs. Raymond of Aguilers, *"Liber" de Raymond d'Aguilers*, 39. On churches dedicated to military saints in Constantinople and its vicinity, see Janin, "Églises byzantines des saints militaires."

22. Quoted in Good, *Cult of Saint George*, 34.

23. Riley-Smith, "First Crusade and St. Peter," 57; MacGregor, "Negotiating Knightly Piety," 323.

24. "Epistula Patriarchae Hierosolymitani et aliorum episcoporum ad occidentales," in Hagenmeyer, *Kreuzzugsbriefe*, 146–49.

25. Taviani-Carozzi, *Terreur du monde*, 375.

26. Erdmann did not develop this theory, however, writing, "establishing the precise source of this motif hardly matters to our study." Erdmann, *Origin of the Idea*, 280–81.

27. On Norman mercenaries in the Byzantine military, see Simpson, "Three Sources of Military Unrest"; Shepard, "Uses of the Franks"; Beech, "Norman-Italian Adventurer"; McQueen, "Relations Between the Normans and Byzantium"; van Houts, "Normandy and Byzantium"; Jeffreys, "Western Infiltration"; and Nicol, "Symbiosis and Integration."

28. Anna Comnena, *Alexiad*, 329. Recent works on the *Alexiad* include Frankopan, "Turning Latin into Greek"; Neville, *Heroes and Romans*, 182–93; Macrides, "Pen and the Sword"; and Howard-Johnston, "Anna Komnene and the *Alexiad*."

29. See Pryor and Jeffreys, "Alexios, Bohemond"; France, "Departure of Tatikios," 141; Shepard, "When Greek Meets Greek," 201, 247–48.

30. Nicol, "Symbiosis and Integration."

31. Shepard, "When Greek Meets Greek," 256.

32. Loud, *Age of Robert Guiscard*, 212. See also Kolia-Dermitzake, "Michael VII Doukas."

33. Savvides, *Byzantino Normannica*, 38.

34. Loud, *Age of Robert Guiscard*, 211; Harris, *Byzantium and the Crusades*, 38; Shepard, "When Greek Meets Greek," 259.

35. Amatus of Montecassino, *History of the Normans*, 178; *Storia de' Normanni*, 318–20.

36. Russo, "Expansion normande"; Russo, *Boemondo*, 20–28; Savvides, *Byzantino Normannica*; Smith, "Nobilissimus and Warleader"; Rösch, "'Kreuzzug' Bohemunds."

37. Anna Comnena, *Alexiad*, 135–36.

38. Most modern historians do believe that Guiscard entertained hopes of capturing Constantinople; see Chalandon, *Histoire de la domination normande*, 1:258; Martin, *Italies normandes*, 363; Taviani-Carozzi, *Terreur du monde*, 449; Hanawalt, "Norman Views of Eastern Christendom," 116; and Savvides, *Byzantino Normannica*, 47. For a dissenting (and more convincing) opinion, see McQueen, "Relations Between the Normans and Byzantium," 439.

39. Anna Comnena, *Alexiad*, 146. On the battle, see Savvides, *Byzantino Normannica*, 52–53.

40. Orderic Vitalis, *Ecclesiastical History*, 4:18–19.

41. Haldon, *Warfare, State, and Society*, 32.

42. Orderic Vitalis, *Ecclesiastical History*, 4:18–19.

43. Anna Comnena, *Alexiad*, 169.

44. Ibid., 182.

45. Shepard, "When Greek Meets Greek." See also Harris, *Byzantium and the Crusades*, 67–71; Asbridge, *Creation of the Principality of Antioch*, 24–46, 185–277; Lilie, *Byzantium and the Crusader States*, 31–43.
46. Anna Comnena, *Alexiad*, 323.
47. Shepard, "When Greek Meets Greek," 206, 238, 241.
48. Ibid., 270.
49. Anna Comnena, *Alexiad*, 343.
50. *Gesta Francorum*, 34. For discussion of this episode, see France, "Departure of Tatikios."
51. Raymond of Aguilers, *Historia Francorum*, 37; *"Liber" de Raymond d'Aguilers*, 55–56.
52. Shepard, "When Greek Meets Greek," 271.
53. Raymond of Aguilers, *Historia Francorum*, 37; *"Liber" de Raymond d'Aguilers*, 56.
54. Shepard, "When Greek Meets Greek," 271.
55. *Gesta Francorum*, 45. See also Raymond of Aguilers, *Historia Francorum*, 37; *"Liber" de Raymond d'Aguilers*, 55.
56. Shepard, "When Greek Meets Greek," 274. For an edition of the charter, see *Liber privilegiorum*, 40–41. Another important source associated with Bohemond's activities in the aftermath of the battle of Antioch, a letter written by crusaders to Urban II and dated September 11, 1098, is probably not genuine, so I have omitted it from the present discussion. See Pryor and Jeffreys, "Alexios, Bohemond."
57. *Gesta Francorum*, 72.
58. On Bohemond as a storyteller, see Paul, "Warlord's Wisdom," 556–60.
59. Walter, "Thracian Horseman," 663.
60. Erdmann, *Origin of the Idea*, 279. On the cult of Saint George and the Monomachos family, see Cheynet, "Par saint Georges, par saint Michel," 120–21.
61. Kazhdan and Epstein, *Change in Byzantine Culture*, 110–19.
62. Angold, *Byzantine Empire*, 156.
63. Walter, "Thracian Horseman," 662.
64. Hendy, *Coinage and Money*, 41–45, plates 1.9–12. As further proof of Alexius's special interest in Saint Demetrius, Anna Comnena mentions that Alexius attended "a ceremony in honor of the great martyr Demetrius" in Thessaloniki in January 1107. *Alexiad*, 380.
65. The successors of Alexius I—John II and Manuel I—continued the tradition, also minting coins with a representation of Saint Demetrius, although with a slightly altered iconography. They also added new saints to the repertoire, with John II first minting coins with a likeness of Saint George and Manuel I with one of Saint Theodore. Hendy, *Coinage and Money*, 43, 437–38. Manuel I worked particularly hard to strengthen his connection with military saints by removing an icon of Saint Theodore from Corinth and moving the cover from the "tomb" of Saint Demetrius from Thessaloniki to Constantinople. Magdalino, *Empire of Manuel I Komnenos*, 178–79. Unfortunately, saints did not always come to Emperor Manuel's aid when summoned. According to Niketas Choniates, before Manuel's campaign against the Turks in 1176, a certain Byzantine reported having had a dream in which the icon of the Virgin Mary addressed an unseen audience: "The emperor is now in the utmost danger. . . . Who will go forth in my name to assist him?" The Virgin's interlocutors debated whether either Saint George or Saint Theodore could help the emperor, but they concluded that "no one could avert the impending evil." Niketas Choniates, *O City of Byzantium*, 107–8.
66. Metcalf, *Coinage of the Crusades*, 28. On intercultural exchange in the principality of Antioch, see Russo, *Normanni del mezzogiorno*.
67. Ibn al-Athir, *Chronicle of Ibn al-Athir*, 2:323.
68. Ralph of Caen, *History of the Normans*, 42; *Gesta Tancredi in Expeditione*, 22–23.

69. Quoted in Jones, *Saint Nicholas of Myra*, 178. For discussion, see also Leib, *Rome, Kiev et Byzance*, 51–74.

70. Jones, *Saint Nicholas of Myra*, 181, 184.

71. Geary, *Furta Sacra*, 126.

72. Chibnall, *Normans*, 95.

73. Oldfield, "Urban Government in Southern Italy," 590; Gadolin, "Prince Bohemond's Death and Apotheosis," 135; Yewdale, *Bohemond I*, 133.

74. *Hystoria de via et recuperatione Antiochiae*, 89.

75. Yewdale, *Bohemond I*, 115–31; Asbridge, *Creation of the Principality of Antioch*, 99–103.

76. Bohemond's predilection for the church of Saint Nicholas was so strong that Albert of Aachen even claims, mistakenly, that Bohemond was buried in it: "In this year Bohemond, Tancred's uncle, was attacked by illness and departed this life; he was buried according to Christian rite at Bari, the town of blessed Nicolas." Albert of Aachen, *Historia Ierosolimitana*, 824–25. According to Gadolin, it is possible that Bohemond's "remains might have been awaiting last rites" in the church of Saint Nicholas. Gadolin, "Prince Bohemond's Death and Apotheosis," 130.

77. Gadolin, "Prince Bohemond's Death and Apotheosis," 130.

78. See Krautheimer, "Note on Justinian's Church."

79. He arrived around April 10 and left probably around May 7, 1097. Shepard, "When Greek Meets Greek," 210.

80. McQueen, "Relations Between the Normans and Byzantium," 471–73; Epstein, "Date and Significance of the Cathedral," 79–90; Gadolin, "Prince Bohemond's Death and Apotheosis."

81. Epstein, "Date and Significance of the Cathedral," 87.

82. It is perhaps this close association of the church with Byzantine emperors that made Mehmed the Conqueror raze it in 1461 for the construction of the Fethiye Mosque.

83. Gadolin, "Prince Bohemond's Death and Apotheosis," 141.

84. Epstein, "Date and Significance of the Cathedral," 88.

85. Both inscriptions are translated in their entirety in Epstein, "Date and Significance of the Cathedral," 86. On the inscriptions, see also Donne, "Inscrizioni del Mausoleo." For a different interpretation of the reasons for this unusual choice of burial place for Bohemond, see Russo, *Boemondo*, 199–200.

86. On this image, see Tronzo, *Cultures of His Kingdom*, 140–41; Houben, *Roger II of Sicily*, 113–15; Kitzinger, "On the Portrait of Roger II." On representations of William II of Sicily (grandson of Roger II) at Monreale, see Borsook, *Messages in Mosaic*, 3. For an overview of Norman art in Sicily, see Demus, *Mosaics of Norman Sicily*. On Roger, see also Wieruszowski, "Roger II of Sicily."

87. Tronzo, *Cultures of His Kingdom*, 141. This is not the first representation of a Norman leader in Byzantine attire. At Salerno, for example, Robert Guiscard minted a coin featuring his likeness "in Byzantine robes and crown, holding a cross-scepter and a double orb." Grierson, "Salernitan Coinage," 48. Compare coins minted by Tancred in Hanawalt, "Norman Views of Eastern Christendom," 120.

88. The motive for Roger I's "patronage of Greek culture . . . may have been to ensure the support of all his Christian subjects in an island whose population was still largely Muslim. But as a result, Byzantine influence upon the intellectual and artistic development of Sicily was to be dominant through much of the twelfth century." Douglas, *Norman Achievement*, 201.

89. Kitzinger, "On the Portrait of Roger II," 320.

90. Roger "sent envoys to emperor John who was still alive and asked to obtain a bride of imperial blood for his son. The embassy did not achieve its goal when John died.

Sometime later he communicated with Manuel who then governed the empire and made the same requests. Therefore Basil, by surname Xeros, went to Sicily to discuss this with Roger. But seduced by gold, he promised him some unwelcome things, chief of which was that in the future the emperor and Roger were to be on an equal plane of greatness." Kinnamos, *Deeds of John and Manuel Comnenus*, 75. See also Kitzinger, "On the Portrait of Roger II," 320; Houben, *Roger II of Sicily*, 84–85.

91. "There were those who then advised the king . . . to write to King Roger, who was then vigorously attacking the empire, and, aided by his fleet, to attack Constantinople itself." Odo of Deuil, *De profectione Ludovici VII*, 58–59.

92. Houben, *Roger II of Sicily*, 85.

93. Magdalino, *Empire of Manuel I Komnenos*, 51. To quote Ernst Kitzinger, "there is reason to believe that during and after the Second Crusade he [Roger] hatched far-reaching plans of ousting the Comnenian dynasty and setting up a Latin Kingdom on the Bosphorus." Kitzinger, "On the Portrait of Roger II," 320. Along the same lines, according to Roberto Salvini, the mosaics of Maria dell'Ammiraglio and similar Byzantinizing projects reflect the overarching aim of the Normans "to match and possibly absorb the Empire on the Bosphorus." Salvini, "Monuments of Norman Art," 67.

94. Houben, *Roger II of Sicily*, 86.

95. Tronzo, *Cultures of His Kingdom*, 141.

96. Similarly, Anne Derbes has explored the polyvalence of Western attitudes toward Byzantium in her discussion of Italian *duecento* paintings. She argues that *maniera greca* implied at once a "tacit recognition of the prestige of Byzantium and a wish to appropriate that prestige," but also a celebration of the conquest of Constantinople during the Fourth Crusade, in 1204, and of "the colonial status of the East." Derbes, *Picturing the Passion*, 15.

97. Niketas Choniates, *O City of Byzantium*, 45.

98. Robert of Clari, *Conquest of Constantinople*, 90–91; *Conquête de Constantinople*, 148–51.

99. Among numerous other spoils that the Venetians brought back to Constantinople was a bas-relief representation of Saint Demetrius, which they inserted in the façade of the Cathedral of San Marco. Demus, *Church of San Marco*, 128–35; Belting, *Likeness and Presence*, 195–96.

100. Stephenson, *Byzantium's Balkan Frontier*, 288–90.

101. Niketas Choniates, *O City of Byzantium*, 205.

102. Stephenson, *Byzantium's Balkan Frontier*, 293, 290. See also the episode of the Venetians acquiring a relic of Saint Stephen in Constantinople, in Italikos, *Lettres et discours*, 234–36; Angold, *Byzantine Empire*, 233.

103. *Povest' vremennykh let*, 44–45 (my translation).

104. Runciman, "Byzantium and the Crusades," 15.

105. Ciggaar, *Western Travellers to Constantinople*, 14.

106. Macrides, "Constantinople," 196.

107. Kazhdan and Epstein, *Change in Byzantine Culture*, 167.

108. Nicol, "Byzantine View of Western Europe," 315–16.

109. Riley-Smith, "First Crusade and St. Peter," 57. See also Daly, "Christian Fraternity."

110. Brown, "Eastern and Western Christendom," 5. See also Dunn, "Eastern Influence on Western Monasticism."

CHAPTER 4

1. Loud, *Age of Robert Guiscard*, 156–57.

2. Geoffrey Malaterra, *Deeds of Count Roger*, 109–10; *De rebus gestis Rogerii Calabriae*, 44.

3. Geoffrey Malaterra, *Deeds of Count Roger*, 102; *De rebus gestis Rogerii Calabriae*, 204; Wolf, *Making History*, 146. On Malaterra, see also Lucas-Avenel, "Récit de Geoffroi Malaterra."

4. On the *Gesta Francorum*, see Bull, "Relationship Between the *Gesta Francorum*"; Niskanen, "Origins of the *Gesta Francorum*"; Paul, "Warlord's Wisdom"; Carrier, "Pour en finir avec les *Gesta Francorum*"; Flori, "De l'anonyme normand à Tudebode"; Rubenstein, "What Is the Gesta Francorum?"; Albu, "Probing the Passions of a Norman"; France, "Anonymous *Gesta Francorum*"; France, "Use of the Anonymous *Gesta Francorum*"; Morris, "*Gesta Francorum* as Narrative History"; Wolf, "Bohemond and the *Gesta Francorum*"; and Jamison, "Some Notes on the *Anonymi Gesta Francorum*."

5. Loud, *Age of Robert Guiscard*, 164.

6. On Geoffrey Malaterra and his chronicle, see, among others, Lucas-Avenel, "Récit de Geoffroi Malaterra"; Wolf, *Making History*, 143–71; Capitani, "Specific Motivations."

7. For the use of the term "dominus" by the author, see Rubenstein, "What Is the Gesta Francorum," 185.

8. France, "Anonymous *Gesta Francorum*," 54. Most recently, Nicholas Paul has mentioned that "some passages in the *Gesta Francorum*" clearly "lionized Bohemond or favored his side against Alexios Komnenos." Paul, "Warlord's Wisdom," 545. According to Hans Mayer, the *Gesta Francorum* "thoroughly idealized Bohemond." Mayer, *Crusades*, 43. Harold S. Fink calls the *Gesta Francorum* "a pro-Norman chronicle of the First Crusade." Fink, "Foundation of the Latin States," 391. On Bohemond, see Russo, *Boemondo*; Flori, *Bohémond d'Antioche*; Yewdale, *Bohemond I*.

9. Wolf, "Bohemond and the *Gesta Francorum*," 213.

10. *Gesta Francorum*, 56.

11. Albu, *Normans and Their Histories*, 160.

12. Rubenstein, "What Is the Gesta Francorum," 187.

13. For a different perspective, see Hodgson, "Reinventing Normans as Crusaders," 121.

14. Loud, *Age of Robert Guiscard*, 156.

15. *Gesta Francorum*, 69.

16. France, "Normans and Crusading," 90.

17. Erdmann, *Origin of the Idea*, 134.

18. Taviani-Carozzi, *Terreur du monde*, 376. See also Chevedden, "Crusade from the First."

19. Loud, *Age of Robert Guiscard*, 164.

20. Erdmann, *Origin of the Idea*, 27.

21. On Paul the Deacon and historiographical traditions at Montecassino, see Pohl, "History in Fragments"; Goffart, *Narrators of Barbarian History*, 329–431.

22. Amatus of Montecassino, *History of the Normans*, 41; *Storia de' Normanni*, 4.

23. Paul the Deacon, *Historia Romana*, 197.

24. Paul the Deacon, *History of the Lombards*, 82–83; *Historia Langobardorum*, 121–22. The relics of Saint Sabinus were discovered at Canosa in 1091. On the cult of Saint Sabinus in southern Italy in the late eleventh century, see Gadolin, "Prince Bohemond's Death and Apotheosis," 132. On Bohemond and Canosa, see Russo, *Boemondo*, 201–3.

25. Martin, *Normands et le culte de saint Michel*; Callahan, "Cult of St. Michael the Archangel," 182. For recent works on the pilgrimage site of Monte Gargano, see Piemontese, *San Michele e il suo sanctuario*; Carletti and Otranto, *Culto e insediamenti micaelici*.

26. Johnson, *Saint Michael the Archangel*, 41. This was not the only connection between two pilgrimage sites dedicated to Saint Michael. William of Volpiano, who visited Monte Gargano around 995, later oversaw the reform of several monasteries in Normandy, including Mont-Saint-Michel. Loud, *Age of Robert Guiscard*, 65.

27. William of Apulia, *Gesta Roberti Wiscardi*, 99–100. On the early settlement of the Normans in Italy, see Hoffmann, "Anfänge der Normannen in Süditalien"; Joranson,

"Inception of the Career of the Normans"; France, "Occasion of the Coming of the Normans."

28. Martin, *Normands et le culte de Saint Michel*, 347.

29. Callahan, "Cult of St. Michael the Archangel," 181.

30. Erdmann, *Origin of the Idea*, 21. See also Callahan, "Cult of St. Michael the Archangel," 182.

31. Douglas, *Norman Achievement*, 40.

32. Bouet and Desbordes, *Chroniques latines*, 113. See also Otranto, "'Liber de apparatione'"; Everett, *"Liber de Apparitione S. Michaelis"*; Johnson, *Saint Michael the Archangel*, 37.

33. Bouet and Desbordes, *Chroniques latines*, 128–31.

34. Some historians argue that this account echoes specific campaigns between the Lombards and the Byzantines and their allies. According to Nicholas Everett, however, "the author seems determined to keep the setting of the text in the distant and somewhat foggy past." Everett, *"Liber de Apparitione S. Michaelis,"* 370. See also Otranto, "'Liber de apparatione,'" 225; Johnson, *Saint Michael the Archangel*, 40. On the Lombards' wars against the Byzantines, see Christie, *Lombards*, 73–91.

35. Cowdrey, "Mahdia Campaign of 1087," 26. Peter's sword is perhaps an allusion to the passage in the Gospel of John in which he cuts off the ear of a high priest's servant who comes to arrest Christ (John 18:10).

36. Ibid., 2.

37. Erdmann, *Origin of the Idea*, 293; Cowdrey, "Mahdia Campaign of 1087," 3. See also Marshall, "Crusading Motivations," 45.

38. On historical writing at Fleury, see Bautier, "École historique"; Bautier, "Place de l'abbaye de Fleury-sur-Loire."

39. Head, *Hagiography and the Cult of Saints*, 52–53.

40. On Hugh, see Nelson, *Charles the Bald*; and McKitterick, *Frankish Kingdoms*.

41. *Miracles de Saint Benoît*, 89, quoted in translation in Head, *Hagiography and the Cult of Saints*, 53.

42. Abbo, *Viking Attacks on Paris*, 68–69. For an analysis of Abbo's work, see MacLean, *Kingship and Politics*, 55–64.

43. *Translatio Sancti Germani Parisiensis*, 92; Nelson, *Charles the Bald*, 152.

44. Abbo, *Viking Attacks on Paris*, 68–69.

45. Ibid.

46. Ibid., 70–71.

47. Augustine, "De cura pro mortuis gerenda," 510–11. For discussion, see chapter 2.

48. Abbo, *Viking Attacks on Paris*, 78–79.

49. Ibid., 74–75.

50. Simeon of Durham, *Historia de sancto Cuthberto*, 1:204–6.

51. Simpson, "King Alfred/St. Cuthbert Episode"; Smyth, *King Alfred the Great*, 343; Hare, "Apparitions and War," 79. The *Life of St. Neot*, written in the late tenth century, features a story nearly identical to that in the *History of Saint Cuthbert*, but it replaces Saint Cuthbert with Saint Neot. Simpson, "King Alfred/St. Cuthbert Episode," 410; Hare, "Apparitions and War" 79.

52. Adomnán, *Adomnán's Life of Columba*, 14–15. For discussion of Adomnán, see Fraser, "Adomnán and the Morality of War," 99–100.

53. Bede the Venerable, *Historia ecclesiastica gentis Anglorum*, 1:356–59.

54. Orderic Vitalis, *Ecclesiastical History*, 2:100–101.

55. Ibid., 2:126–29.

56. Loud, "How 'Norman' Was the Norman Conquest," 30. See also Ménager, "Inventaire des familles normandes"; Beech, "Remarkable Life of Ansger."

57. France, "Normans and Crusading."

58. On the concept of ethnic or national identity in the Middle Ages, see Carozzi and Taviani-Carozzi, *Peuples du Moyen Âge*; Forde, Johnson, and Murray, *Concepts of National Identity*.
59. William of Poitiers, *Gesta Guillelmi*, 156–57.
60. Baldric of Bourgueil, *Oeuvres poétiques*, 205; translation in Davis, *Normans and Their Myth*, 65.
61. Aelred of Rievaulx, "Battle of the Standard," in *Historical Works*, 252–53.
62. Haskins, *Normans in European History*, 247.
63. Jamison, *Sicilian Norman Kingdom*, 42. David C. Douglas has taken a similar view: "Despite their individual features, all the enterprises undertaken by the Normans between 1050 and 1100 can be regarded as forming part of a single movement . . . . Contemporary writers seem in fact to have been very conscious of this." Douglas, *Norman Achievement*, 110.
64. Davis, *Normans and Their Myth*, 87–88.
65. Drell, "Cultural Syncretism and Ethnic Identity."
66. Webber, *Evolution of Norman Identity*, 63, 84.
67. Johnson, "Normandy and Norman Identity," 95, 100.
68. Loud, "'Gens Normannorum,'" 114. In support of this view, see also Marjorie Chibnall's *Normans*: "The Norman people were the product, not of blood, but of history" (3).
69. Loud, "'Gens Normannorum,'" 116.
70. Amatus of Montecassino, *History of the Normans*, 46; *Storia de' Normanni*, 9–11.
71. Loud, "'Gens Normannorum,'" 111.
72. Geoffrey Malaterra, *Deeds of Count Roger*, 52; *De rebus gestis Rogerii Calabriae*, 8.
73. Albu, "Bohemond and the Rooster," 161.
74. Dudo of Saint-Quentin, *History of the Normans*, 16, 119; *De moribus et actis primorum Normanniae*, 131, 244.
75. William of Apulia, *Gesta Roberti Wiscardi*, 138–39, 148–49.
76. Amory, "Viking Hasting in Franco-Scandinavian Legend," 270; Mathieu's preface to William of Apulia, *Gesta Roberti Wiscardi*, 46–52.
77. Anna Comnena, *Alexiad*, 367; see also Albu, "Bohemond and the Rooster."
78. Webber, *Evolution of Norman Identity*, 43.
79. As Cassandra Potts puts it, "To shake off their image as bloodthirsty pagans, the Norman rulers made a determined effort to associate their authority with the religious traditions of the land. Their Viking heritage was not forgotten—indeed, it was used to perpetuate their reputation as outstanding warriors." Potts, "*Atque unum ex diversis gentibus populum*," 152. On Norman historical writing, see also Shopkow, *History and Community*.
80. Dudo of Saint-Quentin, *History of the Normans*, 15–16; *De moribus et actis primorum Normanniae*, 129–30.
81. Van Houts, *Gesta Normannorum Ducum*, 1:16–17.
82. Dudo of Saint-Quentin, *History of the Normans*, 17; *De moribus et actis primorum Normanniae*, 132.
83. Van Houts, *Gesta Normannorum Ducum*, 1:20–21, 52–53, 22–23.
84. Dudo of Saint-Quentin, *History of the Normans*, 22; *De moribus et actis primorum Normanniae*, 137.
85. Van Houts, *Gesta Normannorum Ducum*, 1:22–23.
86. Geoffrey Malaterra, *Deeds of Count Roger*, 70; *De rebus gestis Rogerii Calabriae*, 21.
87. Geoffrey Malaterra, *Deeds of Count Roger*, 51; *De rebus gestis Rogerii Calabriae*, 7.
88. Amatus of Montecassino, *Storia de' Normanni*, 223; *History of the Normans*, 133.
89. Loud, "'Gens Normannorum,'" 115.
90. On the Cadalan schism, see Cowdrey, *Pope Gregory VII*, 50–51; Cowdrey, *Age of Abbot Desiderius*, 118–19.
91. Cowdrey, *Age of Abbot Desiderius*, 119.

92. On Benzo, see Robinson, *Authority and Resistance*, 70–75 and passim.

93. Benzo of Alba, *Sieben Bücher an Kaiser Heinrich IV*, 258. The skirmish took place in Rome, and the supporters of Cadalus outmaneuvered the Normans by concealing a part of their forces in the vicinity of what Benzo called "Opus Praxitelis." Since antiquity, a pair of colossal statues of horse tamers stood near the site of the Baths of Constantine on the Quirinal Hill in Rome. In the Middle Ages, one bore the inscription "Opus Praxitelis" and the other, "Opus Fidiae." The statues represent Castor and Pollux, even though a medieval guide to Rome, *Mirabilia Urbis Romae*, offers a different, more fanciful interpretation. *Marvels of Rome*, 18–19. One is tempted to think that Benzo knew the correct interpretation and also the historical tradition. On Benzo, see Stroll, *Popes and Antipopes*, 17–19.

94. Amatus of Montecassino, *History of the Normans*, 83; *Storia de' Normanni*, 109.

95. Amatus of Montecassino, *History of the Normans*, 83; *Storia de' Normanni*, 109–10.

96. Amatus of Montecassino, *History of the Normans*, 83; *Storia de' Normanni*, 110. It is true that subsequent relations between Montecassino and the Normans were, for the most part, mutually beneficial. Loud, "Introduction," in Amatus, *History of the Normans*, 27; Loud, "How 'Norman' Was the Norman Conquest," 27.

97. Amatus of Montecassino, *History of the Normans*, 99–100; *Storia de' Normanni*, 151. On the cult of Saint Matthew in southern Italy, see Galdi, *Santi, territori, poteri*. On the battle, see Taviani-Carozzi, "Léon IX et les Normands."

98. On Andrew of Fleury, see Head, "Andrew of Fleury and the Peace League."

99. Vidier, *Historiographie à Saint-Benoît-sur-Loire*, 206.

100. *Miracles de Saint Benoît*, 187–91.

101. Abbo, *Viking Attacks on Paris*, 62–63.

102. See Har-Peled, "Animalité, pureté et croisade."

103. Wolf, *Making History*, 94. See also Kolia-Dermitzake, "Michael VII Doukas," 256.

104. Loud, *Age of Robert Guiscard*, 5.

CHAPTER 5

1. On Maccabees in the context of the Crusades, see Russo, "Continuité et transformations"; Russo, "Maccabei e crociati"; Lapina, "Maccabees and the Battle of Antioch"; Gouguenheim, "Maccabées"; Morton, "Defense of the Holy Land"; Lapina, "Anti-Jewish Rhetoric"; Fischer, "Books of the Maccabees"; and Auffarth, *Irdische Wege*, 123–50. On receptions of the Maccabees in the Middle Ages more generally, see Keller, "*Machabaeorum pugnae*"; Dunbabin, "Maccabees as Exemplars"; Robinson, "Bible in the Investiture Contest"; and McGrath, "Romance of the Maccabees." On visual representations of the Maccabees, see Reeve, "Painted Chamber"; Hess, "Bodenmosaik von S. Colombano"; and Ligato, "Iconografia della prima crociata." On medieval exegesis in the context of the Crusades more generally, see Smith, "Glossing the Holy War"; Buc, "Vengeance de Dieu"; Cole, "'O God, the Heathens'"; Cole, *Preaching of the Crusades*; Rousset, *Origines et les caractères*; and Alphandéry, "Citations bibliques."

2. Nirenberg, *Anti-Judaism*, 82.

3. Origen, "Homilies on Joshua," quoted in Caspary, *Politics and Exegesis*, 19.

4. Smith, *War and the Making of Medieval Monastic Culture*, 167.

5. Berkeley, "Some Misapprehensions of Christian Typology," 3, 5.

6. Auerbach, *Figura*, 58.

7. Berkeley, "Some Misapprehensions of Christian Typology," 7. See also Emmerson, "*Figura* and the Medieval Typological Imagination," 14; Hollander, "Typology and Secular Literature," 9.

8. Guibert of Nogent, *Deeds of God*, 28; *Dei gesta per Francos*, 87.

9. See Cohen, "'Slay Them Not.'"
10. See Bar-Kochva, *Judas Maccabaeus*; Gera, *Judaea and Mediterranean Politics*.
11. See Pate and Kennard, *Deliverance Now and Not Yet*; Nauroy, "Du combat de la piété"; Nauroy, "Frères Maccabées"; Deléani, "Typologie du martyre chrétien"; Deléani, "Exempla bibliques du martyre"; and Frend, *Martyrdom and Persecution*.
12. Jerome, *Commentarius in Ecclesiasten*, col. 1066.
13. Augustine of Hippo, "Sermo 300," col. 1377; "Sermon 300," 276.
14. Augustine of Hippo, "Sermo 300," col. 1379. On the Maccabees and Antioch as the place of their martyrdom and burial, see Rouwhorst, "Cult of the Seven Maccabean Brothers"; Joslyn-Siemiatkoski, *Christian Memories*; Ziadé, *Martyrs Maccabées*; Schatkin, "Maccabean Martyrs."
15. Ambrose of Milan, *De officiis*, 232–37.
16. Dunbabin, "Maccabees as Exemplars," 32.
17. William of Poitiers, *Gesta Guillelmi*, 90–91.
18. *Annals of Fulda*, 57; Morton, "Defense of the Holy Land," 278.
19. Smith, *War and the Making of Medieval Monastic Culture*, 102; Cowdrey, "Pope Gregory VII and the Bearing of Arms"; Cowdrey, "Martyrdom and the First Crusade," 47–48; Erdmann, *Origin of the Idea*.
20. Bernold of St. Blasien, "Chronicle," 266; "Chronikon," 425–26.
21. Andreas of Strumi, *Vita S. Arialdi*, 1059–60. See Erdmann, *Origin of the Idea*, 141–42; Smith, *War and the Making of Medieval Monastic Culture*, 15.
22. Bonizo of Sutri, "Liber ad Amicum," 1:599; "To a Friend," 215. Münsch, "Hate Preachers and Religious Warriors," 171; Morton, "Defense of the Holy Land," 279.
23. Bonizo of Sutri, "Liber ad Amicum," 1:605; "To a Friend," 229–31.
24. Robinson, "Introduction," *Papal Reform of the Eleventh Century*, 51. In 1095, Pope Urban II was present at the burial of Erlembald's relics in the monastery of San Dionisio in Milan. Cowdrey, "Martyrdom and the First Crusade," 49.
25. Manegold of Lautenbach, *Ad Geberhardum*, 1:399. For discussion, see Münsch, "Hate Preachers and Religious Warriors," 168; and Erdmann, *Origin of the Idea*, 234–36.
26. Caffaro, *De liberatione civitatum orientis*, 103.
27. Fulcher of Chartres, *History of the Expedition*, 58; *Historia Hierosolymitana*, 117.
28. Bonizo of Sutri, "To a Friend," 161.
29. On martyrdom and the First Crusade, see Riley-Smith, "Death on the First Crusade"; Cowdrey, "Martyrdom and the First Crusade"; Flori, "Mort et martyre des guerriers"; Morris, "Martyrs on the Field of Battle."
30. Fulcher of Chartres, *History of the Expedition*, 58; *Historia Hierosolymitana*, 117.
31. See Flori, "Mort et martyre des guerriers."
32. For Maccabees in the Armenian exegetical tradition, see Morton, "Defense of the Holy Land."
33. *Gesta Francorum*, 77–78.
34. Albert of Aachen, *Historia Ierosolimitana*, 196; Robert the Monk, *Historia Iherosolimitana*, 771. In fact, Antiochus was founded by Seleucus, the general of Alexander the Great, who named it after his father. Fulcher of Chartres was the best informed when he wrote that Antioch was founded by "Seleucus, son of Antiochus." Fulcher of Chartres, *Historia Hierosolymitana*, 215–16.
35. Guibert of Nogent, *Deeds of God*, 110; *Dei gesta per Francos*, 240.
36. William of Malmesbury, *Gesta regum Anglorum*, 1:638–39.
37. Gilo of Paris, *Historia vie Hierosolimitane*, 160–61.
38. Ibid., 95, 97.
39. Ralph of Caen, *History of the Normans*, 127; *Gesta Tancredi in Expeditione*, 93.
40. Ntedika, *Évocation de l'au-delà*, 90.

41. Fetellus, *Description of Jerusalem*, 52.
42. See Weiss, "*Hec est Domus Domini*"; Schein, *Gateway to the Heavenly City*, 96.
43. Jerome, *Commentariorum in Esaiam*, 73A:740.
44. Ralph of Caen, *History of the Normans*, 149–50; *Gesta Tancredi in Expeditione*, 112.
45. Schein, *Gateway to the Heavenly City*, 97.
46. For Baldwin I, see Sandro de Sandoli, *Corpus inscriptionum Crucesignatorum*, 57. For subsequent kings, see Morton, "Defense of the Holy Land," 285. At least in part because of their association with the Temple, Maccabees appear frequently in the documents concerning the Templars. See, for example, Barber and Bate, *Templars: Selected Sources*, 64–65.
47. Schein, *Gateway to the Heavenly City*, 105.
48. Orderic Vitalis, *Ecclesiastical History*, 5:348–49.
49. For Joab, see 2 Sam. 2:12–32, 3:22–32, 8:16, 11:6–25, 12:26–29, 18:5–19:3; 1 Kings 2:5, 28–34. Abishai was David's nephew and devoted and loyal follower (1 Sam. 26:4–12; 2 Sam. 2:17–24, 18:1–13). Banaiah or Benaiah is the name of five characters in the Old Testament. Orderic must be referring to the son of Jehoiada, the chief priest. David named Banaiah the chief of his bodyguard of Cherethites and Pelethites. Solomon raised him to the rank of commander-in-chief (1 Chron. 11:22, 18:17, 27:5; 2 Sam. 8:18, 23:20–22; 1 Kings 1:8, 10, 26, 32, 2:25, 29, 30, 34, 35, 4:4). For Uriah, see 2 Sam. 11:2–12:14. For the Ethites, see Ezra, 9:1.
50. Orderic Vitalis, *Ecclesiastical History*, 6:107.
51. See, for example, Cowdrey, "Mahdia Campaign of 1087," 26.
52. Fulcher of Chartres, *History of the Expedition*, 214; *Historia Hierosolymitana*, 589. Orderic refers to Fulcher of Chartres's chronicle in the preface to his work, but he makes little use of it (*Ecclesiastical History*, 5:6–7; see also discussion on p. xiv). For another reference to the Maccabees' victory in spite of being outnumbered, see Cowdrey, "Mahdia Campaign of 1087," 26.
53. Saul and his three sons were killed in the battle against the Philistines on Mount Gilboa (1 Sam. 31); Josiah was slain in battle at Meggiddo in Mesopotamia (1 Kings 22; 2 Chron. 35). On the death of Judas Maccabeus, see 1 Macc. 9:18.
54. *Chronicle of the Third Crusade*, 366–67; *Itinerarium Peregrinorum*, 422.
55. See, among others, Schroeder, *Topos der Nine Worthies*.
56. Raymond of Aguilers, *Historia Francorum*, 35; "*Liber*" *de Raymond d'Aguilers*, 53.
57. Raymond of Aguilers, *Historia Francorum*, 95; "*Liber*" *de Raymond d'Aguilers*, 115.
58. See Pastoureau, "Homme et le porc"; Fabre-Vassas, *Bête singulière*.
59. Guibert of Nogent, *Deeds of God*, 124; *Dei gesta per Francos*, 267 (hereafter cited parenthetically in the text by page number in Levine's English translation followed by page number in the original Latin).
60. Quoted in Bynum, *Holy Feast and Holy Fast*, 36.
61. On attitudes toward sexuality in Christianity and Judaism, see Boyarin, *Carnal Israel*; Brown, *Body and Society*.
62. On Bernard of Clairvaux and the Jews, see Chazan, *Medieval Stereotypes and Modern Antisemitism*, 42–46; Berger, "Attitude of St. Bernard of Clairvaux."
63. Quoted in Barber and Bate, *Templars: Selected Sources*, 224–25; Bernard of Clairvaux, *Liber ad Milites Templi*, 3:222.
64. It is possible that, in his description of the Jewish Temple, Bernard wanted the reader to recall the description of the Dome of the Rock as crusaders found it when they took Jerusalem. Ralph of Caen, for example, claimed that there was found "an image of Mohamet, entirely covered with gems, purple cloth and shining gold." *History of the Normans*, 144; *Gesta Tancredi in Expeditione*, 93. I would like to thank Nicholas Morton for suggesting this idea.

65. Christians' derogatory association of Islam with sexuality predates the First Crusade by several centuries. For example, *Risâlat al-Kindi,* written in Arabic in the ninth century, claims that Muhammad "had the sexual powers of forty men" and lists his fifteen wives. Tolan, *Saracens,* 60–62.

66. Ekkehard of Aura, *Hierosolymita,* 18–19; translation in McGinn, *Visions of the End,* 92.

67. Josephus, *Jewish War,* 3:463.

68. Baldric of Bourgueil refers to Josephus by name in his recollection of the conquest of Jerusalem by Titus and Vespasian. Baldric of Bourgueil, *Historia Ierosolimitana,* 5. One compiled manuscript (Rouen, Bibliothèque municipale, MS 1125) includes both Baldric's and Josephus's works; see Biddlecombe's introduction, ibid., lxxix. On Flavius Josephus in the Middle Ages more generally, see Akbari, *Idols in the East,* 123.

69. See, for example, the forged encyclical of Sergius IV, in Schaller, "Zur Kreuzzugsenzyklika Papst Sergius IV," 150–51; Throop, *Crusading as an Act of Vengeance,* 45–46.

70. *Chanson d'Antioche,* 516. The supposed vengeance of Vespasian became the subject of a widely known poem, *La Venjance Nostre Seigneur,* the earliest manuscript of which dates from ca. 1200. See *Oldest Version of the Twelfth-Century Poem.*

71. Throop, *Crusading as an Act of Vengeance,* 82–83.

72. Baldric of Bourgueil's chronicle also reveals a positive attitude toward the Roman conquest of Jerusalem. In his chronicle, the conquest precedes Jerusalem's rebuilding as a Christian city. Although Titus and Vespasian were not directly responsible for the reconstruction of the Christian Jerusalem, their destruction of the Jewish Jerusalem made it possible. It is likely, then, that Baldric was not only inviting a comparison between the Romans and the crusaders but also justifying the brutal conquest of Muslim Jerusalem by the crusaders, since this also led to its reconstruction as a Christian city. Baldric of Bourgueil, *Historia Ierosolimitana,* 5.

73. *Chanson d'Antioche,* 916.

74. Peter Tudebode, *Historia de Hierosolymitano itinere,* 120; English translation in the Hills' 1974 edition, 97.

75. William of Malmesbury, *Gesta regum Anglorum,* 1:645.

76. For discussion of the tension between the two kinds of anti-Jewish violence, see Nirenberg, "Figures of Thought."

77. For reclassification of the Jews, see Cohen, "Muslim Connection," 143–44. In some cases, Jews had already been grouped with other non-Christians in the patristic era. Origen, for example, claimed that there were three classes of people. The Jews and the pagans were "hylics" (from *hylē,* matter), while Christians were either psychics (from *psychē,* soul) or pneumatics (from *pneuma,* spirit), depending on their level of spirituality. Nirenberg, "Christian Sovereignty and the Jewish Flesh," 169.

78. Guibert of Nogent, *Monodies,* 97; *Autobiographie,* 246–49. For a similar description of crusaders' actions in a Hebrew source, see Eidelberg's translation of *The Jews and the Crusaders,* 26. The causes and circumstances of the massacre at Rouen and of those in the Rhineland continue to be hotly debated. Recent articles include Haverkampf, "Martyrs in Rivalry"; Chazan, "'Let not a remnant or a residue escape'"; Bronstein, "Crusades and the Jews"; Nirenberg, "Rhineland Massacres of Jews"; and Riley-Smith, "Christian Violence and the Crusades."

79. See Cohen, "'Slay Them Not.'"

80. See, for example, Gaposchkin, "Louis IX, Crusade, and the Promise."

81. The manuscript is now located in the Biblioteca Medicea Laurenziana in Florence. See Huygens's introduction, in Guibert of Nogent, *Dei gesta per Francos,* 26.

CHAPTER 6

1. *Gesta Francorum*, 62.
2. Watkins, *History and the Supernatural*, 48.
3. Van Houts, *Gesta Normannorum Ducum*, 2:162–63.
4. *Gesta Stephani*, 50–51.
5. Van Houts, *Gesta Normannorum Ducum*, 2:162–63.
6. *Gesta Stephani*, 50–51.
7. Rubenstein, *Armies of Heaven*, 155.
8. Watkins, *History and the Supernatural*, 50.
9. Raymond of Aguilers, *"Liber" de Raymond d'Aguilers*, 151; *Historia Francorum*, 41.
10. Brown, "Where Do Cardinal Direction Terms Come From," 143.
11. Ibid., 122. Angelika Mietzner and Helma Pasch are less sure on this point: "We are, however, reluctant to have Brown's claim confirmed that knowledge about cardinal direction is a fairly recent factor in many parts of the world. All we know is that the scientific cardinal directions are a recent introduction in most African countries." Mietzner and Pasch, "Expressions of Cardinal Directions," 14.
12. Brown, "Where Do Cardinal Direction Terms Come From," 145. Recent research has confirmed this hypothesis; see Mietzner and Pasch, "Expressions of Cardinal Directions." For a different point of view, see Gordon, "Sacred Directions, Orientation," 211.
13. Said, *Orientalism*, 12.
14. Ibid., 2–3.
15. Tolan, *Saracens*, xviii.
16. Kinoshita, *Medieval Boundaries*, 6.
17. Meserve, *Empires of Islam*, 10–11.
18. Akbari, *Idols in the East*, 12. See also Akbari, "From Due East to True North" and "Alexander in the Orient." Another "easy conflation" took place in scholarship between the binary of Greece/Persia and that of East/West. Said is not the only one to date the binary to the time of Aeschylus. Many modern scholars associate the first description of the world as divided into two poles along the east-west axis with the Greco-Persian wars of the fifth century B.C. According to Denys Hay, for example, "In so far as the Greeks had a sense of fundamental continental differences, they lay between East and West, between Persian and Greek, between Asia and Europe." Hay, *Europe*, 2–3. More generally, Nancy Bisaha argues that "the myth of East and West as polar opposites was introduced over two thousand years ago by the Greeks and adapted by the Romans." Bisaha, *Creating East and West*, 2. Finally, Anthony Pagden writes, "The East as Herodotus knew it, the lands that lay between the European peninsula and the Ganges, was inhabited by a large number of varied peoples.... Yet, for all their size and variety, they all seemed to have something in common, something that set them apart from the peoples of Europe, of the West." Pagden, *Worlds at War*, xi. However, this binary is not found in ancient sources. It is true that Herodotus describes the conflict as juxtaposing Europe and Asia: "The Persians claim Asia for their own, and the foreign nations that dwell in it; Europe and the Greek race they hold to be separate from them." Herodotus, *Works*, 1:7. But Herodotus makes no reference to the East or the West.
19. Akbari, "From Due East to True North," 29.
20. Hugh of Saint Victor, *De arca Noe morali*, 678.
21. Otto of Freising, *Chronicle of Universal History*, 322–23 (see also 94–95); Otto's *Ottonis Episcopi Frisingensis Chronica*, 227–28 (see also 7–8).
22. Otto of Freising, *Chronicle of Universal History*, 167; *Ottonis Episcopi Frisingensis Chronica*, 82. On both the fourfold and a related sixfold model of history, see Rubenstein, "Lambert of Saint-Omer."
23. For discussion of Daniel's sources, see Momigliano, "Origins of Universal History."

24. Jerome, *In Danielem*, cols. 503–4.
25. Gerald of Wales, *Expugnatio Hibernica*, 75.
26. Ibid., 236–37.
27. Wright, *Geographical Lore*, 235. See also Glacken, *Traces on the Rhodian Shore*; Hay, *Europe*. More recently, Scafi has written about "the fundamental east-west progression underlying the *mappae mundi*." Scafi, *Mapping Paradise*, 127.
28. McKenzie, "Westward Progression of History," 335.
29. Quoted in Wright, *Geographical Lore*, 234.
30. McKenzie, "Westward Progression of History," 342.
31. Assmann, *Death and Salvation in Ancient Egypt*, 150.
32. This expression became popular during the First World War but appeared as early as the late sixteenth century. According to Eric Partridge, "The basic idea is that of the setting sun; pioneering in North America might have contributed." Partridge, "Dictionary of Slang," 337. It is also possible that the expression originated in the westward journey that a condemned criminal would make from Newgate Prison to the gallows at Tyburn. Green, *Slang Down the Ages*, 343.
33. Augustine, *De civitate Dei*, 27.
34. Cyril of Jerusalem, *St. Cyril of Jerusalem's Lectures*, 54. At about the same time, referring to the prophecy of Malachi, Saint Jerome explained the mystery of baptism in a similar manner: "In the mysteries we renounce him who is in the West and who together with our sins becomes for us as one dead; then turning towards the East, we enter into a covenant with the Sun of Righteousness and promise that we will serve him." Jerome, "In Amos," col. 1068; translation in Rahner, *Greek Myths and Christian Mystery*, 124.
35. See Scafi, *Mapping Paradise*, 35; Wright, *Geographical Lore*, 261–63.
36. "Constitutions of the Holy Apostles," 421.
37. Gordon, "Sacred Directions, Orientation," 216. See also Sauer, *Symbolik des Kirchengebäudes*. In the seventh century, Isidore of Seville wrote that "paradise is a place in the East." Isidore of Seville, *Etymologies*, 285. In the eighth century, Bede the Venerable revealed his awareness of the discrepancy between the two translations: "where our edition . . . has the phrase 'from the beginning,' the phrase 'to the East' appears instead in the old translation. From this some wish it to be understood that paradise is located in the eastern part of the world." Bede the Venerable, *On Genesis*, 111.
38. According to Eusebius of Caesarea, Emperor Constantine taught his subjects to revere "the Day of Salvation," which also "bears the names of Light Day and Sun Day." Eusebius of Caesarea, *Life of Constantine*, 159. Ambrose of Milan, referring to the prophecy of Malachi (4:2), described the creation of the sun in the following manner: "God the Father says: 'Let the Sun be made,' and the Son [Christ] made the sun, for it is fitting that the 'Sun of Justice' should make the sun of the world." Ambrose of Milan, *Hexameron*, 125. See also Berrens, *Sonnenkult und Kaisertum*; Rahner, *Greek Myths and Christian Mystery*.
39. For more on this subject, see Fischer, *Oriens—Occidens—Europa*. See also Gordon, "Sacred Directions, Orientation"; Baritz, "Idea of the West."
40. Friedman, "Cultural Conflicts," 75.
41. Lactantius, *Divine Institutes*, 135.
42. Orosius, *Seven Books of History*, 46.
43. Ibid., 44.
44. Avitus of Vienne, *Letters and Selected Prose*, 147; *Epistolae*, col. 285.
45. Avitus of Vienne, *Letters and Selected Prose*, 370; *Epistolae*, cols. 257–58.
46. On *translatio* in the premodern period, see Lusignan, "Université de Paris"; Nordholt, *Myth of the West*; Stahuljak, *Bloodless Genealogies*; Jongkees, "Translatio studii"; and Goez, *Translatio Imperii*.
47. Nicholas I, *Epistolae*, 949.

48. Glaber, *Rodulfi Glabri Historiarum*, 40–43. According to Glaber, then, the East that was behind Christ's back enjoyed less divine favor than the West that he was facing. The origin was less important than the destination.

49. Robert the Monk, *History of the First Crusade*, 101; *Historia Iherosolimitana*, 21.

50. Guibert de Nogent, *Deeds of God*, 35; *Dei gesta per Francos*, 99 (hereafter cited in the text by page number in Levine's English translation followed by page number in the original Latin).

51. On Islam as a Christian heresy, see Tolan, *Saracens*, 135–69.

52. Purkis, *Crusading Spirituality*, 48. See also Riley-Smith, "Death on the First Crusade."

53. *Gesta Francorum*, 1–2. On Urban II and the *vita apostolica*, see Cowdrey, "Pope Urban II and the Idea of Crusade."

54. Raymond of Aguilers, *Historia Francorum*, 128; "Liber" *de Raymond d'Aguilers*, 151. On crusaders as apostles, see also Lapina, "Paintings of Berzé-la-Ville"; Katzenellenbogen, "Central Tympanum at Vézelay."

55. Fulcher of Chartres, *History of the Expedition*, 271; *Historia Hierosolymitana*, 748.

56. Robert the Monk, *History of the First Crusade*, 90; *Historia Iherosolimitana*, 13.

57. Ibid.

58. Robert emphasizes the northern origins of crusaders in his description of their battle against the emir of Babylon: "Our men [crusaders] blew away the flanks and wings of the army as easily as the north wind dissipates cloud or a sudden gust a heap of straw." *History of the First Crusade*, 209; *Historia Iherosolimitana*, 106. The imagery comes from Isaiah 40:24. It is important to note that for Robert, the North could be a negative cardinal point. For example, he describes a certain Rainald, who "concluded a secret treaty with the Turks," as follows: "Alas! Alas! Cowardly soldier that he was, from the North and not from the South.... It was only fitting that he deserved to lose God's grace and fall to the lot of he who chose to reside in the North." *History of the First Crusade*, 86; *Historia Iherosolimitana*, 10–11. This passage refers to a prophecy of Isaiah, who describes Lucifer falling from heaven and sitting on the "mount of assembly" in the North (Isa. 14:12–13).

59. Robert places an important biblical reference in the mouth of Kerbogha's mother: "The soothsayers, mages and diviners, the oracles of our divine powers and the words of the prophets (in which it is said: 'from the east and from the west, from the north and from the south shall your coast be. There shall no man be able to stand before you') all agree." *History of the First Crusade*, 156; *Historia Iherosolimitana*, 63. The source of the passage is Joshua 1:4–5.

60. Hasegawa, "Orbits of Ancient and Medieval Comets."

61. Fulcher of Chartres, *History of the Expedition*, 89; *Historia Hierosolymitana*, 203–5.

62. For a different interpretation, see Rubenstein, *Armies of Heaven*, 155.

63. Fulcher of Chartres, *History of the Expedition*, 95; *Historia Hierosolymitana*, 224.

64. Ralph of Caen, *History of the Normans*, 83; *Gesta Tancredi in Expeditione*, 55–56.

65. Robert the Monk, *History of the First Crusade*, 146; *Historia Iherosolimitana*, 54.

66. Robert the Monk, *History of the First Crusade*, 164; *Historia Iherosolimitana*, 69.

67. Ralph of Caen, *History of the Normans*, 109; *Gesta Tancredi in Expeditione*, 77.

68. Ralph of Caen, *History of the Normans*, 109; *Gesta Tancredi in Expeditione*, 78.

69. Ralph of Caen, *History of the Normans*, 109–10; *Gesta Tancredi*, 78. Here, once again, we see a close association between the North and the West.

70. Goldreich, *Climate of Israel*, 140–41.

71. For another examples of harmful eastern wind, see Jonah 4:8: "And it came to pass, when the sun did arise, that God prepared a vehement east wind; and the sun beat upon the head of Jonah, that he fainted, and wished in himself to die, and said, It is better for me to die than to live."

72. Two recent studies have examined the situation in the Middle East in the decades leading up to the First Crusade and have demonstrated that the region was hardly prosperous. Ronnie Ellenblum has argued that between 950 and 1072 the region suffered numerous climatic disasters, particularly droughts and cold spells, which led to hunger, violence, and the decline of urban centers, and accelerated Islamization. Although climatic disasters became rarer toward the end of the century, their impact was to be felt for decades if not centuries. Ellenblum, *Collapse of the Eastern Mediterranean*. For a new assessment of the situation in Byzantium on the eve of the First Crusade, see Frankopan, *First Crusade*.

73. Rubenstein, "Lambert of Saint-Omer," 71.

CONCLUSION

1. See Sweetenham's introduction to Robert the Monk, *History of the First Crusade*, 8–11.
2. Gabrieli, *Arab Historians of the Crusades*, 8.
3. Riches, *St. George*, 133.
4. *Koran Interpreted*, 89, 198.
5. Ibn Ishaq, *Life of Muhammad*, 303.
6. Ibid., 310.
7. Cornell, "Fruit of the Tree of Knowledge," 75.
8. Ibn Ishaq, *Life of Muhammad*, 303–4.
9. On the revival of jihad in response to the Crusades, see Hillenbrand, *Crusades*, 103–12.
10. O'Callaghan, *Reconquest and Crusade*, 197.
11. Fletcher, *Saint James's Catapult*, 298–99.
12. O'Callaghan, *Reconquest and Crusade*, 195–96; Kendrick, *Saint James in Spain*, 19–24, 63.
13. O'Callaghan, *Reconquest and Crusade*, 196.
14. Abel-Turby, "New World Augustinians and Franciscans"; Weckmann, *Medieval Heritage of Mexico*, 157–66.
15. García, "Santiago Mataindios."
16. Beliles and McDowell, *America's Providential History*, 9–10.
17. See, for example, Nordholt, *Myth of the West*; Dickey, "*Translatio Imperii* and *Translatio Religionis*"; Gerbi, *Dispute of the New World*; Tuveson, *Redeemer Nation*; Tuveson, *Millennium and Utopia*; Baritz, "Idea of the West"; and Bercovitch, *Puritan Origins*.
18. Quoted in Neill, *English Colonization of America*, 178.
19. Edwards, *Compleat History or Survey*, 2:691.
20. Jackson, *Letters of the Lewis and Clark Expedition*, 1:47.
21. Hegel, *Philosophy of History*, 103–4.
22. Nirenberg, "Islam and the West," 251.

Bibliography

LIST OF ABBREVIATIONS

CCCM Corpus Christianorum Continuatio Mediaevalis
MGH   *Monumenta Germaniae Historica* (with the following divisions)
Ldl   *Libelli de lite imperatorum et pontificum saeculis XI. et XII. conscripti*
SS   *Scriptores*
PL   *Patrologiae cursus completus, series Latina*, ed. J.-P. Migne, 221 vols. Paris, 1855–61.

PRIMARY SOURCES

Abbo of Saint-Germain-des-Prés. *Viking Attacks on Paris: The "Bella parisiacae urbis" of Abbo of Saint-Germain-des-Prés*. Edited and translated by Nirmal Dass. Paris, 2007.
Adomnán. *Adomnán's Life of Columba*. Edited and translated by Alan Orr Anderson and Marjorie Ogilvie Anderson. Oxford, 1991.
Aelfric. *Aelfric's Homilies on Judith, Esther, and the Maccabees*. Edited by Stuart D. Lee. http://users.ox.ac.uk/~stuart/kings/.
Aelred of Rievaulx. *The Historical Works*. Translated by Jane Patricia Freeland. Edited by Marsha L. Dutton. Cistercian Fathers Series 56. Kalamazoo, 2005.
Albert of Aachen. *Historia Ierosolimitana*. Edited and translated by Susan B. Edgington. Oxford, 2007.
Amatus of Montecassino. *The History of the Normans*. Translated by Prescott N. Dunbar. Woodbridge, UK, 2004.
———. *Storia de' Normanni di Amato di Montecassino*. Edited by Vincenzo de Bartholomeis. Rome, 1935.
Ambrose of Milan. *De officiis*. Edited and translated by Ivor J. Davidson. Oxford, 2001.
———. *Hexameron, Paradise, and Cain and Abel*. Translated by John J. Savage. New York, 1961.
Anastasius Bibliothecarius. "Passio sancti Demetrii martyris." *PL* 129, cols. 715–26.
Andreas of Strumi. *Vita S. Arialdi*. Edited by F. Baethgen. MGH SS 30.2, 1047–75.
Anna Comnena. *The Alexiad*. Translated by Edgar Robert Ashton Sewter. London, 2003.
The Annals of Fulda. Translated by Timothy Reuter. Manchester, 1992.
Anselm of Canterbury. *La conception virginale et le péché originel*. Edited and translated by Michel Corbin, Alain Galonnier, Paul Gilbert, Antoine Lauras, and Rémi de Ravinel. Paris, 1990.
Arnulf of Lièges. *Gesta episcoporum Tungrensium, Traiectensium et Leodiensium*. Edited by G. H. Pertz. MGH SS, vol. 7. Hanover, 1846.
Augustine of Hippo. *De civitate Dei*. PL 41.
———. "De cura pro mortuis gerenda." In Oeuvres de Saint Augustin, Première série: Opuscules, II, Problèmes moraux, 457–523. Edited and translated by Gustave Combès. Paris, 1948.

———. "Homélies sur l'Évangile de Saint Jean, LXXX–CIII." In *Oeuvres de Saint Augustin*, 9ᵉ série, *Traités sur saint Jean*, vol. 74B. Translated by Marie-François Berrouard. Paris, 1998.

———. "Sermo 300: In solemnitate martyrum Machabaeorum." *PL* 38, cols. 1376–80.

———. "Sermon 300: On the solemnity of the Maccabee martyrs." In *The Works of Saint Augustine: A Translation for the Twenty-First Century; Part III—Sermons*, trans. Edmund Hill, vol. 8, *Sermons 273–305A*, 276–81. New York, 1994.

———. *Tractates on the Gospel of John*. Translated by John W. Rettig. Washington, D.C., 1994.

Avitus of Vienne. *Epistolae*. *PL* 59, cols. 199–290.

———. *Letters and Selected Prose*. Translated by Danuta Shanzer and Ian Wood. Liverpool, 2002.

Baldric of Bourgueil. *Historia Ierosolimitana*. Edited by Steven Biddlecombe. Woodbridge, UK, 2014.

———. *Les oeuvres poétiques de Baudri de Bourgueil*. Edited by Phyllis Abrahams. Paris, 1926.

Barber, Malcolm, and Keith Bate, trans. *The Templars: Selected Sources*. Manchester, 2002.

Bartolf of Nangis. "Gesta Francorum Iherusalem expugnantium." *Recueil des Historiens des Croisades: Historiens Occidentaux*, 3:487–543. Paris, 1866.

Bede the Venerable. *Historia ecclesiastica gentis Anglorum*. Edited and translated by Michael Lapidge, Pierre Monat, and Philippe Robin. 3 vols. Sources Chre'tiennes, vol. 489. Paris, 2005.

———. *On Genesis*. Translated by Calvin B. Kendall. Liverpool, 2008.

Beliles, Mark A., and Steven K. McDowell. *America's Providential History: Including Biblical Principles of Education, Government, Politics, Economics, and Family Life*. 2nd ed. Charlottesville, 1991.

Benzo of Alba. *Sieben Bücher an Kaiser Heinrich IV.* Edited and translated by Hans Seyffert. Hanover, 1996.

Bernard of Angers. *The Book of Sainte Foy*. Translated by Pamela Sheingorn and Robert L. A. Clark. Philadelphia, 1995.

———. *Liber miraculorum sancte fidis*. Edited by Auguste Bouillet. Paris, 1897.

Bernard of Clairvaux. *Liber ad Milites Templi de laude novae militia*. In *S. Bernardi Opera*, ed. Jean Leclercq and Henri Rochais, 7 vols., 3:205–39. Rome, 1957–72.

Bernold of St. Blasien. "Chronicle." In *Eleventh-Century Germany: The Swabian Chronicles*, trans. Ian Stuart Robinson, 245–337. Manchester, 2008.

———. "Die Chronikon Bertholds von Reichenau und Bernolds von Konstanz." Edited by Ian Stuart Robinson. Scriptores rerum Germanicarum in usum scholarum, new ser., 14. Hanover, 2003.

Bonizo of Sutri. "Liber ad Amicum." *MGH Ldl*, 1:568–620. Hanover, 1891.

———. "To a Friend." In *The Papal Reform of the Eleventh Century: Lives of Pope Leo IX and Pope Gregory VII*, trans. Ian Stuart Robinson, 158–261. Manchester, 2004.

Bouet, Pierre, and Olivier Desbordes, eds. *Chroniques latines du Mont Saint-Michel (IXe–XIIe siècles)*. Caen, 2009.

Caffaro. *De liberatione civitatum orientis*. In *Annali Genovesi di Caffaro e de' suoi continuatori*, ed. Luigi Tommaso Belgrano, 98–124. Rome, 1890.

Certain, Eugène de, ed. *Les miracles de Saint Benoît écrits par Adrevald, Aimon, André, Raoul Tortaire et Hugues de Sainte Marie, moines de Fleury*. Paris, 1858.

La Chanson d'Antioche. Edited and translated by Bernard Guidot. Paris, 2011.

The Chanson d'Antioche. Translated by Susan B. Edgington and Carol Sweetenham. Farnham, 2011.

Chronicle of the Third Crusade: A Translation of the "Itinerarium Peregrinorum et Gesta Regis Ricardi." Translated by Helen J. Nicholson. Crusade Texts in Translation. Aldershot, 1997.
Chronicon Paschale, 284–628 AD. Translated by Michael Whitby and Mary Whitby. Liverpool, 1989.
Cicero. *The Nature of the Gods.* Edited and translated by P. G. Walsh. Oxford, 1997.
Constantine Porphyregenitus. *De administrando imperio.* Edited and translated by Gyula Moravcsik and Romilly James Heald Jenkins. Washington, D.C., 1967.
"Constitutions of the Holy Apostles." Translation revised by James Donaldson. In *Lactantius, Venantius, Asterius, Victorinus, Dionysius, Apostolic Teaching and Constitutions, Homily, and Liturgies*, 385–508. The Ante-Nicene Fathers: Translation of the Writings of the Fathers Down to A.D. 325, vol. 7. New York, 1888.
Cyril of Jerusalem. *St. Cyril of Jerusalem's Lectures on the Christian Sacraments: The Procatechesis and the Five Mystagogical Catecheses.* Edited and translated by F. L. Cross. 1951. Reprint, Crestwood, New York, 1986.
Dionysius of Halicarnassus. *The Roman Antiquities.* Edited and translated by Earnest Cary. 7 vols. Cambridge, Mass., 1937–50.
Dudo of Saint-Quentin. *De moribus et actis primorum Normanniae ducum, auctore Dudone Sancti Quintini decano.* Edited by Jules Lasir. Caen, 1965.
——. *History of the Normans.* Translated by Eric Christiansen. Woodbridge, UK, 1998.
Edwards, John. *A Compleat History or Survey of All the Dispensations and Methods of Religion.* 2 vols. London, 1699.
Ekkehard of Aura. *Hierosolymita.* Recueil des Historiens des Croisades: Historiens Occidentaux, 5:1–40. Paris, 1895.
Eusebius of Caesarea. *Life of Constantine.* Translated by Averil Cameron and Stuart G. Hill. Oxford, 1999.
Festugière, André-Jean, ed. and trans. *Vie de Théodore de Sykéôn.* 2 vols. Brussels, 1970.
Fetellus. *Description of Jerusalem and the Holy Land by Fetellus (c. 1130).* Translated by J. R. MacPherson. Palestine Pilgrims' Text Society, vol. 5. New York, 1892.
Frontinus, Sextus Julius. *The Strategems.* Edited and translated by Charles E. Bennett. London, 1925.
Fulcher of Chartres. *Fulcheri Carnotensis Historia Hierosolymitana (1095–1127).* Edited by Heinrich Hagenmeyer. Heidelberg, 1913.
——. *A History of the Expedition to Jerusalem.* Translated by Harold S. Fink. Knoxville, Tenn., 1969.
Gabrieli, Francesco. *Arab Historians of the Crusades.* Translated by E. J. Costello. Los Angeles, 1984.
Geoffrey Malaterra. *The Deeds of Count Roger of Calabria and Sicily and of His Brother Duke Robert Guiscard.* Translated by Kenneth Baxter Wolf. Ann Arbor, 2005.
——. *De rebus gestis Rogerii Calabriae et Siciliae Comitis et Roberti Guiscardi ducis fratris eius.* Edited by Ernesto Pontieri. Rerum Italicarum Scriptores, 2nd ed., vol. 5, part 1. Bologna, 1928.
Gerald of Wales. *Expugnatio Hibernica: The Conquest of Ireland.* Edited and translated by A. B. Scott and Francis Xavier Martin. Dublin, 1978.
Gesta Francorum et aliorum Hierosolimitanorum: The Deeds of the Franks and the Other Pilgrims to Jerusalem. Edited and translated by Rosalind Hill. London, 1962.
Gesta Stephani. Edited and translated by Kenneth Reginald Potter. Oxford, 1976.
Gilo of Paris. *The "Historia vie Hierosolimitane" of Gilo of Paris and a Second, Anonymous Author.* Edited and translated by Christopher Wallace Grocock and Elizabeth Siberry. Oxford, 1997.

Glaber, Raoul. *Rodulfi Glabri Historiarum libri quinque: The Five Books of the Histories.* Edited and translated by Neithard Bulst, John France, and Paul Reynolds. Oxford, 1989.
Guibert of Nogent. *Autobiographie.* Edited and translated by Edmond-René Labande. Paris, 1981.
———. *The Deeds of God Through the Franks.* Translated by Robert Levine. Woodbridge, UK, 1997.
———. *Dei gesta per Francos.* Edited by Robert Burchard Constantijn Huygens. CCCM, vol. 127A. Turnhout, 1996.
———. *Liber quo ordine sermo fieri debeat.* Edited by Robert Burchard Constantijn Huygens. CCCM, vol. 127. Turnhout, 1993.
———. *Monodies.* Translated by Joseph McAlhany and Jay Rubenstein. London, 2011.
Hagenmeyer, Heinrich, ed. *Die Kreuzzugsbriefe aus den Jahren 1088–1100.* Innsbruck, 1901.
Hall, Martin, and Jonathan Phillips. *Caffaro, Genoa, and the Twelfth-Century Crusades.* Crusade Texts in Translation. Aldershot, 2013.
Hegel, Georg Wilhelm Friedrich. *The Philosophy of History.* Translated by J. Sibree. New York, 1956.
Henry of Huntington. *Historia Anglorum: The History of the English People.* Edited and translated by Diana Greenway. Oxford, 1996.
Herodotus. *The Works of Herodotus.* Edited and translated by Alfred Denis Godley. 4 vols. Cambridge, Mass., 1981–94.
History of the Patriarchs of the Coptic Church of Alexandria. Edited and translated by Basil T. A. Evetts. 4 vols. Paris, 1948–59.
Homer. *The Iliad of Homer.* Translated by Ennis Rees. Oxford, 1991.
Horace. *Satires, Epistles, and Ars Poetica.* Translated by Henry Rushton Fairclough. Cambridge, Mass., 1991.
Hugh of Saint Victor. *De arca Noe morali.* PL 176, cols. 617–80.
Hystoria de via et recuperatione Antiochiae atque Ierusolymarum (olim Tudebodus imitatus et continuatus): I Normanni d'Italia alla prima Crociata in una cronaca cassinese. Edited by Edoardo D'Angelo. Florence, 2009.
Ibn al-Athir. *The Chronicle of Ibn al-Athir for the Crusading Period.* Translated by Donald Sidney Richards. 3 vols. Crusade Texts in Translation. Aldershot, 2010.
Ibn Ishaq, Muhammad. *The Life of Muhammad: A Translation of Ibn Ishaq's Sirat Rasul Allah.* Translated by Alfred Guillaume. Oxford, 1955.
Isidore of Seville. *The Etymologies.* Translated by Stephen A. Barney, W. J. Lewis, J. A. Beach, and Oliver Berghof. Cambridge, 2006.
Italikos, Michael. *Lettres et discours.* Edited and translated by Paul Gautier. Paris, 1972.
Itinerarium Peregrinorum et Gesta Regis Ricardi. Edited by William Stubbs. London, 1864.
Jackson, Donald, ed. *Letters of the Lewis and Clark Expedition, with Related Documents, 1783–1854.* Urbana, 1962.
Jerome. *Commentariorum in Esaiam.* Edited by Marcus Adriaen and Germain Morin. Corpus Christianorum, Series Latina, 73–73A.
———. *Commentarius in Ecclesiasten.* PL 23, cols. 1009–1116.
———. *In Amos.* PL 25, cols. 989–1096.
———. *In Danielem.* PL 25, cols. 491–584.
The Jews and the Crusaders: The Hebrew Chronicles of the First and Second Crusades. Translated by Shlomo Eidelberg. Madison, 1977.
John Scotus Eriugena. *Homélie sur le prologue de Jean.* Edited by Édouard Jeauneau. Sources Chrétiennes, vol. 151. Paris, 1969.
Josephus, Flavius. *Jewish War.* Translated by H. St. J. Thackeray. 3 vols. London, 1961–68.

Kierkegaard, Søren. *Philosophical Fragments*. Translated by Howard V. Hong and Edna H. Hong. Princeton, 1985.
Kinnamos, John. *Deeds of John and Manuel Comnenus*. Translated by Charles M. Brand. New York, 1976.
The Koran Interpreted. Translated by Arthur J. Arberry. London, 1955.
Lactantius. *The Divine Institutes*. Translated by Mary Francis McDonald. Washington, D.C., 1964.
Lemerle, Paul, ed. and trans. *Les plus anciens recueils des miracles de Saint Démétrius et la pénétration des slaves dans les Balkans*. Paris, 1979.
Leo the Deacon. *The History of Leo the Deacon: Byzantine Military Expansion in the Tenth Century*. Translated by Alice-Mary Talbot and Denis F. Sullivan. Dumbarton Oaks Studies, vol. 41. Washington, D.C., 2005.
Liber privilegiorum ecclesiae Ianuensis. Edited by D. Puncuh. Genoa, 1962.
Manegold of Lautenbach. *Ad Geberhardum*. MGH Ldl, 1:300–430. Hanover, 1891.
The Marvels of Rome/Mirabilia Urbis Romae. Translated by Francis Morgan Nichols. New York, 1986.
McCarthy, Thomas John Henry, trans. *Chronicles of the Investiture Contest: Frutolf of Michelsberg and His Continuators*. Manchester, UK, 2014.
Nicholas I. *Epistolae*. PL 119, cols. 769–1182.
Niketas Choniates. *O City of Byzantium: Annals of Niketas Choniates*. Translated by Harry J. Magoulias. Detroit, 1984.
Odo of Deuil. *De profectione Ludovici VII in orientem*. Edited and translated by Virginia Gingerick Berry. New York, 1948.
The Oldest Version of the Twelfth-Century Poem, La Venjance Nostre Seigneur. Edited by Loyal A. T. Gryting. Ann Arbor, 1952.
Orderic Vitalis. *The Ecclesiastical History of Orderic Vitalis*. Edited and translated by Marjorie Chibnall. 6 vols. Oxford, 1969–80.
Orosius, Paulus. *The Seven Books of History Against the Pagans*. Translated by Roy J. Deferrari. Washington, D.C., 1964.
Otto of Freising. *A Chronicle of Universal History to the Year 1146 AD*. Translated by Charles Christopher Mierow. 2nd ed. New York, 2002.
———. *Ottonis Episcopi Frisingensis Chronica sive Historia de Duabus Civitatibus*. Edited by Adolf Hofmeister. Hanover, 1912.
Paul the Deacon. *Historia Langobardorum*. Edited by Ludwig Bethmann and Georg Waitz. MGH, Scriptores rerum Langobardicarum et Italicarum saec, VI–XI. Hanover, 1878.
———. *Historia Romana*. Edited by Amadeo Crivelucci. Rome, 1914.
———. *History of the Lombards*. Translated by W. D. Foulke. Philadelphia, 1974.
Pausanias. *Description of Greece*. Edited and translated by W. H. S. Jones. 5 vols. London, 1918–35.
P'awstos Buzand. *The Epic Histories Attributed to P'awstos Buzand*. Edited by Nina G. Garsoïan. Harvard Armenian Texts and Studies, vol. 8. Cambridge, Mass., 1989.
Peter Damian. *Die Briefe*. Edited by Kurt Reindel. 4 vols. Munich, 1988.
———. *Letters*. Translated by Owen J. Blum. 6 vols. Fathers of the Church, Medieval Continuation. Washington, D.C., 1989–2005.
Peter the Venerable. *Letters*. Edited by Giles Constable. 2 vols. Cambridge, Mass., 1967.
Peter Tudebode. *Historia de Hierosolymitano itinere*. Translated by John Hugh Hill and Laurita Lyttleton Hill. Memoirs of the American Philosophical Society, vol. 101. Philadelphia, 1974.
———. *Historia de Hierosolymitano itinere*. Edited by John Hugh Hill and Laurita Lyttleton Hill. Paris, 1977.

Plutarch. *Lives*. Translated by Bernadotte Perrin. 10 vols. London, 1914–26.
Polyaenus. *Strategems of War*. Translated by R. Sheperd. 1793. Reprint, Chicago, 1974.
Povest' vremennykh let [The Russian Primary Chronicle]. In *Nachalo Russkoi Literatury: XI–Nachalo XII Veka* [The Beginnings of Russian Literature: Eleventh–Early Twelfth Centuries], ed. Lev Aleksandrovich Dmitriev and Dmitrii Sergeevich Likhachev, 23–277. Moscow, 1978.
Rabanus Maurus. *Commentaria in libros Machabaeorum*. PL 109, cols. 1125–1256.
Ralph of Caen. *Gesta Tancredi in Expeditione Hierosolymitana*. Edited by Edoardo D'Angelo. CCCM, vol. 231. Turnhout, 2011.
———. *The Gesta Tancredi of Ralph of Caen: A History of the Normans on the First Crusade*. Translated by Bernard S. Bachrach and David Stewart Bachrach. Crusade Texts in Translation. Aldershot, 2005.
Raymond of Aguilers. *Historia Francorum qui ceperunt Iherusalem*. Translated by John Hugh Hill and Laurita L. Hill. Philadelphia, 1968.
———. *Le "Liber" de Raymond d'Aguilers*. Edited by John Hugh Hill and Laurita L. Hill. Paris, 1969.
Robert of Clari. *The Conquest of Constantinople*. Translated by Edgar Holmes McNeal. New York, 1936.
———. *La Conquête de Constantinople*. Edited and translated by Jean Dufournet. Paris, 2004.
Robert the Monk. *Historia Iherosolimitana*. Edited by Damien Kempf and Marcus G. Bull. Woodbridge, UK, 2013.
———. *History of the First Crusade*. Translated by Carol Sweetenham. Crusade Texts in Translation. Aldershot, 2005.
Sandro de Sandoli. *Corpus inscriptionum Crucesignatorum Terrae Sanctae*. Jerusalem, 1974.
Simeon of Durham. *Historia de sancto Cuthberto, Symeonis monachi opera omnia*. Edited by Thomas Arnold. 2 vols. London, 1882–85.
Skylitzes, John. *A Synopsis of Byzantine History, 811–1057*. Translated by John Wortley. Cambridge, 2010.
Socrates Scholasticus. *The Ecclesiastical History of Socrates Scholasticus*. Translation revised by A. C. Zenos. In *Socrates, Sozomenus: Church Histories*, ed. Philip Schaff and Henry Wace, 1–178. A Select Library of Nicene and Post-Nicene Fathers of the Christian Church, 2nd ser., vol. 2. New York, 1891.
Sozomen, Salminius Hermias. *The Ecclesiastical History*. Translation revised by Chester D. Hatranft. In *Socrates, Sozomenus: Church Histories*, ed. Philip Schaff and Henry Wace, 236–427. A Select Library of Nicene and Post-Nicene Fathers of the Christian Church, 2nd ser., vol. 2. New York, 1891.
Theodoret. *The Ecclesiastical History*. Translated by Blomfield Jackson. In *Theodoret, Jerome, Gennadius, Rufinus: Historical Writings, Etc.*, ed. Philip Schaff and Henry Wace, 33–159. A Select Library of Nicene and Post-Nicene Fathers of the Christian Church, 2nd ser., vol. 3. New York, 1892.
Translatio Sancti Germani Parisiensis. Analecta Bollandiana 2 (1883): 69–98.
Valerius Maximus. *Memorable Deeds and Sayings*. Translated by H. J. Walker. Indianapolis, 2004.
van Houts, Elisabeth M. C., ed. and trans. *The Gesta Normannorum Ducum of William of Jumièges, Orderic Vitalis, and Robert of Torigni*. 2 vols. Oxford Medieval Texts. Oxford, 1992–95.
Walter the Chancellor. *The Antiochene Wars*. Translated by Thomas S. Asbridge and Susan B. Edgington. Crusade Texts in Translation. Aldershot, 1999.
———. *Bella Antiochena*. Edited by Heinrich Hagenmeyer. Innsbruck, 1896.

William of Apulia. *Gesta Roberti Wiscardi.* Edited by Marguerite Mathieu. Palermo, 1961.
William of Malmesbury. *Gesta regum Anglorum.* Edited and translated by R. A. B. Manors, Rodney M. Thomson, and Michael Winterbottom. 2 vols. Oxford, 1998.
William of Newburgh. *The History of English Affairs.* Edited and translated by P. G. Walsh and M. J. Kennedy. Warminster, 1988.
William of Poitiers. *The Gesta Guillelmi.* Edited and translated by R. H. C. Davis and Marjorie Chibnall. Oxford, 1998.
William of Tyre. *Chronique.* Edited by Robert Burchard Constantijn Huygens. 2 vols. CCCM, vols. 63–63A. Turnhout, 1986.
———. *A History of Deeds Done Beyond the Sea.* Translated by Emily Atwater Babcock and A. C. Krey. 2 vols. New York, 1943.
Xenophon. *Hellenica.* Edited and translated by Carleton L. Brownson. 2 vols. London, 1918–21.
Zosimus. *New History.* Translated by Ronald T. Ridley. Byzantina Australiensia, vol. 2. Sydney, 1982.

SECONDARY SOURCES

Abel-Turby, Mickey. "The New World Augustinians and Franciscans in Philosophical Opposition: The Visual Statement." *Colonial Latin American Review* 5 (1996): 7–23.
Ainsworth, Peter. "Contemporary and 'Eyewitness' History." In *Historiography in the Middle Ages,* ed. Deborah Mauskopf Deliyannis, 249–76. Leiden, 2003.
Akbari, Suzanne Conklin. "Alexander in the Orient: Bodies and Boundaries in the *Roman de toute chevalerie*." In *Postcolonial Approaches to the European Middle Ages: Translating Cultures*, ed. Ananya Jahanara Kabir and Deanne Williams, 105–26. Cambridge, 2005.
———. "From Due East to True North: Orientalism and Orientation." In *The Postcolonial Middle Ages*, ed. Jeffrey Jerome Cohen, 19–34. New York, 2000.
———. *Idols in the East: European Representations of Islam and the Orient.* Ithaca, 2009.
Albu, Emily. "Bohemond and the Rooster: Byzantines, Normans, and the Artful Ruse." In *Anna Komnene and Her Times*, ed. Thalia Gouma-Peterson, 157–68. New York, 2000.
———. *The Normans and Their Histories: Propaganda, Myth, and Subversion.* Woodbridge, UK, 2001.
———. "Probing the Passions of a Norman on Crusade: The *Gesta Francorum et Aliorum Hierosolimitanorum*." *Anglo-Norman Studies* 27 (2004): 1–15.
Allen, Richard Hinckley. *Star Names: Their Lore and Meaning.* 1899. Reprint, New York, 1963.
Alphandéry, Paul. "Les citations bibliques chez les historiens de la première croisade." *Revue d'Histoire des Religions* 99 (1929): 137–57.
Amory, Frederic. "The Viking Hasting in Franco-Scandinavian Legend." In *Saints, Scholars, and Heroes: Studies in Medieval Culture in Honor of Charles W. Jones*, ed. Margot H. King and Wesley M. Stevens, 2 vols., 2:265–86. Collegeville, Minn., 1971.
Angelidi, Christine, and Titos Papamastorakis. "Picturing the Spiritual Protector: From Blanchernitissa to Hodegetria." In *Images of the Mother of God: Perceptions of the Theotokos in Byzantium*, ed. Maria Vassilaki, 209–23. Aldershot, 2005.
Angold, Michael. *The Byzantine Empire, 1025–1204: A Political History.* 2nd ed. London, 1997.
Asbridge, Thomas S. *The Creation of the Principality of Antioch, 1098–1130.* Woodbridge, UK, 2000.

———. *The First Crusade: A New History*. 2nd edition. London, 2005.
———. "The Holy Lance of Antioch: Power, Devotion, and Memory on the First Crusade." *Reading Medieval Studies* 33 (2007): 3–36.
Assmann, Jan. *Death and Salvation in Ancient Egypt*. Ithaca, 2001.
Auerbach, Erich. *Figura*. Paris, 2003.
Auffarth, Christoph. *Irdische Wege und himmlischer Lohn: Kreuzzug, Jerusalem, und Fegefeuer in religionswissenschaftlicher Perspektive*. Göttingen, 2002.
Baritz, Loren. "The Idea of the West." *American Historical Review* 66, no. 3 (1961): 618–40.
Bar-Kochva, Bezalel. *Judas Maccabaeus: The Jewish Struggle Against the Seleucids*. Cambridge, 1989.
Bartlett, Robert. *Trial by Fire and Water: The Medieval Judicial Ordeal*. New York, 1986.
Bautier, Robert-Henri. "L'école historique de l'abbaye de Fleury d'Aimon à Hugues de Fleury." In *Histoires de France, Historiens de France*, ed. Yves-Marie Bercé and Philippe Contamine, 59–72. Paris, 1994.
———. "La place de l'abbaye de Fleury-sur-Loire dans l'historiographie française du IXe au XIIe siècle." In *Études ligériennes d'histoire et d'archéologie médiévales*, ed. René Louis, 25–33. Auxerre, 1975.
Baynes, Norman H. "The Death of Julian the Apostate in a Christian Legend." *Journal of Roman Studies* 27 (1937): 22–29.
Beech, George T. "A Norman-Italian Adventurer in the East: Richard of Salerno, 1097–1112." *Anglo-Norman Studies* 15 (1993): 25–40.
———. "The Remarkable Life of Ansger, a Breton Monk and Poet from the Loire Valley Who Became Bishop of Catania in Sicily, 1091–1124." *Viator* 45 (2014): 149–74.
Beer, Jeanette M. A. *Narrative Conventions of Truth in the Middle Ages*. Geneva, 1981.
Bellomo, Elena. *A servizio di Dio e del Santo Sepolcro: Caffaro e l'Oriente latino*. Padua, 2003.
Belting, Hans. *Likeness and Presence: A History of the Image Before the Era of Art*. Chicago, 1994.
Bengston, Jonathan. "Saint George and the Formation of English Nationalism." *Journal of Medieval and Early Medieval Studies* 27 (1997): 317–40.
Bercovitch, Sacvan. *The Puritan Origins of the American Self*. New Haven, 1975.
Berger, David. "The Attitude of St. Bernard of Clairvaux Toward the Jews." *Proceedings of the American Academy for Jewish Research* 40 (1972): 89–108.
Berkeley, David S. "Some Misapprehensions of Christian Typology in Recent Literary Scholarship." *Studies in English Literature, 1500–1900* 18 (1978): 3–12.
Berrens, Stephan. *Sonnenkult und Kaisertum von den Severern bis zu Constantin I. (193–337 n. Chr)*. Stuttgart, 2004.
Biddlecombe, Steven. "Baldric of Bourgueil and the *Familia Christi*." In *Writing the Early Crusades: Text, Transmission, and Memory*, ed. Marcus Bull and Damien Kempf, 9–23. Woodbridge, UK, 2014.
Binon, Ste'phane. *Essai sur le cycle de saint Mercure, martyr de Dèce et meurtrier de l'empereur Julien*. Paris, 1937.
Bisaha, Nancy. *Creating East and West: Renaissance Humanists and the Ottoman Turks*. Philadelphia, 2006.
Borsook, Eve. *Messages in Mosaic: The Royal Programmes of Norman Sicily (1130–1187)*. Woodbridge, UK, 1990.
Bowersock, G. W. *Julian the Apostate*. Cambridge, Mass., 1978.
Boyarin, Daniel. *Carnal Israel: Reading Sex in Talmudic Culture*. Berkeley, 1993.
Braun, Rene', and Jean Richer, eds. *L'empereur Julien de l'histoire à la légende*. Paris, 1978.
Bronstein, Judith. "The Crusades and the Jews: Some Reflections on the 1096 Massacre." *History Compass* 5 (2007): 1268–79.

Brown, Cecil H. "Where Do Cardinal Direction Terms Come From?" *Anthropological Linguistics* 25, no. 2 (1983): 121–61.
Brown, Peter. *Augustine of Hippo: A Biography*. Berkeley, 1967.
———. *The Body and Society: Men, Women, and Sexual Renunciation in Early Christianity*. New York, 1988.
———. "Eastern and Western Christendom in Late Antiquity: A Parting of the Ways." In *The Orthodox Churches and the West*, ed. Derek Baker, 1–24. Studies in Church History 13. Oxford, 1976.
———. "Society and the Supernatural: A Medieval Change." In Brown, *Society and the Holy in Late Antiquity*, 302–32. London, 1982.
Browning, Robert. *The Emperor Julian*. Berkeley, 1976.
Buc, Philippe. *L'ambiguïté du livre, prince, pouvoir et peuple dans les commentaires de la Bible au Moyen Âge*. Paris, 1994.
———. "La vengeance de Dieu: De l'exégèse patristique à la réforme ecclésiastique et à la première croisade." In *La vengeance, 400–1200*, ed. Dominique Barthélemy, François Bougard, and Régine Le Jan, 451–86. Rome, 2006.
Bull, Marcus. "The Relationship Between the *Gesta Francorum* and Peter Tudebode's *Historia de Hierosolymitano Itinere*: The Evidence of a Hitherto Unexamined Manuscript (St. Catharine's College, Cambridge, 3)." *Crusades* 11 (2012): 1–17.
———. "The Roots of Lay Enthusiasm for the First Crusade." *History* 78 (1993): 353–72.
———. "Views of Muslims and of Jerusalem in Miracle Stories, c. 1000–c. 1200: Reflections on the Study of First Crusaders' Motivations." In *The Experience of Crusading*, vol. 1, *Western Perspectives*, ed. Marcus Bull and Norman Housley, 13–38. Cambridge, 2003.
———. "The Western Narratives of the First Crusade." In *Christian-Muslims Relations: A Bibliographical History*, ed. David Thomas and Alex Mallett, 6 vols. to date, 3:15–25. Leiden, 2009–.
Bull, Marcus, and Damien Kempf, eds. *Writing the Early Crusades: Text, Transmission, and Memory*. Woodbridge, UK, 2014.
Bynum, C. Walker. *Holy Feast and Holy Fast: The Religious Significance of Food to Medieval Women*. Berkeley, 1987.
Callahan, Daniel. "The Cult of St. Michael the Archangel and the 'Terrors of the Year 1000.'" In *The Apocalyptic Year 1000: Religious Expectation and Social Change, 950–1050*, ed. Richard Allen Landes, Andrew Gow, and David C. van Meter, 181–204. Oxford, 2003.
Cameron, Averil. "Elites and Icons in Late Sixth-Century Byzantium." *Past and Present* 84 (1979): 3–35.
Capitani, Ovidio. "Specific Motivations and Continuing Themes in the Norman Chronicles of Southern Italy in the Eleventh and Twelfth Centuries." In Ovidio Capitani, Giuseppe Galasso, and Roberto Salvini, *The Normans in Sicily and Southern Italy*, 1–46. Oxford, 1977.
Carletti, Carlo, and Giorgio Otranto, eds. *Culto e insediamenti micaelici nell'Italia meridionale fra tarda antichità e medioevo*. Bari, 1994.
Carozzi, Claude, and Huguette Taviani-Carozzi, eds. *Peuples du Moyen Âge: Problèmes d'identification*. Aix-en-Provence, 1996.
Carrier, Marc. "Pour en finir avec les *Gesta Francorum*: Une réflexion historiographique sur l'état des rapports entre Grecs et Latins au début du XIIe siècle et sur l'apport nouveau d'Albert d'Aix." *Crusades* 7 (2008): 13–34.
Caspary, Gerard E. *Politics and Exegesis: Origen and the Two Swords*. Berkeley, 1979.
Chalandon, Ferdinand. *Histoire de la domination normande en Italie et en Sicile*. 2 vols. Paris, 1907.

Chaurand, Jacques. "La conception de l'histoire de Guibert of Nogent." *Cahiers de Civilisation Médiévale* 8 (1965): 381–95.
Chazan, Robert. "'Let not a remnant or a residue escape': Millenarian Enthusiasm in the First Crusade." *Speculum* 84 (2009): 289–313.
———. *Medieval Stereotypes and Modern Antisemitism*. London, 1997.
Chenu, Marie-Dominique. *La théologie au douzième siècle*. Paris, 1957.
Chevedden, Paul E. "'A Crusade from the First': The Norman Conquest of Islamic Sicily, 1060–1091." *Al-Masaq: Islam and the Medieval Mediterranean* 22 (2010): 191–225.
Cheynet, Jean-Claude. "Le culte de saint Théodore chez les officiers de l'armée d'Orient." In *Vyzantio kratos kai koinōnia: Mnēmē Nikou Oikonomidē* [Byzantium: State and Society; In Memory of Nikos Oikonomides], ed. Anna Avramea, Angeliki E. Laiou, Euangelos K. Chrysos, and Nicolas Oikonomide's, 137–54. Athens, 2003.
———. "Par saint Georges, par saint Michel." *Travaux et mémoires: Mélanges G. Dagron* 14 (2002): 114–34.
Chibnall, Marjorie. *The Normans*. Oxford, 2001.
Chrétien, Jean-Louis. "Neuf propositions sur le concept chrétien de témoignage." *Philosophie* 88 (2005): 75–94.
———. *Saint Augustin et les actes de parole*. Paris, 2002.
Christe, Yves. *L'Apocalypse de Jean: Sens et développement de ses visions synthétiques*. Paris, 1996.
Christie, Neil. *The Lombards: The Ancient Longobards*. Oxford, 1995.
Ciggaar, Krijnie Nelly. *Western Travellers to Constantinople: The West and Byzantium, 962-1204; Cultural and Political Relations*. Leiden, 1998.
Cizek, Alexandre. "L'historia comme témoignage oculaire: Quelques implications et conséquences de la définition de l'historiographie chez Isidore de Séville." In *Histoire et littérature au Moyen Âge: Actes du colloque du Centre d'Études Médiévales de l'Université de Picardie, Amiens, 20-24 mars 1985*, ed. Danielle Buschinger, 69–84. Göppingen, 1991.
Clarke, David. *The Angels of Mons: Phantom Soldiers and Ghostly Guardians*. Chichester, 2004.
Cohen, Jeremy. "The Muslim Connection, or On the Changing Role of the Jew in High Medieval Theology." In *From Witness to Witchcraft: Jews and Judaism in Medieval Christian Thought*, ed. Jeremy Cohen, 141–62. Wiesbaden, 1996.
———. "'Slay Them Not': Augustine and the Jews in Modern Scholarship." *Medieval Encounters* 4 (1998): 78–92.
Cole, Penny J. "'O God, the Heathens Have Come into Your Inheritance' (Ps. 78:1): The Theme of Religious Pollution in Crusade Documents, 1095–1188." In *Crusaders and Muslims in Twelfth-Century Syria*, ed. Maya Shatzmiller, 84–111. Leiden, 1993.
———. *The Preaching of the Crusades to the Holy Land, 1095-1270*. Cambridge, Mass., 1991.
Constable, Giles. "The Historiography of the Crusades." In *The Crusades from the Perspective of Byzantium and the Muslim World*, ed. Angeliki E. Laiou and Roy P. Mottahedeh, 1–22. Washington, D.C., 2001.
Cormack, Robert, and Stavros Mihalarias. "A Crusader Painting of St. George: 'Maniera greca' or 'lingua franca'?" *Burlington Magazine* 126 (1984): 132–41.
Cormack, Robin. "The Making of a Patron Saint: The Powers of Art and Ritual in Byzantine Thessaloniki." In *World Art: Themes of Unity in Diversity; Acts of the XXVIth International Congress of the History of Art*, ed. Irving Lavin, 3 vols., 3:547–57. University Park, 1989.

Cornell, Vincent J. "Fruit of the Tree of Knowledge: The Relationship Between Faith and Practice in Islam." In *The Oxford History of Islam*, ed. John L. Esposito, 63–105. Oxford, 1999.

Cowdrey, H. E. J. *The Age of Abbot Desiderius: Montecassino, the Papacy, and the Normans in the Eleventh and Early Twelfth Centuries.* Oxford, 1983.

———. "The Mahdia Campaign of 1087." *English Historical Review* 92 (1977): 1–29.

———. "Martyrdom and the First Crusade." In *Crusade and Settlement: Papers Read at the First Conference of the Society for the Study of the Crusades and the Latin East*, ed. Peter W. Edbury, 46–56. Cardiff, 1985.

———. *Pope Gregory VII.* Oxford, 1998.

———. "Pope Gregory VII and the Bearing of Arms." In *Montjoie: Studies in Crusade History in Honor of Hans Eberhard Mayer*, ed. Benjamin Z. Kedar, Jonathan Riley-Smith, and Rudolf Hiestand, 23–35. Aldershot, 1997.

———. "Pope Urban II and the Idea of Crusade." *Studi Medievali*, 3rd ser., 36 (1995): 721–42.

Crane, Ronald S. "Anglican Apologetics and the Idea of Progress, 1699–1745." In Crane, *The Idea of the Humanities and Other Essays Critical and Historical*, 214–87. Chicago, 1967.

Cutler, Allan Harris, and Helen Elmquist Cutler. *The Jew as Ally of the Muslim.* Notre Dame, 1986.

Daly, William. "Christian Fraternity, the Crusaders, and the Security of Constantinople, 1097–1204: The Precarious Survival of an Ideal." *Medieval Studies* 22 (1960): 43–91.

Damian-Grint, Peter. *The New Historians of the Twelfth-Century Renaissance: Inventing Vernacular Authority.* Woodbridge, UK, 1999.

Daniel, Norman. *Islam and the West: The Making of an Image.* Edinburgh, 1960.

Davis, R. H. C. *The Normans and Their Myth.* London, 1976.

Dehoux, Esther. "*Con avès non, vasal al ceval blanc?* Sur quelques apparitions des saints guerriers lors de combats, notamment dans la *Chanson d'Aspremont*." In *L'epopea normanna e il territorio*, 23–114. Reggio Calabria, 2007.

———. "Iconographie de l'archange et réforme grégorienne en Aquitaine septentrionale (Xe–XIIIe siècle)." In *Rappresentationi del Monte e dell'arcangelo san Michele nella letteratura e nelle arti*, ed. Pierre Bouet, Giorgio Otranto, André Vauchez, and Catherine Vincent, 109–33. Bari, 2011.

———. "Représenter le martyre: Images de saint Georges et de saint Maurice dans le regnum Francorum (IXe–XIIIe siècle)." In *Corps outragés, corps saccagés: Regards croisés de l'antiquité au Moyen Âge*, ed. Lydie Bodiou, Véronique Mehl, and Myriam Soria, 117–37. Turnhout, 2012.

———. "Saint Michel, saint Pierre et les sarrasins: Guerre, organisation sociale et préoccupations eschatologiques (IXe siècle–début du XIIe siècle)." In *L'arcangelo Michele dalla storia alla leggenda*, ed. Giampetro Casiraghi, 77–102. Stresa, 2012.

Deléani-Nigoul, Simone. "Les exempla bibliques du martyre." In *Le monde latin et la Bible*, ed. Jacques Fontaine and Charles Pietri, 243–60. Paris, 1985.

———. "Une typologie du martyre chrétien: La *Passion* des frères Maccabées et de leur mère selon saint Cyprien." In *Figures de l'Ancien Testament chez les Pères*, 189–213. Cahiers de Biblia Patristica 3. Strasbourg, 1989.

Delehaye, Hippolyte. *Les légendes grecques des saints militaires.* 1909. Reprint, New York, 1975.

Demus, Otto. *The Church of San Marco in Venice: History, Architecture, Sculpture.* Washington, D.C., 1960.

———. *The Mosaics of Norman Sicily.* London, 1949.

Derbes, Anne. *Picturing the Passion in Late Medieval Italy: Narrative Painting, Franciscan Ideologies, and the Levant.* Cambridge, 1996.

Deschamps, Paul. "La légende de Saint George et les combats des Croisés dans les peintures murales du Moyen Âge." *Monuments et Mémoires* 44 (1950): 109–23.

Dickey, Lawrence. "*Translatio Imperii* and *Translatio Religionis*: The 'Geography of Salvation' in Russian and American Messianic Thinking." In *The Cultural Gradient: The Transmission of Ideas in Europe, 1789–1991*, ed. Catherine Evtuhov and Stephen Kotkin, 13–32. Lanham, Md., 2003.

Didi-Huberman, Georges, Riccardo Garbetta, and Manuela Morgaine. *Saint George et le dragon: Versions d'une légende.* Paris 1994.

Dijk, Hans van, and Willem Noomen, eds. *Aspects de l'épopée romane: Mentalités, idéologies, intertextualités.* Groningen, 1995.

Donne, Fulvio Delle. "Le inscrizioni del mausoleo di Boemondo d'Altavilla a Canosa." *Archivo Normanno-Svevo* 3 (2011–12): 9–18.

Douglas, David C. *Norman Achievement, 1050–1100.* Berkeley, 1969.

Drell, Joanna. "Cultural Syncretism and Ethnic Identity: The Norman 'Conquest' of Southern Italy and Sicily." *Journal of Medieval History* 26 (1999): 187–202.

Dunbabin, Jean. "The Maccabees as Exemplars in the Tenth and Eleventh Centuries." In *The Bible in the Medieval World: Essays in Memory of Beryl Smalley*, ed. Katherine Walsh and Diana Wood, 31–41. Oxford, 1985.

Duncalf, Frederic. "First Crusade: Clermont to Constantinople." In *A History of the Crusades*, ed. Kenneth Meyer Setton, 6 vols., 1:253–79. Madison, 1969–89.

Dunn, Marilyn. "Eastern Influence on Western Monasticism in the Eleventh and Twelfth Centuries." In *Byzantium and the West, c. 850–1200*, ed. James Howard-Johnston, 245–59. Amsterdam, 1988.

Edgington, Susan B. "Albert of Aachen and the *chansons de geste*." In *The Crusades and Their Sources: Essays Presented to Bernard Hamilton*, ed. John France and William G. Zajac, 23–37. Aldershot, 1998.

———. "Albert of Aachen Reappraised." In *From Clermont to Jerusalem: The Crusades and Crusader Societies, 1095–1500; Selected Proceedings of the International Medieval Congress, University of Leeds, 10–13 July 1995*, ed. Alan V. Murray, 55–68. Turnhout, 1998.

———. "The First Crusade: Reviewing the Evidence." In *The First Crusade: Origins and Impact*, ed. J. P. Phillips, 55–77. Manchester, 1997.

Ellenblum, Ronnie. *The Collapse of the Eastern Mediterranean: Climate Change and the Decline of the East, 950–1072.* Cambridge, 2012.

Emmerson, Richard K. "*Figura* and the Medieval Typological Imagination." In *Typology and English Medieval Literature*, ed. Hugh T. Keenan, 7–42. New York, 1992.

Epstein, Ann Wharton. "The Date and Significance of the Cathedral of Canosa in Apulia, South Italy." *Dumbarton Oaks Papers* 37 (1983): 79–90.

Erdmann, Carl. *The Origin of the Idea of Crusade.* Translated by Marshall W. Baldwin and Walter Goffart. Princeton, 1977.

Everett, Nicholas. "The *Liber de Apparitione S. Michaelis in Monte Gargano* and the Hagiography of Dispossession." *Analecta Bollandiana* 120 (2002): 364–91.

Fabre-Vassas, Claudine. *La bête singulière: Les juifs, les chrétiens et le cochon.* Paris, 1994.

Fink, Harold S. "The Foundation of the Latin States, 1099–1144." In *A History of the Crusades*, ed. Kenneth Meyer Setton, 6 vols., 1:368–409. Madison, 1969–89.

Fischer, Jürgen. *Oriens—Occidens—Europa: Begriff und Gedanke "Europa" in der späten Antike und im frühen Mittelalter.* Wiesbaden, 1957.

Fischer, Mary. "The Books of the Maccabees and the Teutonic Order." *Crusades* 4 (2005): 59–72.

Fletcher, Richard. "Reconquest and Crusade in Spain, c. 1050–1150." *Transactions of the Royal Historical Society*, 5th ser., 37 (1987): 31–47.

———. *Saint James's Catapult: The Life and Times of Diego Gelmírez of Santiago de Compostela*. Oxford, 1984.

Flori, Jean. *Bohémond d'Antioche: Chevalier d'aventure*. Paris, 2007.

———. *Chroniqueurs et propagandistes: Introduction critique aux sources de la première croisade*. Geneva, 2010.

———. "De l'anonyme normand à Tudebode et aux *Gesta Francorum*: L'impact de la propagande de Bohémond sur la critique textuelle des sources de la première croisade." *Revue d'Histoire Ecclésiastique* 102 (2007): 717–46.

———. *La guerre sainte: La formation de l'ide'e de croisade dans l'Occident chre'tien*. Paris, 2001.

———. "Mort et martyre des guerriers vers 1100: L'exemple de la première croisade." *Cahiers de Civilisation Médiévale* 34 (1991): 121–39.

Folda, Jaroslav. "Mounted Warrior Saints in Crusader Icons: Images of the Knighthoods of Christ." In *Knighthoods of Christ: Essays on the History of the Crusades and the Knights Templar, Presented to Malcolm Barber*, ed. Norman Housley, 87–107. Aldershot, 2007.

Fontaine, Jacques. *Isidore de Séville et la culture classique dans l'espace wisigothique*. 2nd ed. 2 vols. Paris, 1983.

Forde, Simon, Lesley Johnson, and Alan V. Murray, eds. *Concepts of National Identity in the Middle Ages*. Leeds, 1995.

Forrai, Réka. "The Interpreter of the Popes: The Translation Project of Anastasius Bibliothecarius." PhD diss., Central European University, Budapest, 2008.

France, John. "The Anonymous *Gesta Francorum* and the *Historia Francorum qui ceperunt Iherusalem* of Raymond of Aguilers and the *Historia de Hierosolymitano itinere* of Peter Tudebode: An Analysis of the Textual Relationship Between Primary Sources for the First Crusade." In *The Crusades and Their Sources: Essays Presented to Bernard Hamilton*, ed. John France and William G. Zajac, 39–69. Aldershot, 1998.

———. "Byzantium in Western Chronicles Before the First Crusade." In *Knighthoods of Christ: Essays on the History of the Crusades and the Knights Templar, Presented to Malcolm Barber*, ed. Norman Housley, 3–16. Aldershot, 2007.

———. "The Departure of Tatikios from the Crusader Army." *Bulletin of the Institute of Historical Research* 44 (1971): 137–47.

———. "Holy War and Holy Men: Erdmann and the Lives of the Saints." In *The Experience of Crusading: Western Approaches*, ed. Marcus Bull and Norman Housley, 193–208. Cambridge, 2003.

———. "The Normans and Crusading." In *The Normans and Their Adversaries at War*, ed. Richard Philip Abels and Bernard S. Bachrach, 87–101. Woodbridge, UK, 2001.

———. "The Occasion of the Coming of the Normans to Italy." *Journal of Medieval History* 17 (1991): 185–205.

———. "Patronage and the Appeal of the First Crusade." In *The First Crusade: Origins and Impact*, ed. Jonathan Phillips, 5–17. Manchester, 1997.

———. "The Text of the Account of the Capture of Jerusalem in the Ripoll Manuscript, Bibliothèque Nationale (Latin) 5132." *English Historical Review* 102 (1988): 640–58.

———. "The Use of the Anonymous *Gesta Francorum* in the Early Twelfth-Century Sources for the First Crusade." In *From Clermont to Jerusalem: The Crusades and Crusader Societies, 1095–1500; Selected Proceedings of the International Medieval Congress, University of Leeds, 10–13 July 1995*, ed. Alan V. Murray, 29–42. Turnhout, 1998.

———. *Victory in the East: A Military History of the First Crusade*. Cambridge, 1994.
Frankopan, Peter. *The First Crusade: A Call from the East*. London, 2012.
———. "Turning Latin into Greek: Anna Komnene and the *Gesta Roberti Wiscardi*." *Journal of Medieval History* 39 (2013): 80–99.
Fraser, James E. "Adomnán and the Morality of War." In *Adomnán of Iona: Theologian, Lawmaker, Peacemaker*, ed. Jonathan M. Wooding, with Rodney Aist, Thomas Owen Clancy, and Thomas O'Loughlin, 95–111. Dublin, 2010.
Frend, William Hugh Clifford. *Martyrdom and Persecution in the Early Church: A Study of a Conflict from the Maccabees to Donatus*. Garden City, N.Y., 1965.
———. "Martyrdom in East and West: The Saga of St. George of Nobatia and England." In *Martyrs and Martyrologies*, ed. Diana Wood, 47–56. Studies in Church History 30. Oxford, 1993.
Frendo, Joseph D. C. "The Miracles of St. Demetrius and the Capture of Thessaloniki: An Examination of the Purpose, Significance, and Authenticity of John Kaminiates' *De Expugnatione Thessalonicae*." *Byzantinoslavica* 58 (1997): 205–24.
Friedman, John B. "Cultural Conflicts in Medieval World Maps." In *Implicit Understandings: Observing, Reporting, and Reflecting on the Encounters Between Europeans and Other Peoples in the Early Modern Era*, ed. Stuart B. Schwartz, 64–95. Cambridge, 1994.
Gadolin, Anitra R. "Prince Bohemond's Death and Apotheosis." *Byzantion* 52 (1982): 124–53.
Galdi, Amalia. *Santi, territori, poteri e uomini nella Campagnia medievale (secc. XI–XII)*. Salerno, 2004.
Gaposchkin, M. Cecilia. "Louis IX, Crusade, and the Promise of Joshua in the Holy Land." *Journal of Medieval History* 34 (2008): 245–74.
García, Javier Domínguez. "Santiago Mataindios: La continuación de un discurso medieval en la Nueva España." *Nueva Revista de Filología Hispánica* 54 (2006): 33–56.
Geanakoplos, Deno John. *Interaction of the "Sibling" Byzantine and Western Cultures in the Middle Ages and Italian Renaissance*. New Haven, 1976.
Geary, Patrick J. *Furta Sacra: The Theft of Relics in the Central Middle Ages*. Princeton, 1978.
———. *Phantoms of Remembrance: Memory and Oblivion at the End of the First Millennium*. Princeton, 1995.
Gera, Dov. *Judaea and Mediterranean Politics, 219 to 161 BC*. Leiden, 1998.
Gerbi, Antonello. *The Dispute of the New World: The History of a Polemic, 1750–1900*. Translated by Jeremy Moyle. Pittsburgh, 1973.
Giese, Wolfgang. "Die 'lancea Domini' von Antiochia." In *Fälschungen im Mittelalter: Internationaler Kongreß der Monumenta Germaniae Historica, München, 16.–19. September 1986; 5 Fingierte Briefe, Frömmigkeit und Fälschung. Realienfälschungen*, ed. Wolfram Setz, 5 vols., 5:485–504. Hanover, 1998.
Glacken, Clarence J. *Traces on the Rhodian Shore: Nature and Culture in Western Thought from Ancient Times to the End of the Eighteenth Century*. Berkeley, 1967.
Goar, Robert Jefferson. *Cicero and the State Religion*. Amsterdam, 1972.
Goez, Werner. *Translatio Imperii: Ein Beitrag zur Geschichte des Geschichtsdenkens und der politischen Theorien im Mittelalter und in der frühen Neuzeit*. Tübingen, 1958.
Goffart, Walter. *The Narrators of Barbarian History (A.D. 550–800): Jordanes, Gregory of Tours, Bede, and Paul the Deacon*. Princeton, 1988.
Goldreich, Yair. *The Climate of Israel: Observation, Research, and Application*. New York, 2003.
Good, Jonathan. *The Cult of Saint George in Medieval England*. Woodbridge, UK, 2009.
Gordon, Burton L. "Sacred Directions, Orientation, and the Top of the Map." *History of Religions* 10, no. 3 (1971): 211–27.

Goss, Vladimir P., and Christine V. Bornstein, eds. *The Meeting of Two Worlds: Cultural Exchange Between East and West During the Period of the Crusades*. Kalamazoo, 1986.
Gouguenheim, Sylvain. "Les Maccabées, modèles des guerriers chrétiens des origines au XIIe siècle." *Cahiers de Civilisation Médiévale* 54 (2011): 3–20.
Gouma-Peterson, Thalia, ed. *Anna Komnene and Her Times*. New York, 2000.
Green, Jonathon. *Slang Down the Ages: The Historical Development of Slang*. London, 1993.
Grierson, Philip. "The Salernitan Coinage of Gisulf II (1052–1077) and Robert Guiscard (1077–1085)." *Papers of the British School of Rome* 24 (1956): 37–59.
Grotowski, Piotr. *Arms and Armour of the Warrior Saints: Tradition and Innovation in Byzantine Iconography (843–1261)*. Translated by Richard Brzezinski. Leiden, 2010.
Guenée, Bernard. *Histoire et culture historique dans l'Occident médiéval*. Paris, 1980.
Hagenmeyer, Heinrich. *Chronologie de la première croisade, 1094–1100*. 1902. Reprint, Hildesheim, 1973.
Haldon, John. *Warfare, State, and Society in the Byzantine World, 565–1024*. London, 1999.
Hamilton, Sarah. *The Practice of Penance, 900–1050*. Woodbridge, UK, 2001.
Hanak, Walter K. "The Infamous Svjatoslav: Master of Duplicity in War and Peace." *Peace and War in Byzantium: Essays in Honor of George T. Dennis*, ed. Timothy S. Miller and John W. Nesbitt, 138–51. Washington, D.C., 1995.
Hanawalt, Emily Albu. "Norman Views of Eastern Christendom: From the First Crusade to the Principality of Antioch." In *The Meeting of Two Worlds: Cultural Exchange Between East and West During the Period of the Crusades*, ed. Vladimir P. Goss and Christine V. Bornstein, 115–21. Kalamazoo, 1986.
Harari, Yuval Noah. "Eyewitnessing in Accounts of the First Crusade: The *Gesta Francorum* and Other Contemporary Narratives." *Crusades* 3 (2004): 77–99.
Hare, Kent J. "Apparitions and War in Anglo-Saxon England." In *The Circle of War in the Middle Ages: Essays in Military and Naval History*, ed. Donald J. Kagay and L. J. Andrew Villalon, 76–86. Woodbridge, UK, 1999.
Har-Peled, Misgav. "Animalité, pureté et croisade: Étude sur la transformation des églises en étables par les musulmans durant les croisades (XIIe–XIIIe siècles)." *Cahiers de Civilisation Médiévale* 52 (2009): 113–36.
Harris, Jonathan. *Byzantium and the Crusades*. London, 2003.
Hartog, François. *Évidence de l'histoire: Ce que voient les historiens*. Paris, 2005.
Hasegawa, Ichiro. "Orbits of Ancient and Medieval Comets." *Publications of the Astronomical Society of Japan* 31 (1979): 257–70.
Haskins, Charles Homer. *The Normans in European History*. Boston, 1915.
Haverkampf, Eva. "Martyrs in Rivalry: The 1096 Jewish Martyrs and the Thebean Legion." *Jewish History* 23 (2009): 319–42.
Hay, Denys. *Europe: The Emergence of an Idea*. Edinburgh, 1957.
Head, Thomas. "Andrew of Fleury and the Peace League of Bourges." *Historical Reflections/Réflexions Historiques* 14 (1987): 513–29.
———. *Hagiography and the Cult of Saints: The Diocese of Orléans, 800–1200*. Cambridge, 1990.
Hendy, Michael F. *Coinage and Money in the Byzantine Empire, 1081–1261*. Washington, D.C., 1969.
Hess, Rosmarie. "Das Bodenmosaik von S. Colombano in Bobbio." *Arte Medievale* 2 (1988): 103–40.
Hiestand, R. "Il cronista medievale e il suo pubblico: Alcune osservazioni in margine alla storiografia delle crociate." *Annali della Facoltà di Lettere e Filosofia dell'Università di Napoli*, new ser., 25 (1984–85): 207–27.
Hill, Joyce. "Aelfric, Gelasius, and St. George." *Mediaevalia* 11 (1985): 1–17.

Hillenbrand, Carole. *The Crusades: Islamic Perspectives*. Edinburgh, 1999.
Hodgson, Natasha. "Reinventing Normans as Crusaders? Ralph of Caen's *Gesta Tancredi*." *Anglo-Norman Studies* 30 (2008): 117-32.
Hoffmann, Hartmut. "Die Anfänge der Normannen in Süditalien." *Quellen und Forschungen aus Italianischen Archiven und Bibliotheken* 47 (1967): 95-144.
Holdsworth, Christopher. "'An Airier Aristocracy': The Saints at War." *Transactions of the Royal Historical Society*, 6th ser., 6 (1996): 103-22.
Hollander, Robert. "Typology and Secular Literature: Some Medieval Problems and Examples." In *Literary Uses of Typology from the Late Middle Ages to the Present*, ed. Earl Miner, 3-19. Princeton, 1977.
Houben, Hubert. *Roger II of Sicily: A Ruler Between East and West*. Translated by Graham A. Loud and Diane Milburn. Cambridge, 2002.
Housley, Norman. *Fighting for the Cross: Crusading to the Holy Land*. New Haven, 2008.
Howard-Johnston, James. "Anna Komnene and the *Alexiad*." In *Alexios I Komnenos*, ed. Margaret Mullett and Dion Smythe, 232-302. Belfast, 1996.
———, ed. *Byzantium and the West, c. 850-1200*. Amsterdam, 1988.
Howell, David. "St. George as Intercessor." *Byzantion* 39 (1969): 121-36.
Huber, P. Michael. "Zur Georgslegende." *Festschrift zum 12. Deutschen Neuphilologentag in München*, ed. Eugen Stollreither, 174-235. Erlangen, 1906.
Hunt, Harold Arthur Kinross. *The Humanism of Cicero*. Melbourne, 1954.
Hyams, P. "Trial by Ordeal: The Key to Proof in the Early Common Law." In *On the Laws and Customs of England: Essays in Honor of Samuel E. Thorne*, ed. Morris S. Arnold, Thomas A. Green, Sally A. Scully, and Stephen White, 90-126. Chapel Hill, 1981.
Immerzeel, Mat. "Divine Cavalry: Mounted Saints in Middle Eastern Christian Art." In *East and West in the Crusader States: Context, Contacts, and Confrontations*, ed. Krijnie Ciggaar and Herman Teule, 3 vols., 3:265-86. Louvain, 1996-2003.
———. "Holy Horsemen and Crusader Banners: Equestrian Saints in Wall Paintings in Lebanon and Syria." *Eastern Christian Art* 1 (2004): 29-60.
Jamison, Evelyn. *The Sicilian Norman Kingdom in the Mind of Anglo-Norman Contemporaries*. London, 1938.
———. "Some Notes on the *Anonymi Gesta Francorum*." In *Studies in French Language and Mediaeval Literature Presented to Professor Mildred K. Pope by Pupils, Colleagues, and Friends*, 183-208. Manchester, 1939.
Janin, R. "Les églises byzantines des saints militaires." *Echos d'Orient* 33 (1934): 163-80, 331-42; 34 (1935): 56-70.
Janson, Tore. *Latin Prose Prefaces: Studies in Literary Conventions*. Stockholm, 1964.
Jeffreys, Elizabeth. "Western Infiltration of the Byzantine Aristocracy: Some Suggestions." In *The Byzantine Aristocracy: IX to XIII Centuries*, ed. Michael Angold, 202-10. Oxford, 1984.
Jenkins, Romilly James Heald. "The Bronze Athena at Byzantium." *Journal of Hellenic Studies* 67 (1947): 31-33.
Johnson, Ewan. "Normandy and Norman Identity in Southern Italian Chronicles." *Anglo-Norman Studies* 27 (2005): 85-100.
Johnson, James Turner. *The Holy War Idea in Western and Islamic Traditions*. University Park, 1997.
Johnson, Richard F. *Saint Michael the Archangel in Medieval English Legend*. Woodbridge, UK, 2005.
Jones, Charles W. *Saint Nicholas of Myra, Bari, and Manhattan: Biography of a Legend*. Chicago, 1978.

Jongkees, A. G. "*Translatio studii*: Les avatars d'un thème médiéval." In *Miscellanea Mediaevalia in Memoriam Jan Frederik Niermeyer*, ed. D. P. Blok, A. Bruckner, G. Van Herwijnen, T. S. Jansma, C. van de Kieft, H. van Werveke, and Ph. Wolff, 41–51. Groningen, 1967.

Joranson, Einar. "The Inception of the Career of the Normans in Italy: Legend and History." *Speculum* 23 (1948): 353–96.

Joslyn-Siemiatkoski, Daniel. *Christian Memories of the Maccabean Martyrs*. New York, 2009.

Kaeuper, Richard W. *Holy Warriors: The Religious Ideology of Chivalry*. Philadelphia, 2009.

Kantorowicz, Ernst H. *Laudes Regiae: A Study of Liturgical Acclamations and Medieval Ruler Worship*. Berkeley, 1958.

Katzenellenbogen, Adolf. "The Central Tympanum at Vézelay: Its Encyclopedic Meaning and Its Relation to the First Crusade." *Art Bulletin* 26, no. 3 (1944): 141–51.

Kazhdan, Alexander P., ed. *Oxford Dictionary of Byzantium*. 3 vols. Oxford, 1991.

Kazhdan, Alexander P., and Ann Wharton Epstein. *Change in Byzantine Culture in the Eleventh and Twelfth Centuries*. Berkeley, 1985.

Keller, Hagen. "*Machabaeorum pugnae*: Zum Stellenwert eines biblischen Vorbilds in Widukinds Deutung der ottonischen Königsherrschaft." In *Iconologia sacra: Mythos, Bildkunst, und Dichtung in der Religions- und Socialgeschichte Alteuropas*, ed. Karl Hauck, Hagen Keller, and Nikolaus Staubach, 417–37. Berlin, 1994.

Kendrick, Thomas Downing. *Saint James in Spain*. London, 1960.

King, Noel Quinton. *The Emperor Theodosius and the Establishment of Christianity*. London, 1961.

Kinoshita, Sharon. *Medieval Boundaries: Rethinking Difference in Old French Literature*. Philadelphia, 2006.

Kitzinger, Ernst. "On the Portrait of Roger II in the Martorana in Palermo." In Kitzinger, *The Art of Byzantium and the Medieval West: Selected Studies*, 320–26. Bloomington, 1976.

Klein, Holger. "Eastern Objects and Western Desires." *Dumbarton Oaks Papers* 58 (2004): 283–314.

Kolbaba, Tia. "Fighting for Christianity: Holy War in the Byzantine Empire." *Byzantion* 68 (1998): 194–221.

Kolia-Dermitzake, Athina. "Michael VII Doukas and the Byzantine-Norman Marriage Negotiations." *Byzantinoslavica* 58 (1997): 251–68.

Kovács, Péter. *Marcus Aurelius' Rain Miracle and the Marcomannic Wars*. Leiden, 2009.

Krautheimer, Richard. "A Note on Justinian's Church of the Holy Apostles in Constantinople." In Krautheimer, *Studies in Early Christian, Medieval, and Renaissance Art*, 197–201. London, 1969.

Laborderie, Oliver de. "Richard the Lionheart and the Birth of a National Cult of St. George in England: Origins and Development of a Legend." *Nottingham Medieval Studies* 39 (1995): 37–52.

Lacoste, Jean-Yves, ed. *Dictionnaire critique de théologie*. Paris, 1998.

Laiou, Angeliki E., and Roy P. Mottahedeh, eds. *The Crusades from the Perspective of Byzantium and the Muslim World*. Washington, D.C., 2001.

Lapina, Elizabeth. "Anti-Jewish Rhetoric in Guibert of Nogent's *Dei Gesta per Francos*." *Journal of Medieval History* 35 (2009): 239–53.

———. "Maccabees and the Battle of Antioch (1098)." In *Dying for the Faith, Killing for the Faith: Old-Testament Faith-Warriors (Maccabees 1 and 2) in Cultural Perspective*, ed. Gabriela Signori, 147–59. Leiden, 2012.

———. "The Paintings of Berzé-la-Ville in the Context of the First Crusade and the Reconquista." *Journal of Medieval History* 31 (2005): 309–26.

———. "La représentation de la bataille d'Antioche (1098) sur les peintures murales de Poncé-sur-le-Loir." *Cahiers de Civilisation Médiévale* 52 (2009): 137–57.

———. "St. Demetrius of Thessaloniki: Patron Saint of Crusaders." *Viator: Medieval and Renaissance Studies* 40 (2009): 93–112.

Leib, Bernard. *Rome, Kiev et Byzance à la fin du XIe siècle*. 1924. Reprint, New York, 1968.

Levine, Robert. "The Pious Traitor: Rhetorical Reinventions of the Fall of Antioch." *Mittellateinisches Jahrbuch* 33 (1998): 59–80.

Ligato, Giuseppe. "Iconografia della prima crociata nel mosaico di Bobbio." In *Il Concilio di Piacenza e le Crociate*, 213–24. Piacenza, 1996.

Lilie, Ralph-Johannes. *Byzantium and the Crusader States, 1096–1204*. Oxford, 1993.

Loud, Graham A. *The Age of Robert Guiscard: Southern Italy and the Norman Conquest*. London, 2000.

———. "The 'Gens Normannorum': Myth or Reality?" *Anglo-Norman Studies* 4 (1982): 104–16.

———. "How 'Norman' Was the Norman Conquest of Southern Italy?" *Nottingham Medieval Studies* 25 (1981): 3–34.

Lucas-Avenel, Marie-Agnès. "Le récit de Geoffroi Malaterra ou la légitimation de Roger, Grand Comte de Sicile." *Anglo-Norman Studies* 34 (2012): 169–92.

Lusignan, Serge. "L'Université de Paris comme composante de l'identité du royaume de France: Étude sur le thème de la *Translatio Studii*." In *L'identité régionale et conscience nationale en France et en Allemagne du Moyen Âge à l'époque moderne*, ed. Rainer Babel and Jean-Marie Moeglin, 59–72. Sigmaringen, 1997.

MacEvitt, Christopher. *The Crusades and the Christian World of the East*. Philadelphia, 2008.

MacGregor, James B. "The Ministry of Gerold d'Avranches: Warrior Saints and Knightly Piety on the Eve of the First Crusade." *Journal of Medieval History* 29 (2003): 219–37.

———. "Negotiating Knightly Piety: The Cult of the Warrior-Saints in the West, ca. 1070–ca. 1200." *Church History: Studies in Christianity and Culture* 73 (2004): 317–45.

———. "*Salue martir spes anglorum*: English Devotion to Saint George in the Middle Ages." PhD diss., University of Cincinnati, 2002.

MacLean, Simon. *Kingship and Politics in the Late Ninth Century: Charles the Fat and the End of the Carolingian Empire*. Cambridge, 2003.

Macrides, Ruth J. "Constantinople: The Crusaders' Gaze." In *Travel in the Byzantine World*, ed. Ruth J. Macrides, 193–212. Aldershot, 2002.

———. "The Pen and the Sword: Who Wrote the *Alexiad*?" In *Anna Komnene and Her Times*, ed. Thalia Gouma-Peterson, 63–81. New York, 2000.

Magdalino, Paul. *The Empire of Manuel I Komnenos, 1143–1180*. 2nd ed. Cambridge, 2002.

———. "St. Demetrios and Leo VI." *Byzantinoslavica* 51 (1990): 198–201.

Marshall, Christopher J. "The Crusading Motivations of the Italian City Republics in the Latin East, ca. 1096–1104." *Rivista di Bizantinistica* 1 (1991): 41–68.

Martin, Jean-Marie. *Italies normandes: XIe–XIIe siècles*. Paris, 1994.

———. "Les Normands et le culte de saint Michel en Italie du Sud." In *Culte et pèlerinages à Saint Michel en Occident: Les trois monts dédiés à l'archange*, ed. Pierre Bouet, Giorgio Otranto, and André Vauchez, 341–64. Rome, 2003.

Mayer, Hans. *The Crusades*. 2nd ed. Oxford, 1988.

McGinn, Bernard. *Visions of the End: Apocalyptic Traditions in the Middle Ages*. New York, 1979.

McGrath, Robert L. "The Romance of the Maccabees in Medieval Art and Literature." PhD diss., Princeton University, 1963.

McGrath, Stamatina. "The Battle of Dorostolon (971): Rhetoric and Reality." In *Peace and War in Byzantium: Essays in Honor of George T. Dennis*, ed. Timothy S. Miller and John W. Nesbitt, 152–64. Washington, D.C., 1995.

McKenzie, Stephen. "The Westward Progression of History on Medieval Mappaemundi: An Investigation of the Evidence." In *The Hereford World Map: Medieval World Maps and Their Context*, ed. P. D. A. Harvey, 335–44. London, 2006.

McKitterick, Rosamond. *The Frankish Kingdoms Under the Carolingians, 751–987*. London, 1983.

McQueen, William B. "Relations Between the Normans and Byzantium, 1071–1112." *Byzantion* 66 (1986): 427–76.

Ménager, Leon-Robert. "Inventaire des familles normandes et franques emigrées en Italie méridionale et en Sicile (XIe–XIIe siécles)." In *Roberto il Guiscardo e il suo tempo: Atti delle prime giornate normanno-sveve*, 279–410. Bari, 1991.

Meserve, Margaret. *Empires of Islam in Renaissance Historical Thought*. Cambridge, 2008.

Metcalf, David M. *Coinage of the Crusades and the Latin East in the Ashmolean Museum, Oxford*. London, 1995.

Mietzner, Angelika, and Helma Pasch. "Expressions of Cardinal Directions in Nilotic and in Ubangian Lanuguages." *SKASE Journal of Theoretical Linguistics* 4, no. 3 (2004). http://www.skase.sk/Volumes/JTL10/pdf_doc/2.pdf.

Momigliano, Arnaldo. "The Origins of Universal History." In Momigliano, *On Pagans, Jews, and Christians*, 31–57. Middletown, Conn., 1987.

Morris, Colin. "The Aims and Spirituality of the Crusade as Seen Through the Eyes of Albert of Aix." *Reading Medieval Studies* 16 (1990): 99–117.

———. "The *Gesta Francorum* as Narrative History." *Reading Medieval Studies* 19 (1993): 55–71.

———. "Martyrs on the Field of Battle Before and During the First Crusade." In *Martyrs and Martyrologies*, ed. Diana Wood, 93–105. Studies in Church History 30. Oxford, 1993.

———. *The Papal Monarchy*. Oxford, 1989.

———. "Policy and Visions: The Case of the Holy Lance at Antioch." In *War and Government in the Middle Ages: Essays in Honour of J. O. Prestwich*, ed. John Gillingham and James C. Holt, 33–45. Cambridge, 1984.

Morton, Nicholas. "The Defense of the Holy Land and the Memory of the Maccabees." *Journal of Medieval History* 36 (2010): 275–93.

Münsch, Oliver. "Hate Preachers and Religious Warriors: Violence in the *Libelli de Lite* of the Late Eleventh Century." In *Dying for the Faith, Killing for the Faith: Old-Testament Faith-Warriors (Maccabees 1 and 2) in Cultural Perspective*, ed. Gabriela Signori, 161–75. Leiden, 2012.

Nauroy, Gérard. "Du combat de la piété à la confession du sang: Ambroise de Milan, lecteur critique du *IV Livres des Maccabées*." *Revue d'Histoire et de Philosophie Religieuses* 70 (1990–91): 49–68.

———. "Les frères Maccabées dans l'exégèse d'Ambroise de Milan ou la conversion de la sagesse judéo-hellénique aux valeurs du martyre chrétien." In *Figures de l'Ancien Testament chez les Pères*, 215–45. Cahiers de Biblia Patristica 3. Strasbourg, 1989.

Neill, Edward D. *The English Colonization of America in the Seventeenth Century*. London, 1871.

Nelson, Janet L. *Charles the Bald*. London, 1992.

Neville, Leonora. *Heroes and Romans in Twelfth-Century Byzantium: The Material for History of Nikephoros Bryennios*. Cambridge, 2012.

Nichols, Stephen. *Romanesque Signs: Early Medieval Narrative and Iconography*. New Haven, 1983.

Nicholson, Helen. *Templars, Hospitallers, and Teutonic Knights: Images of the Military Orders, 1128–1291*. Leicester, 1993.
Nicol, Donald MacGillivray. "The Byzantine View of Western Europe." *Greek, Roman, and Byzantine Studies* 8 (1967): 315–39.
———. *Byzantium: Its Ecclesiastical History and Relations with the Western World*. London, 1972.
———. "Symbiosis and Integration: Some Greco-Latin Families in Byzantium in the Eleventh to Thirteenth Centuries." *Byzantinische Forschungen* 7 (1979): 113–36.
Nirenberg, David. *Anti-Judaism: The Western Tradition*. New York, 2013.
———. "Christian Sovereignty and the Jewish Flesh." In *Rethinking the Medieval Senses*, ed. Stephen G. Nichols, Andreas Kablitz, and Alison Calhoun, 154–85. Baltimore, 2008.
———. "Figures of Thought and Figures of Flesh: 'Jews' and 'Judaism' in Late Medieval Spanish Poetry and Politics." *Speculum* 81 (2006): 398–426.
———. "Islam and the West: Two Dialectical Fantasies." In *Islam in the West*, ed. David Westerlund and Ingvar Svanberg, vol. 4, *Politics and Law*, 249–75. Critical Concepts in Islamic Studies. London, 2011.
———. "The Rhineland Massacres of Jews in the First Crusade: Memories Medieval and Modern." In *Medieval Concepts of the Past: Ritual, Memory, Historiography*, ed. Gerd Althoff, Johannes Fried, and Patrick J. Geary, 279–310. Cambridge, 2002.
Niskanen, Samu. "The Origins of the *Gesta Francorum* and Two Related Texts: Their Textual and Literary Character." *Sacris Eruditi* 51 (2012): 287–316.
Nordholt, J. W. Schulte. *The Myth of the West: America as the Last Empire*. Translated by Herbert Harvey Rowen. Grand Rapids, 1995.
Norwich, John Julius. *The Normans in the South, 1016–1130*. 2nd ed. London 1981.
Ntedika, Joseph. *L'évocation de l'au-delà dans la prière pour les morts: Étude de patristique et de liturgie latine*. Kinshasa, 1971.
Obolensky, Dimitri. "The Cult of St. Demetrios of Thessaloniki in the History of Byzantine-Slav Relations." *Balkan Studies* 15 (1974): 3–20.
O'Callaghan, Joseph F. *Reconquest and Crusade in Medieval Spain*. Philadelphia, 2003.
Oldfield, Paul. "Urban Government in Southern Italy, c. 1085–c. 1127." *English Historical Review* 122 (2007): 579–608.
Otranto, Giorgio. "Il 'Liber de apparatione,' il Santuario di san Michele sul Gargano e i Longobardi del Ducato di Benevento." In *Sanctuari e politica nel mondo antico*, ed. Marta Sordi, 210–43. Milan, 1983.
Ovčarov, Nikolaj. "Sur l'iconographie de St. Georges aux XIe–XIIe siècles." *Byzantinoslavica* 52 (1991): 121–29.
Pagden, Anthony. *Worlds at War: The 2,500-Year Struggle Between East and West*. New York, 2008.
Partridge, Eric. *A Dictionary of Slang and Unconventional English*. 5th ed. London, 1963.
Pastoureau, Michel. "L'homme et le porc: Une histoire symbolique." In Pastoureau, *Couleurs, Images, Symboles: Études d'histoire et d'anthropologie*, 237–83. Paris, 1989.
Pate, C. Marvin, and Douglas W. Kennard. *Deliverance Now and Not Yet: The New Testament and the Great Tribulation*. New York, 2003.
Paul, Nicholas. *To Follow in Their Footsteps: The Crusades and Family Memory in the High Middle Ages*. Ithaca, 2013.
———. "A Warlord's Wisdom: Literacy and Propaganda at the Time of the First Crusade." *Speculum* 85 (2010): 534–66.
Pentcheva, Bissera V. *Icons and Power: The Mother of God in Byzantium*. University Park, 2006.

———. "The Supernatural Protector of Constantinople: The Virgin and Her Icons in the Tradition of the Avar Siege." *Byzantine and Modern Greek Studies* 26 (2002): 2–41.
Piemontese, Giuseppe. *San Michele e il suo sanctuario*. Foggia, 1997.
Pohl, Walter. "History in Fragments: Montecassino's Politics of Memory." *Early Medieval Europe* 10 (2001): 343–74.
Potts, Cassandra. "*Atque unum ex diversis gentibus populum effecit*: Historical Tradition and Norman Identity." *Anglo-Norman Studies* 18 (1996): 139–52.
Powell, James. "Myth, Legend, Propaganda, History: The First Crusade, 1140–c. 1300." In *Autour de la première croisade*, ed. Michel Balard, 127–41. Paris, 1996.
Pryor, John H., and Michael J. Jeffreys. "Alexios, Bohemond, and Byzantium's Euphrates Frontier." *Crusades* 11 (2012): 31–86.
Purkis, William J. *Crusading Spirituality in the Holy Land and Iberia, c. 1095–c. 1187*. Woodbridge, UK, 2008.
Rahner, Hugo. *Greek Myths and Christian Mystery*. London, 1963.
Ramey, Lynn Tart. *Christian, Saracen, and Genre in Medieval French Literature*. New York, 2001.
Reeve, Matthew M. "The Painted Chamber at Westminster, Edward I, and the Crusade." *Viator* 37 (2006): 189–221.
Rice, Geoffrey. "A Note on the Battle of Antioch." *Parergon* 25 (1979): 3–8.
Riches, S. *St. George: Hero, Martyr, and Myth*. Stroud, 2000.
Riley-Smith, Jonathan. "Christian Violence and the Crusades." In *Religious Violence Between Christians and Jews: Medieval Roots, Modern Perspectives*, ed. Anna Sapir Abulafia, 3–20. Basingstoke, 2002.
———. "Death on the First Crusade." In *The End of Strife: Papers Selected from the Proceedings of the Colloquium of the Commission Internationale d'Histoire Eccle'siastique Compare'e Held at the University of Durham, 2 to 9 September 1981*, ed. David M. Loades, 14–31. Edinburgh, 1984.
———. "Early Crusaders to the East and the Cost of Crusading." In *Cross-Cultural Convergences in the Crusader Period: Essays Presented to Aryeh Graboïs on his Sixty-Fifth Birthday*, ed. Michael Goodich, Sophia Menache, and Sylvia Schein, 237–57. New York, 1995.
———. "Erdmann and the Historiography of the Crusades, 1935–1995." In *La primera cruzada, novecientos años después: El Concilio de Clermont y los orígenes del movimiento cruzado*, ed. Luis García-Guijarro Ramos, 17–29. Madrid, 1998.
———. "The First Crusade and St. Peter." In *Outremer: Studies in the History of the Crusading Kingdom of Jerusalem Presented to Joshua Prawer*, ed. B. Z. Kedar, H. E. Mayer, and R. C. Smail, 41–63. Jerusalem, 1982.
———. *The First Crusade and the Idea of Crusading*. Philadelphia, 1986.
———. *What Were the Crusades?* 2nd ed. London, 1992.
Robinson, Ian Stuart. *Authority and Resistance in the Investiture Contest: The Polemical Literature of the Late Eleventh Century*. Manchester, 1978.
———. "The Bible in the Investiture Contest: The South German Gregorian Circle." In *The Bible in the Medieval World: Essays in Memory of Beryl Smalley*, ed. Katherine Walsh and Diana Wood, 61–84. Oxford, 1985.
———. *The Papal Reform of the Eleventh Century: Lives of Pope Leo IX and Pope Gregory VII*. Manchester, 2004.
Rösch, G. "Der 'Kreuzzug' Bohemunds gegen Dyrrachion 1107–8 in der latinischen Tradition des 12. Jahrhunderts." *Römische Historische Mitteilungen* 26 (1984): 181–90.
Rousset, Paul. *Les origines et les caractères de la première croisade*. Neuchâtel, 1945.

Rouwhorst, Gerard. "The Cult of the Seven Maccabean Brothers and Their Mother in Christian Tradition." In *Saints and Role Models in Judaism and Christianity*, ed. Marcel Poorthuis and Joshua Schwartz, 183–204. Leiden, 2004.

Rubenstein, Jay. *Armies of Heaven: The First Crusade and the Quest for Apocalypse*. New York, 2011.

———. "Guibert of Nogent, Albert of Aachen, and Fulcher of Chartres: Three Crusade Chronicles Intersect." In *Writing the Early Crusades: Text, Transmission, and Memory*, ed. Marcus Bull and Damien Kempf, 24–37. Woodbridge, UK, 2014.

———. *Guibert of Nogent: Portrait of a Medieval Mind*. New York, 2002.

———. "Lambert of Saint-Omer and the Apocalyptic First Crusade." In *Remembering the Crusades: Myth, Image, and Identity*, ed. Nicholas Paul and Suzanne Yeager, 69–95. Baltimore, 2012.

———. "Putting History to Use: Three Crusade Chronicles in Context." *Viator* 35 (2004): 131–68.

———. "What Is the *Gesta Francorum*, and Who Was Peter Tudebode?" *Revue Mabillon* 16 (2005): 179–204.

Runciman, Steven. "Byzantium and the Crusades." In *The Meeting of Two Worlds: Cultural Exchange Between East and West During the Period of the Crusades*, ed. Vladimir P. Goss and Christine V. Bornstein, 15–22. Kalamazoo, 1986.

———. "The Holy Lance Found at Antioch." *Analecta Bollandiana* 68 (1950): 197–209.

Russell, Eugenia. *St. Demetrius of Thessalonica: Cult and Devotion in the Middle Ages*. Oxford, 2010.

Russo, Luigi. *Boemondo: Figlio del Guiscardo e principe di Antiochia*. Ariano Irpino, 2009.

———. "Continuité et transformations de la typologie des Maccabées jusqu'aux origines du mouvement des croisades." In *La typologie biblique comme forme de pensée dans l'historiographie médiévale*, ed. Marek Thue Kretschmer, 53–75. Textes et Études du Moyen Âge 75. Barcelona, 2015.

———. "L'expansion normande contre Byzance (XIème–XIIème siècles): Réflexions sur une question toujours ouverte." In *911–2011: Penser les mondes normands médiévaux*, ed. David Bates and Pierre Bauduin. Forthcoming.

———. "Maccabei e crociati: Spunti per una riflessione sull'utilizzo della tipologia biblica nelle fonti della 'prima crociata.'" In *Auctor et auctoritas in Latinis Medii Aevi litteris: Author and Authorship in Medieval Latin Literature*, ed. Edoardo D'Angelo and Jan Ziolkowski, 979–94. Florence, 2014.

———. *I Normanni del Mezzogiorno e il movimento crociato*. Bari, 2014.

———. "Recherche sull''Historia Iherosolimitana' di Roberto di Reims." *Studi Medievali*, 3rd ser., 43 (2002): 651–91.

———. "Ricerche sui cronisti della 'Prima crociata.'" PhD diss., Università degli Studi di Torino, 2001.

Said, Edward W. *Orientalism: Western Conceptions of the Orient*. 25th anniversary ed. London, 2003.

Salvini, Roberto. "Monuments of Norman Art in Sicily and Southern Italy." In Ovidio Capitani, Giuseppe Galasso, and Roberto Salvini, *The Normans in Sicily and Southern Italy*, 64–92. Oxford, 1977.

Sauer, Joseph. *Symbolik des Kirchengebäudes und seiner Ausstattung in der Auffassung des Mittelalters: Mit Berückischtigung von Honorius Augustodunensis Sicardus und Durandus*. 2nd ed. Münster, 1964.

Savvides, Alexios G. C. *Byzantino Normannica: The Norman Capture of Italy (to AD 1081) and the First Two Invasions of Byzantium (AD 1081–1085 and 1107–1108)*. Louvain, 2007.

Scafi, Alessandro. *Mapping Paradise: A History of Heaven on Earth*. Chicago, 2006.

Schaller, Hans Martin. "Zur Kreuzzugsenzyklika Papst Sergius IV." In *Papsttum, Kirche, und Recht im Mittelalter: Festschrift für Horst Fuhrmann zum 65. Geburtstag*, ed. Hubert Mordek, 135–53. Tübingen, 1991.

Schatkin, Margaret. "The Maccabean Martyrs." *Vigiliae Christianae* 28, no. 2 (1974): 97–113.

Schein, Sylvia. *Gateway to the Heavenly City: Crusader Jerusalem and the Catholic West (1099–1187)*. Aldershot, 2005.

Schlumberger, Gustave Léon. *Un empereur byzantin au dixième siècle, Nicéphore Phocas*. Paris, 1890.

Schmitt, Jean-Claude. *Les revenants: Les vivants et les morts dans la société médiévale*. Paris, 1994.

Schroeder, H. *Der Topos der Nine Worthies in Literatur und bildender Kunst*. Göttingen, 1971.

Schuster, Beate. "Raymond d'Aguilers: Un chanter de l'hérésie avant l'heure?" *Heresis: Revue Semestrielle d'Histoire des Dissidences Médiévales* 36–37 (2002): 161–81.

Setton, Kenneth Meyer, ed. *A History of the Crusades*. 6 vols. Madison, 1969–89.

——. "Saint George's Head." *Speculum* 48 (1973): 1–12.

Shepard, Jonathan. "The Uses of the Franks in Eleventh-Century Byzantium." *Anglo-Norman Studies* 15 (1993): 275–305.

——. "When Greek Meets Greek: Alexius Comnenus and Bohemond in 1097–1098." *Byzantine and Modern Greek Studies* 12 (1988): 185–277.

Shepard, Jonathan, and Simon Franklin, eds. *Byzantine Diplomacy: Papers from the Twenty-Fourth Spring Symposium of Byzantine Studies, Cambridge, March 1990*. Aldershot, 1992.

Shopkow, Leah. *History and Community: Norman Historical Writing in the Eleventh and Twelfth Centuries*. Washington, D.C., 1997.

Simpson, Alicia. "Three Sources of Military Unrest in Eleventh-Century Asia Minor: The Norman Chieftains Hervé Fankopoulos, Robert Crispin, and Roussel de Bailleil." *Mésogeios/Méditerranée* 9–10 (2000): 181–207.

Simpson, Luisella. "The King Alfred/St. Cuthbert Episode in the *Historia de sancto Cuthberto*: Its Significance for Mid-Tenth-Century English History." In *St. Cuthbert, His Cult and His Community to AD 1200*, ed. Gerald Bonner, D. W. Rollason, and Clare Stancliffe, 397–411. Woodbridge, UK, 1989.

Skedros, James C. *Saint Demetrios of Thessaloniki: Civic Patron and Divine Protector, Fourth–Seventh Centuries CE*. Harrisburg, Pa., 1999.

Skoulatos, Basile. "L'auteur anonyme des 'Gesta Francorum' et le monde byzantine." *Byzantion* 50 (1980): 504–32.

Smail, R. C. *Crusading Warfare (1097–1193)*. Cambridge, 1956.

Smith, Katherine Allen. "Glossing the Holy War: Exegetical Constructions of the First Crusade, c. 1095–1146." *Studies in Medieval and Renaissance History*, 3rd ser., 10 (2013): 1–39.

——. *War and the Making of Medieval Monastic Culture*. Woodbridge, UK, 2011.

Smith, Richard Upsher. "Nobilissimus and Warleader: The Opportunity and the Necessity Behind Robert Guiscard's Balkan Expedition." *Byzantion* 70 (2000): 507–26.

Smyth, Alfred P. *King Alfred the Great*. Oxford, 1995.

——. *Warlords and Holy Men: Scotland, AD 80–1000*. London, 1984.

Southern, Richard. *Western Views of Islam*. Cambridge, Mass., 1962.

Spicq, Ceslas, ed. *Léxique théologique du Nouveau Testament*. Fribourg, 1978.

Spiegel, Gabrielle M. "History as Enlightenment: Suger and the Mos Anagogicus." In Spiegel, *The Past as Text: The Theory and Practice of Medieval Historiography*, 163–77. Baltimore, 1997.

———. "Medieval Historiography." In *A Companion to Western Historical Thought*, ed. Lloyd S. Kramer and Sarah C. Maza, 78–98. Oxford, 2002.

———. "Political Utility in Medieval Historiography: A Sketch." In *The Past as Text: The Theory and Practice of Medieval Historiography*, 99–110. Baltimore, 1997.

Stahuljak, Zrinka. *Bloodless Genealogies of the French Middle Ages: Translatio, Kinship, and Metaphor*. Gainesville, Fla., 2005.

Staunton, Michael. *Thomas Becket and His Biographers*. Woodbridge, UK, 2006.

Stephenson, Paul. *Byzantium's Balkan Frontier*. Cambridge, 2000.

Stock, Brian. *Listening for the Text: On the Uses of the Past*. Baltimore, 1990.

Stroll, Mary. *Popes and Antipopes: The Politics of Eleventh-Century Church Reform*. Leiden, 2012.

Swanson, R. N. *Indulgences in Late Medieval England: Passports to Paradise?* Cambridge, 2007.

Taviani-Carozzi, Huguette. "Léon IX et les Normands d'Italie du sud." In *Léon IX et son temps*, ed. Georges Bischoff and Benoît-Michel Tock, 299–329. Turnhout, 2006.

———. *La terreur du monde: Robert Guiscard et la conquête normande en Italie, mythe et histoire*. Paris, 1996.

Thomson, Rodney M. "William of Malmesbury, Historian of Crusade." *Reading Medieval Studies* 23 (1997): 121–34.

Throop, Susanna. *Crusading as an Act of Vengeance, 1095–1216*. Farnham, 2011.

Tolan, John. *Saracens: Islam in the Medieval European Imagination*. New York, 2002.

Tóth, Peter. "Die sirmische Legende des heiligen Demetrius von Thessalonike: Eine lateinische Passionsfassung aus dem mittelalterlichen Ungarn ('BHL' 2127)." *Analecta Bollandiana* 128 (2010): 348–92.

Trites, Allison A. *The New Testament Concept of Witness*. Cambridge, 1977.

Tronzo, William. *The Cultures of His Kingdom: Roger II and the Cappella Palatina in Palermo*. Princeton, 1997.

Tuveson, Ernest Lee. *Millennium and Utopia: A Study in the Background of the Idea of Progress*. New York, 1964.

———. *Redeemer Nation: The Idea of America's Millennial Role*. Chicago, 1968.

Tyerman, Christopher. *The Debate on the Crusades*. Manchester, 2011.

van Dam, Raymond. "The Many Conversions of the Emperor Constantine." In *Conversion in Late Antiquity and the Early Middle Ages: Seeing and Believing*, ed. K. Mills and A. Grafton, 127–51. Rochester, N.Y., 2003.

van Houts, Elisabeth M. C. "Normandy and Byzantium in the Eleventh Century." *Byzantion* 55 (1985): 544–59.

Vidier, Alexandre. *L'historiographie à Saint-Benoît-sur-Loire et les miracles de Saint-Benoît*. Paris, 1965.

Walter, Christopher. "St. Demetrius: The Myroblytos of Thessalonika." *Eastern Church Review* 5 (1973): 157–78.

———. "Theodore, Archetype of the Warrior Saint." *Revue des Études Byzantines* 57 (1999): 163–210.

———. "The Thracian Horseman: Ancestor of the Warrior Saints?" *Byzantinische Forschungen* 14 (1989): 659–73.

———. *The Warrior Saints in Byzantine Art and Tradition*. Aldershot, 2003.

Ward, Benedicta. *Miracles and the Medieval Mind: Theory, Record, and Event, 1100–1225*. London, 1982.

Watkins, Carl. *History and the Supernatural in Medieval England*. Cambridge, 2007.

Webber, Nick. *The Evolution of Norman Identity, 911–1154*. Woodbridge, UK, 2005.

Weckmann, Luis. *The Medieval Heritage of Mexico*. Translated by Frances M. López-Morillas. New York, 1992.

Weiss, Daniel H. "*Hec est Domus Domini Firmiter Edificata:* The Image of the Temple in Crusader Art." *Jewish Art* 23–24 (1997–98): 210–17.
White, Monica. "A Byzantine Tradition Transformed: Military Saints Under the House of Suzdal." *Russian Review* 63 (2004): 493–513.
Wieruszowski, Helen. "Roger II of Sicily, 'Rex-Tyrannus,' in Twelfth-Century Political Thought." *Speculum* 38 (1963): 46–78.
Williams, Ethel C. "Mural Paintings of St. George in England." *Journal of the British Archaeological Association*, 3rd ser., 12 (1949): 19–36.
Wolf, Kenneth Baxter. "Bohemond and the *Gesta Francorum*." *Journal of Medieval History* 17 (1991): 207–16.
———. *Making History: The Normans and Their Historians in Eleventh-Century Italy*. Philadelphia, 1995.
Wright, John Kirtland. *The Geographical Lore of the Time of the Crusades: A Study in the History of Medieval Science and Tradition in Western Europe*. New York, 1925.
Yewdale, Ralph Bailey. *Bohemond I, Prince of Antioch*. 1924. Reprint, Amsterdam, 1970.
Ziadé, Raphaëlle. *Les martyrs Maccabées: De l'histoire juive au culte chrétien; Les homélies de Grégoire de Nazianze et de Jean Chrysostome*. Leiden, 2007.

INDEX

Specific works will generally be found under the author, unless the work is anonymous, in which case it will be located by title. Battles are found under their specific location or name, e.g., "Hastings, battle of."

Abbo, *Bella parisiacae urbis*, 84–85, 95
Abd al-Malik, 109
Abishai, 110–11, 170n49
Achilles, 46–47
Adelarius of Fleury, 83–84, 93
Adhémar of Le Puy, 20, 21–22, 28, 136, 156n54, 161n21
Adomnán of Iona, 85
Adrevald of Fleury, *Miracula sancti Benedicti*, 83, 91
Aelfric of Eynsham, 103
Aelred of Rievaulx, 87
Aeschylus, 125, 126, 172n18
al-Afdal, 66
Saint Agnes, 102
Ainsworth, Peter, 15–16, 154n10
Akbari, Suzanne Conklin, 125–26, 128, 137
Alange, battle of (1299), 148
Alaric, 46–47
Albert of Aachen, *Historia Ierosolimitana*, 10, 13, 160n15, 163n76
Albu, Emily, 89
Alcoraz, battle of (1096), 147
Alexander II, 92, 105
Alexander the Great, 169n34
Alexius I Comnenus, 6, 60–67, 69, 77, 117, 133, 162n64
    Bohemond's relationship with, 62–65
Alexius V, 71
Alfred, king of Wessex, 83, 85, 86
Amatus of Montecassino, *Historia Normannorum*, 59–60, 80, 89, 91, 93–94, 95–96
Ambrose of Milan, *De officiis* and *Hexaemeron*, 102–3, 112, 173n38
Anastasius, 131
Andreas of Strumi, 104–5
Saint Andrew, 47–48
Andrew of Fleury, *Miracula sancti Benedicti*, 94–95
angelic battle interventions. *See* supernatural interventions in battle

Angold, Michael, 65
Anna Comnena, *Alexiad*, 59, 60–61, 62, 63, 90, 162n64
Annals of Fulda, 104
Anselm of Canterbury, *Conception virginale*, 153n7
Anselm of Ribermont, 38
Antichrist, 103, 136
Antioch, battle of (1098)
    celestial phenomena and, 122–23, 138, 139
    wind and, 140–41
    modern historical understanding of, 37–38
Antioch, city
    Maccabean martyrs associated with, 102, 107
    origins of the name, 107, 169n34
Antioch, miracle of saintly interventions in battle of (1098), 37–53
    biblical precursors, 45, 46, 97, 107–8, 114
    Byzantine precursors, 46–52
    early Christian precursors, 44–49
    eyewitnesses and interpreters of, 26–29
    Greek and Roman precursors, 39–46
    medieval hesitancy about recounting, 38–39
    Muslims influenced by, 145–47
Antiochus IV Epiphanes, 101, 102, 107, 114, 118, 119
apocalyptic framework, 45, 123, 126–27, 128, 129, 131, 136, 139, 142
al-Aqsa mosque (Temple Mount, Jerusalem), 110, 116
Archidamus II, 43–44
Ariald the Deacon, 105
Ariulf of Spoleto, 80–81
Arnulf of Chocques, 12–13, 109–10
Asbridge, Thomas, 38, 155n40
Ascalon, battle of (1099), 24–25
Asen and Peter, 72
Athena, 40–41, 46–47
Attila the Hun, 80

Auerbach, Erich, 98
Augustine of Hippo, 120, 130–31, 141
   De civitate Dei, 128
   "De cura pro mortuis gerenda," 45–47, 52, 158n33
   Homily 93, *Tractates on the Gospel of John,* 17, 154n15
   Sermo 300, 101–2
Avitus of Vienne, 131–32, 133

Badr, battle of (624), 146–47
Balbus (Quintus Lucilius Balbus), 42–43
Baldric of Bourgueil, *Historia Ierosolimitana,* 10
   on battle of Antioch, 26, 27
   on eyewitnesses and interpreters, 16, 26, 27, 31, 33–34
   on Josephus, 171n68
   later chroniclers using, 11–12, 56
   reasons for rewriting *Gesta Francorum,* 3–4, 33–34
   on Roman conquest of Jerusalem, 171n72
Baldric of Bourgueil, poem on William the Conqueror, 87
Baldwin of Boulogne (King Baldwin I of Jerusalem), 10, 11, 110–11
Baldwin II, 110, 111
Balkans, Norman invasion of, 60–62, 70
Balsamon, Theodore, 72
Banaiah, 110–11, 170n49
Bari, translation of relics of Saint Nicholas from Myra to, 67–68
Bartolf of Nangis, 157
Basil II, psalter of, 64
Bede the Venerable, *Historia ecclesiastica gentis Anglorum,* 85, 173n37
Beer, Jeanette, 15
Benedict of Nursia, 80, 83–84, 86, 91–95
Benzo of Alba, *Seven books for Emperor Henry IV,* 92–93, 168n93
Bernard of Anges, *Liber miraculorum sancte fidis,* 55
Bernard of Clairvaux, 105, 110
   Liber ad Milites Templi, 116–17, 121, 170n64
Bernard the Monk, *Itinerary,* 12
Bernard of Ripoll, 94
Bernard of Valence, 111
Bernold of St. Blasien, 104, 105
Bethania, anchorite of, 34–35
Beth-Zachariah, battle of, 102
Bisaha, Nancy, 172n18
Saint Blaise, 58
Bohemond of Hauteville

   Alexius I and, 62–65, 74, 77
   association with Byzantium, 59
   in battle of Antioch, 38
   burial place of, 68–69
   church of St. Nicholas in Bari and, 68, 163n76
   connection of Southern Normans to Viking/Northern past and, 86, 87, 90
   death feigned by, 90
   in Geoffrey Malaterra, *De rebus gestis Rogerii Calabriae,* 76
   Gesta Francorum and, 76–78, 165n8
   holy lance, discovery of, 19
   invasion of Balkans with Robert Guiscard, 6, 60–61, 70
   Pirrus and, 27–28
   Ralph of Caen and, 12
Bohemond II, 12, 66
Bonizo of Sutri, 105
Brown, Cecil, 124, 129
Brown, Peter, 73–74
Bruno, 38
Bulgar and Vlach rebellion against Byzantium (1185–86), 72
Bull, Marcus, 9, 11, 16, 157n77
Byzantium
   First Crusade chronicles on, 133–34
   icons, Norman capture of, 71–72
   Lombards and, 80–83, 166n34
   marriages between Normans and Byzantines, 59–60, 163–64n90
   Norman association with, 58–60, 62
   responses of foreigners to, 72–74, 164n96
   supernatural battlefield interventions in, 5–6, 46–52

Cadalan schism, 92, 168n93
Cædwalla, 85
Caesar, 34–35
Caffaro di Rustico, *De liberatione civitatum orientis,* 13, 100, 106, 107, 110
Camerino, battle of (early 7th century), 80–81
Cannae, battle of (216 B.C.), 111
Canosa di Puglia, cathedral of San Sabino, 68–69
cardinal points, medieval references to, 8, 123–28, 130, 132, 136–39, 141, 144, 148, 172n11, 174n58. *See also* East/West dichotomy
Carmen in victoriam Pisanorum, 82–83
Saint Carpophorus, 92
Castor and Pollux (Dioscuri), 41, 42–45, 85, 168n93
celestial phenomena, 117–19, 122–24, 137–40

INDEX ✢ 205

Cerami, battle of (1063), 58, 75–76, 78–79, 81, 83, 92, 93, 96
Chanson d'Antioche, 13–14, 119, 156n54
Charlemagne, 132
Charles the Bald, 83
Charleville poet/Gilo of Paris, *Historia vie Hierosolimitane*, 11, 108
Chaurand, Jacques, 35
Chibnall, Marjorie, 68
Chrétien, Jean-Louis, 17
Chronicon Paschale, 47–48
Cicero
    The Nature of the Gods, 5, 42–43, 44, 45–46, 52
    Robert Guiscard compared, 89
Ciggaar, Krijie Nelly, 73
Civitate, battle of (1053), 93–94
Clavijo, battle of (844), 148
Clermont, Council of (1095), 10, 16, 32, 134, 135, 136
Clovis, 131
Coimbra, taking of (1064), 148
coinage
    with likeness of Robert Guiscard in Byzantine robes, 163n87
    with warrior saints, 65–66, 162n65
Saint Columba, 85
consecration of knights, *ordo* for, 55
Constantine I the Great, 45, 61–62, 69, 74, 86, 133
Constantine IX Monomachos, 58, 65
Constantine X Ducas, 92
Constantine Humbertopoulos, 59
Constantius II, 48
Saints Cosmas and Damian, 44
Cotta, 42–43, 46
Council of Clermont (1095), 10, 16, 32, 134, 135, 136
Cowdrey, H. E. J., 82, 92
Saint Cuthbert, 83, 85, 86, 92
Cyril of Jerusalem, 128–29
Cyrus, 130

Daimbert, 160n18
Damian-Grint, Peter, 15–16
D'Angelo, Edoardo, 11
Daniel, Norman, *Islam and the West*, 125
David, 110–11
Davis, R. H. C., 88
Dead Sea, 29
death
    Vikings and Normans feigning, 89–90
    West associated with, 127, 128–29, 173n32

Delehaye, Hippolyte, 54, 160n3
Saint Demetrius
    Alexius I's special interest in, 65–66, 162n64
    Balkans, Norman invasion of, 62
    in battle of Antioch (*See* Antioch, miracle of saintly interventions in battle of)
    in battle of Dorylaeum, 157n15
    coinage with image of, 65–66, 162n65
    as protector of Thessaloniki, 48–49
    Slavic rebels appropriating, 72
    Venetian *spolia* of bas-relief representation of, 164n99
Derbes, Anna, 164n96
Desiderius, 57
Diomedes, 40–41
Dionysius of Halicarnassus, *Roman Antiquities*, 158n22
Dome of the Rock (As-Sakhrah), 109, 170n54
Dorostolon, battle of (971), 50, 58
Dorylaeum, battle of (1099), 39, 157n15
Douglas, David C., 70167n63
Dudo of Saint-Quentin, *History of the Normans*, 89, 90–91
Durazzo, battle of (1081), 59, 60–62, 64, 67, 74

East/West dichotomy, 7–8, 122–42. *See also* Byzantium
    anti-Muslim discourse and, 125–26, 133–34
    beginnings and Second Coming, East associated with, 128, 129
    cardinal points, medieval references to, 8, 123–28, 130, 132, 136–39, 141, 144, 148, 172n11, 174n58
    celestial phenomena moving West to East, 122–23, 137–40
    death, ending, and hell, West associated with, 127, 128–29, 173n32
    in early modern and modern world, 148–50
    Greek/Persian dichotomy and, 172n18
    history, westward progression of, 126–28, 130–33, 142, 148–50
    Book of Isaiah and, 135–37
    new apostles, crusaders as, 134–35, 144
    superiority of West over East, in First Crusade chronicles, 132–37
    wind out of the east, 140–41, 174n71
Ebrard, 20, 157–58b15
Edgington, Susan, 13, 155n40
Edington, battle of (878), 85
Edwards, John, 149
Edwin, king of Northumbria, 85, 86
Ekkehard of Aura, *Chronicle* and *Hierosolymita*, 13, 117–19

Eleazar, priest, 101–3
Ellenblum, Ronnie, 175n72
Emmaus, Maccabean battle of, 108
Epstein, Ann Wharton, 69, 73
Erdmann, Carl, 5–6, 55, 56, 58, 79, 82, 86, 96, 105, 161n26
Erlembald of Milan, 104–5
eschatology, 7, 45, 123, 126–27, 128, 129, 131, 136, 139, 142
Ethites, 110–11
Eugenius, 44, 45
Eusebius of Caesarea, *Vita Constantini*, 45, 173n38
Saint Eustace, 55
Everett, Nicholas, 166n34
eyewitnesses and interpreters, 4, 15–36
   complementarity of, 23–24
   first-hand chroniclers stressing personal eyewitness, 29–30
   Gesta Francorum, reasons of later chroniclers for rewriting, 32, 33–34
   holy lance, discovery of, 18–22, 30
   medieval views on reliability of first-hand accounts, 15–17
   multiple eyewitnesses to same event, 22–23
   Muslim opponents as, 24–26, 27–28, 156n45
   of saintly interventions in battle of Antioch, 26–29
   second-hand chroniclers on, 30–36
   theological concept of witness and, 17–18, 31, 36

Saint Felix, 46, 85
Ferdinand I, king of León and Castile, 148
Field of Blood, battle of the (1119), 30, 111–12, 145–47
First World War, angels of Mons in, 6
Firuz *See* Pirrus
Flavius Josephus, *Jewish War*, 118, 171n68
Fletcher, Richard, 148
Fontaine, Jacques, 31, 154n2
Fourth Crusade, 71
Saint Foy, 55
France, John, 38, 77, 78, 160n15
Frederick II, Holy Roman Emperor, 90
Frigidus River, battle of (394), 44, 50
Froissart, Jean, 15
Frontinus (Sextus Julius Frontinus), *Stratagems*, 43–44
Frotho, 90
Frutolf of Michelsberg, *World Chronicle*, 13
Fulcher of Chartres, *Historia Hierosolymitana*, 9–10
   celestial phenomena reported by, 123, 138, 139
   on East/West dichotomy, 134–35, 138
   on eyewitnesses and interpreters, 24, 29
   holy lance, discovery of, 20, 21
   new Jews, crusaders viewed as, 100, 105–6, 110, 111–12, 116
   on origins of Antioch, 169n34
   as source for other chroniclers, 11, 12, 26, 32, 170n52

Gabriel, archangel, 146, 147
Gadolin, Anita, 68, 69, 163n76
Geary, Patrick, 67
Geoffrey Malaterra, *De rebus gestis Rogerii Calabriae*, 58, 75–76, 78–79, 81, 83, 89, 91–93, 95–96
Saint George
   Al Khidr and, 147
   in battle of Antioch (*See* Antioch, saintly interventions in battle of)
   in battle of Cerami, 58, 75–76, 79
   in battle of Dorylaeum, 157n15
   coinage with image of, 66, 162n65
   in Delahaye's "état-major," 54
   Jakelin de Mailly mistaken for, 25
   Norman association with military service to Byzantium and, 62
   in Spain, 147–48
George of Antioch, 70
Gerald of Wales, *Conquest of Ireland*, 126, 127, 142, 150
Saint Germain, 83–86, 92, 95
Gerold, clerk at court of Hugh of Avranches, 55, 56
Gesta Francorum, 9
   appropriation of Byzantine warrior saints by crusaders and, 54, 56, 63, 64, 65
   on battle of Antioch, 5, 26, 27, 28, 38, 39, 53, 54, 64
   Bohemond of Hauteville and, 76–78, 165n8
   celestial phenomena reported by, 122, 139
   on East/West dichotomy, 122, 134, 139
   on eyewitnesses and interpreters, 16, 26, 27, 28, 156n56
   Geoffrey Malaterra, *De rebus gestis Rogerii Calabriae* compared, 76, 78
   later chroniclers using, 12, 56
   on Muslims, 117
   Normanitas and, 76–78, 81, 83, 95, 96
   on origins of name of Antioch, 107
   reasons of later chroniclers for rewriting, 3–4, 32, 33–34

relationship to other crusader-chronicles, 9
  rewritings of, 10–11, 14
Gesta Stephani, 122–23
Gideon, 111, 112
Gilo of Paris/Charleville poet, *Historia vie Hierosolimitane*, 11, 108
Gimon of Saint Foy, 55
Glaber, Raoul, *Histories*, 132, 174n48
Godfrey of Bouillon, 11, 110
Godfrey of Lorraine, 92
Graindor de Douai, 14
Greek and Roman accounts of supernatural battle interventions, 39–46, 85, 168n93
Greek/Persian dichotomy, 172n18
Gregory I the Great, pope, *Dialogues*, 22
Gregory VII, pope, formerly Hildebrand, 92, 104, 105
Grocock, Christopher Wallace, 11
Guenée, Bernard, 15, 17
Guibert of Nogent, *Dei gesta per Francos*, 10
  anchorite's vision of taking of Jerusalem in, 34–35
  on battle of Antioch, 26, 114–15
  on East/West dichotomy, 132–36, 141
  on eyewitnesses and interpreters, 22–24, 26, 31–36, 155n39
  holy lance, discovery of, 21–22
  on holy warfare, 1, 2
  on miraculous nature of First Crusade, 1, 3
  Muslims and Jews associated in, 117–18, 120
  new Jews, crusaders as, 97, 99, 100, 107, 113–16, 121
  reasons for rewriting *Gesta Francorum*, 3–4, 33–34
  Robert the Monk and, 11, 157n77
  theological cast of, 14, 33
Guibert of Nogent, *Liber quo ordine sermo fieri debeat*, 31
Guillelmus Bonofilus, 20
Guillelmus Lamus Puer, 20

Haldon, John, 61
Halley's Comet, 122–23
Hannibal of Carthage, 111
Harald Hardrada, 90
Harari, Yuval Noah, 16, 155n39
Haskins, Charles Homer, 87
Hastings, 89, 90
Hastings, battle of (1066), 2
Hattin, battle of (1187), 66
Hay, Denys, 172n18
Heavenfield, battle of (633/634), 85

Hegel, Georg Wilhelm Friedrich, *Philosophy of History*, 149–50
Hendy, Michael, 65
Henry II, king of England, 12, 127
Henry IV, Holy Roman Emperor, 60, 92
Henry of Huntington, *Historia Anglorum*, 12, 28–29
Heracles (hero), 41, 42
Herodotus, 172n18
Hirtius (Aulus Hirtius), 157n81
Historia de via et recuperatione Antiochiae atque Ierusolymarum, 11
history
  theology, relationship to, 3–4, 17–18, 145
  westward progression of, 126–28, 130–33, 142, 148–50
History of the Patriarchs of the Coptic Church of Alexandria, 52
Holdsworth, Christopher, 56
Holy Apostles, church of, Constantinople, 68–69, 163n82
Holy Innocents, 102, 103
holy lance, discovery of, 18–22, 30
Homer, *Iliad*, 39–41, 47
Honorarius II, pope, formerly Peter Cadalus of Parma, 92
Houben, Hubert, 70
Hugh the Abbot (Hugh the Great), 83–84, 91
Hugh of Avranches, 55, 56
Hugh of Saint Victor, 126–27, 128, 142, 150
Hugh of Vermandois, 136

Ibn al-Athir, 37
ibn Ishaq, Muhammad, *Life of Muhammad*, 146–47
icons, Byzantine, Norman capture of, 71–72
Idle River, battle of (616), 85
Ilghazi, 145
Iliad, 39–41, 47
investiture controversy, 99, 105
Isaac II, 72
Isaiah prophecy and East/West dichotomy, 135–37
Isidore of Seville, *Etymologiae*, 15, 16, 31, 115, 173n37
Islam. *See entries at* Muslim
Itinerarium Peregrinorum et Gesta Regis Ricardi, 25–26, 112–13

Jaffa, battle of (1102), 110
Jakelin de Mailly, 25
Saint James, 148
Jamison, Evelyn, 87–88

Janson, Tore, 156–57n76
Jason, high priest, 118
Jefferson, Thomas, 149
Jerez, battle of (1231), 148
Jericho, 108
Jerome, 101, 109, 127, 129, 173n34
Jerusalem. *See also* Temple/Temple Mount
  Roman capture of (A.D. 70), 101, 118–19, 171n72
  siege and capture by crusaders (1099), 108–11, 157–58n15
Jews
  anti-Jewish rhetoric and attacks, 97–101, 113–14, 115, 120, 144
  associated with Muslims, 100–101, 117–20
  classification in patristic era, 171n77
  crusaders compared to (*See* new Jews, crusaders as)
  Roman capture of Jerusalem by (A.D. 70) and, 101, 118–19
Joab, 110–11
Saints John and Philip, 44–45, 49–50
John I Tzimiskes, 50
John II Comnenus, 162–64n90, 162n65
John, king of England, 127
John of Ripoll, 94
John of Salerno, 93–94
John Scotus Eriugena, *Homélie sur la prologue de Jean*, 17
Johnson, Ewan, 88
Josephus, *Jewish War*, 118, 171n68
Josiah, 111, 112, 170n53
Jovian, 51
Judas Maccabeus, 8, 46, 101–5, 108, 110–12, 116, 119. *See also* new Jews, crusaders as
Julian, 50–52, 159n52, 160–61n19
Julius Caesar, 34–35
Justinian I the Great, 68, 69

Kamal ad-Din, *Everything Desirable About the History of Aleppo*, 145–47
Kantorowicz, Ernst, 160n5
Kazhdan, Alexander, 73
Kempf, Damien, 11, 157n77
Kerbogha of Mosul, 18, 37–38, 57, 68, 77, 117, 119, 139, 158n15, 174n59
Al Khidr, 146
Kierkegaard, Søren, 17–18
Kinoshita, Sharon, 125
Kitzinger, Ernst, 70, 164n93
Knights Templar, 110, 116–17, 121, 170n46
Koran, on angelic aid in battle, 146

Lacépède, Bernard, 149
Lactantius, *Divine Institutes*, 44, 130
Lake Regillus, battle of (late 6th or early 5th century B.C.), 42–43
lance, holy, discovery of, 18–22
Last Judgment, 7, 45, 123, 126–27, 128, 129, 131, 136, 139, 142
laudes, 55, 160n5
Saint Lawrence, 102
Leo I the Great, pope, 80
Leo IX, pope, 93
Leo the Deacon, *History*, 50
letters of crusaders, 38
Liber de apparitione Sancti Michaelis, 82, 95, 166n34
Life of St. Neot, 166n51
Lombards, 80–83, 166n34
Loud, Graham, 76, 79, 87, 88, 91–92, 96
Louis VII, king of France, 70

Maccabees, crusaders compared to. *See* new Jews, crusaders as
MacGregor, James, 38, 39, 56
Macrides, Ruth, 73
Magdalino, Paul, 70
Manegold of Lautenbach, 105
Manicheans, 131
Manuel I Comnenus, 70, 162n65, 164n90
Manzikert, battle of (1071), 67
Marathon, battle of (490 B.C.), 43
Saint Mark, 67, 158n15
martyrs. *See also specific martyrs by name*
  early Christian martyrs, crusaders compared to, 115–16
  Maccabean martyrs (*See* new Jews, crusaders as)
Mattathias, 101, 103, 105
Saint Matthew, 93–94
Saint Maurice, 55, 92
Maxentius, 45, 61
Mayer, Hans, 165n8
McKenzie, Stephen, 128
Mehmed the Conqueror, 163n82
Saint Mercurius
  in battle of Antioch (*See* Antioch, miracle of saintly interventions in battle of)
  Julian's vision of, 52
  regicide of Emperor Julian, 50, 51–52, 160–61n19
Meserve, Margaret, 125
Michael Psellus, 58
Saint Michael the Archangel, 81–83, 94–95

Michael V (emperor), 69
Michael VII (emperor), 59–60
Mietzner, Angelika, 172n11
Milvian Bridge, battle of (312), 45, 61, 86
Mons, battle of, 6
Monte Gargano, 81–83, 94–95, 165n26
Mont-Saint-Michel, 81, 165n26
mosaic portrait of Roger II, Santa Maria dell-Ammiraglio, Palermo, 69–71, 164n93
mother of Kerbogha of Mosul, 77, 174n59
Muhammad, prophet, 146
Muslim opponents of crusaders. *See also specific persons*
    East/West dichotomy as anti-Muslim discourse, 125–26, 133–34
    as eyewitnesses and interpreters, 24–26, 27–28, 156n45
    Jews associated with, 100–101, 117–20
    on military ability and God's favor, 77
    saintly intervention in battle of Antioch and, 27–28
    sexual activities associated with, 117, 171n65
    on supernatural battle interventions, 145–47
    Viking invasions and, 95–96
Muslims in Spain, 94–95, 147–48
Myra, translation of relics of Saint Nicholas to Bari from, 67–68

Nebuchadnezzar II, 127
Saint Neot, 166n51
new apostles, crusaders as, 7–8, 134–35, 144
new Jews, crusaders as, 7–8, 97–121, 144
    anxieties and anti-Jewish rhetoric stemming from, 97–101, 113–14, 115, 120, 144
    association of Jews with Muslims and, 100–101, 117–20
    Bernard of Clairvaux and, 105, 110, 116–17, 121
    capture of Jerusalem and crusader attitude toward Temple Mount, 108–11
    First Crusade chronicles, references to Jews in, 105–8, 111–16
Saint Nicholas, translation of relics from Myra to Bari, 67–68
Nicholas I, pope, 132, 133, 134, 141
Nicol, Donald, 73
Nicephorus, *The Translation of Saint Nicholas*, 67
Nikephoros I, 47
Nikephoros III Botaneiates, 80
Niketas Choniates, *O City of Byzantium*, 71–72, 162n65

Nine Worthies, 113
Nirenberg, David, 98, 150
Nola, sack of (410), 46, 85, 158n33
Norman conquest of England, 2, 122–23
Normanitas, promotion of, 75–76
    appropriation of Viking past, 79–80, 83–86
    atrocities committed by Vikings, transformation of, 90–96
    battle of Cerami and, 58, 75–76, 78–79, 81, 83, 92, 93, 96
    character traits regarded as distinctively Norman, 77–78, 89–90
    Geoffrey Malaterra, *De rebus gestis Rogerii Calabriae* and, 58, 75–76, 78–79, 81, 83, 89, 91–93, 95–96
    Muslim wars and Viking invasions, connection between, 95–96
    sense of connection of Southern Normans to Vikings and Normans of Normandy, 86–90
    southern Italian accounts of supernatural intervention and, 80–83
    supernatural interventions for and against Normans of the South, 92–96
Normans of Normandy, affinity with Normans of the South, 87, 88, 89
Normans of the South. *See also* appropriation of Byzantine warrior saints by crusaders; *Normanitas*, promotion of
    Balkans, invasion of, 60–62, 70
    Byzantium, association with, 58–60, 62
    icons, capture of, 71–72
    marriages between Byzantines and, 59–60, 163–64n90
    southern Italian accounts of supernatural intervention familiar to, 80–83
    supernatural interventions for and against, 92–96
    Vikings and Normans of Normandy, sense of connection to, 6–7, 86–90

Odo, king of western Francia, 84
Odo of Deuil, *De profectione Ludovici VII*, 70, 164n91
Oleg, siege of Constantinople by (907), 72
Olympias/Helena, 59
Onias, 108
Orderic Vitalis, *Ecclesiastical History*, 11–12
    on battle of Antioch, 56
    on battle of Durazzo, 61
    on connection of Normans of the South to Northern/Viking past, 86–87

Orderic Vitalis, *Ecclesiastical History* (*continued*)
  on cult of Byzantine warrior saints in Latin West, 55–56
  on eyewitnesses and interpreters, 30–31, 32
  Fulcher's chronicle as source for, 170n52
  new Jews, crusaders as, 110–13
Orientalism, 124–25, 130
Origen, 98, 171n77
Orosius (Paulus Orosius), *Seven Books of History Against the Pagans*, 130–31, 141
Saint Oswald, king of Northumbria, 85, 86, 105
Otto of Freising, 126–27, 128, 142, 150

Pagden, Anthony, 172n18
Palermo, Santa Maria dell-Ammiraglio, mosaic portrait of Roger II, 69–71, 164n93
Pansa (Claudius Vibius Pansa), 157n81
Pansa (Hirtius Pansa), 34–35
Partridge, Eric, 173n32
Pasch, Helma, 172n11
Saint Paul, 44, 109, 113, 132, 135
Paul the Deacon, *Historia Romana* and *Historia Langobardorum*, 80–81
Paul, Nicholas, 165n8
Pausanias, *Description of Greece*, 158n23
Pedro of Aragon, 147
Peregrinatio Antiochie, 9
Pericles, 44
Persian/Greek dichotomy, 172n18
Saint Peter, 44, 57, 80, 82, 85, 94, 104, 132, 135, 166n35
Peter and Asen, 72
Peter Bartholomew, 18–22, 113
Peter Damian, 2
Peter the Hermit, 115
Peter Tudebode, *Historia de Hierosolymitano itinere*, 9, 30, 38, 54, 55, 65, 119, 156n56, 156n72
Phidias, 47
Saints Philip and John, 44–45, 49–50
Phocas (emperor), 48
Photian Schism, 132
Pirrus, 27–28, 64
Plutarch, *Lives*, 43
Postumius (Aulus Postumius), 43
Potts, Cassandra, 167n79
Saint Procopius, 65, 160n3
Publius Vatinius, 42–43
Purkis, William, 134
Pydna, battle of (168 B.C.), 42

Rabanus Maurus, 103
Ragnar the Dane, 84
Ralph of Caen, *Gesta Tancredi*, 12–13
  celestial phenomena reported by, 138–39
  on discovery of holy lance, 18–19, 20–21, 22
  on Dome of the Rock/Temple Mount, 170n64
  on East Wind, 139–40
  imperial tent, Tancred's demand for, 66–67
  new Jews, crusaders as, 108, 109
Raymond of Aguilers, *Historia Francorum qui ceperunt Iherusalem*, 9
  on battle of Antioch, 38–39, 157–58n15
  on battle of Dorylaeum, 39, 157n15
  cardinal points referenced by, 123
  on discovery of holy lance, 18, 19–20, 21–22, 30
  on East/West dichotomy, 134
  on eyewitnesses and interpreters, 24–25, 29, 30
  new Jews, crusaders as, 113
  on siege of Jerusalem, 157n15
  on Tacitius, 63–64
  on unidentified relics found at Antioch, 57
Raymond IV of St. Gilles, count of Toulouse, 9, 136
Raymond of Toulouse, 19, 20–21, 63, 77
regicides, supernatural, 50–53, 160–61n19
Reginald of Evroul, 86–87
Richard I Lionheart (king of England), 112–13
Richard of Capua, 86, 92
Richard le Pèlerin, 14
Richer of Montecassino, 93
Riley-Smith, Jonathan, 3–45, 56, 73
Risâlat al-Kindî, 171n65
Robert of Clari, 71
Robert II (count of Flanders), 10, 117, 136
Robert of Fulda, 104
Robert of Grandmesnil, 86
Robert Guiscard
  association with Byzantium, 58–60
  coinage with likeness in Byzantine robes, 163n87
  Constantinople, hopes of capturing, 161n38
  invasion of Balkans by, 60–61, 70
  promotion of *Normanitas* and, 86, 89, 90, 91, 96
  William of Apulia, *Gesta Roberti Wiscardi*, 81, 89, 96
Robert the Monk, *Historia Iherosolimitana*, 10–11
  on battle of Antioch, 27–28, 29
  celestial phenomena reported by, 138, 139

Chanson d'Antioche and, 13
  on East/West dichotomy, 133, 134, 135–37, 138, 139, 141
  on eyewitnesses and interpreters, 16, 27–28, 29, 32, 33–34
  Guibert of Nogent and, 11, 157n77
  on holy warfare, 2
  on miraculous and significant nature of First Crusade, 1, 3
  on North as cardinal point, 174n58
  reasons for rewriting *Gesta Francorum*, 3–4, 32, 33–34
  surviving manuscripts, 10–11, 145
Robert of Normandy, 10, 87, 136
Roger I of Antioch, 30, 66, 69, 111, 145, 163n88
Roger II of Antioch, 69–71, 163–64n90–91, 165n93
Roger I, count of Sicily, 75–76, 81, 86
Roger II, king of Sicily, 90
Roland, 112
Rollo, 89, 90, 91
Rome and Romans
  classical accounts of supernatural battle interventions, 39–46, 85, 168n93
  East/West dichotomy and, 130–32, 133
  Titus, capture of Jerusalem by (A.D. 70), 101, 118–19, 171n72
Rubenstein, Jay, 10, 33, 37–38, 77, 123, 142
Rudolph of Swabia, 104
Runciman, Steven, 73
The Russian Primary Chronicle, 72

Saint Sabinus, 80–81, 165n24
Said, Edward, *Orientalism*, 124–25, 130
St. George of Mangana, church of, 57–58
St. Nicholas, church of, in Bari, 68, 163n76
Saladin, 66
Salvini, Roberto, 164n93
San Sabino cathedral, Canosa di Puglia, 68–69
Santa Maria dell-Ammiraglio, Palermo, mosaic portrait of Roger II, 69–71, 164n93
Saul, 111, 112, 170n53
Schein, Sylvia, 109, 110
Schmitt, Jean-Claude, 27
Saint Sebastian, 55
Second Coming, 7, 45, 123, 126–27, 128, 129, 131, 136, 139, 142
Second Crusade, 16, 70, 142, 164n93
Segebert and Segevert, 85
Seleucus, 169n34
Sergius IV, pope, 171n69
Sergius, patriarch, 47
Severian, bishop, 128, 129
Shapur I, 48
Shepard, Jonathan, 63
Siberry, Elizabeth, 11
Sicily, Normans in. *See* Normans of the South
Siger, 118
Sigismund of Burgundy, 131, 132
Simancas, battle of (939), 148
Skylitzes, John, *Synopsis of Byzantine History*, 49
Smail, R. C., 37
Smith, Katherine, 98, 159–60n2
Socrates Scholasticus, *Ecclesiastical History*, 50–51
Song of Antioch, 13–14, 119, 156n54
Southern, Richard, *Western Views of Islam*, 125
Sozomen, Salminius Hermias, 51
Spain, supernatural battle interventions against Muslims in, 94–95, 147–48
Spiegel, Gabrielle, 3, 36, 155n35
Spring of Cresson, battle of (1187), 25
Standard, battle of the (1138), 87
Saint Stephen, Venetian acquisition of relic of, 164n102
Stephen of Blois, 10
Stephenson, Paul, 72
Suger, *Vita Ludovici*, 155n35
supernatural interventions in battle. *See also* Antioch, miracle of saintly interventions in battle of
  in Bible, 8, 45, 46, 81, 97, 107–8, 114
  in Byzantium, 5–6, 46–52
  Cerami, Saint George in battle of, 58, 75–76, 79
  early Christian accounts of, 44–49
  Greek and Roman accounts of, 39–46, 85, 168n93
  in Latin West, 6
  Maccabean wars, role of angels in, 8, 97, 107–8, 114
  in Muslim literature, 145–47
  for and against Normans of the South, 92–96
  regicides, 50–53, 160–61n19
  southern Italian accounts, 80–83
  in Spain, 94–95, 147–48
  against Vikings, 6–7, 79–80, 83–86
Svjatoslav, 50
Sweetenham, Carol, 13

Taticius, 63–64
Tall Danith, battle of (1115), 24, 25, 111

Tancred of Hauteville, 12, 66–67, 77, 109–10.
    See also Ralph of Caen, Gesta Tancredi
Taviani-Carozzi, Huguette, 58, 79
Templars, 110, 116–17, 121, 170n46
Temple/Temple Mount
    al-Aqsa mosque, 110, 116
    Bernard of Clairvaux on, 116–17, 170n64
    crusader attitude toward, 109–11
    Dome of the Rock (As-Sakhrah), 109, 170n54
    Ralph of Caen on, 170n64
tent of emperor, Tancred's demand for, 66–67
tent of Kerbogha donated to church of St. Nicholas in Bari, 68
Theban legion, saints of, 55
Saint Theodore (Theodore Stratelates)
    at battle of Antioch, in Peter Tudebode's chronicle, 54, 74
    at battle of Dorostolon, 58
    in Byzantine precursors to saintly intervention at battle of Antioch, 50, 53
    coinage with image of, 162n65
    crusader appropriation of, 54, 55, 57, 58, 61, 62, 65, 71, 74
    Norman invasion of the Balkans and, 61, 62
    regicide of Valens, 50, 161n19
Theodore Synkellos, 47
Saint Theodore Tiron, 160n3
Theodoret of Cyrrhus, *Ecclesiastical History*, 44–45, 47, 159n52
Theodosius, 44, 45
theology
    history, relationship to, 3–4, 17–18, 145
    witness, concept of, 17–18, 31, 36
Theotokos/Virgin Mary, 47, 50, 52, 94, 162n65
Theseus, 41, 43
Titus, capture of Jerusalem by (A.D. 70), 101, 118–19, 171n72
Tolan, John, *Saracens*, 125
Tronzo, William, 70–71
Twisse, William, 149

Urban II, pope, 38, 68, 75, 134, 135, 136, 162n56, 169n24
Uriah, 110–11

Valens, 50, 52, 161n19
Valerius Maximus, *Memorable Deeds and Sayings*, 158n22

Velleius, 42
La Venjance Nostre Seigneur, 171n70
Vespasian, 119, 171n70, 171n72
Vikings
    appropriated by Normans of the South, 6–7, 79–80, 83–86
    atrocities committed by, transformation of, 90–96
    connections drawn between Normans of the South and, 6–7, 79–80, 83–86
    Muslims, connection to wars against, 95–96
Virgin Mary/Theotokos, 47, 50, 52, 94, 162n65
Vlach and Bulgar rebellion against Byzantium (1185–86), 72

Walter Espic, 87
Walter the Chancellor, *The Antiochene Wars*, 24, 29–30, 155n40
Watkins, Carl, 123
Webber, Nick, 88, 90
William I the Conqueror, 2, 87
William II of Sicily, 163n86
William of Apulia, *Gesta Roberti Wiscardi*, 81, 89, 96
William of Jumièges, *Gesta Normannorum Ducum*, 90, 91, 122
William of Malmesbury, *Gesta Regum Anglorum*, 12
    on battle of Antioch, 26–27, 114
    on eyewitnesses and interpreters, 24, 26–27, 30
    new Jews, crusaders viewed as, 97, 107–8, 114, 120
William of Poitiers, *Gesta Guillelmi*, 87, 103–4
William of Tyre, 160n18
William of Volpiano, 165n26
wind out of the east, 140–41, 174n71
witness, theological concept of, 17–18, 31, 36
Wolf, Kenneth, 77, 95–96
World War I, angels of Mons in, 6
Wright, John Kirtland, 127

Xenophon, *Hellenica*, 41–42
Xeros, Basil, 164n90

Zosimus, 46–47

Typeset by
COGHILL COMPOSITION COMPANY

Printed and bound by
SHERIDAN BOOKS

Composed in
MINION PRO

Printed on
NATURES NATURAL

Bound in
ARRESTOX

www.ingramcontent.com/pod-product-compliance
Lightning Source LLC
Chambersburg PA
CBHW021404290426
44108CB00010B/379